WebRTC

APIs and RTCWEB
Protocols of the HTML5
Real-Time Web

WebRTC

APIs and RTCWEB Protocols of the HTML5 Real-Time Web

Alan B. Johnston

Daniel C. Burnett

Third Edition

C:

Digital Codex LLC

∅∅1∅

ISBN-13: 978-0-9859788-6-0
ISBN-10: 0985978864

DEDICATION

For Aidan & Nora, and Craig & Fiona

TABLE OF CONTENTS

LIST OF FIGURES AND TABLES

ACKNOWLEDGMENTS

We would like to thank our technical reviewers Alex Agranovsky, Carol Davids, Emil Ivov, David Kemp, Henry Sinnreich, Harvey Waxman, and Dan York. We would also like to thank Marina Burnett and Chris Comfort for their proofreading and comments. We would also like to thank our families for their encouragement and support.

And finally, we would like to acknowledge our colleagues in W3C and the IETF who are working incredibly hard at creating the WebRTC standards.

PREFACE

The changes in the world of WebRTC are amazing, but they sometimes feels schizophrenic. At times, it is moving forward rapidly, making major strides. At other times, it seems slow and almost glacial in its progress. Interoperability today is superb, and making our demo application work between browsers (Chrome and Firefox) and platforms (Windows and Mac) with voice, video, and the data channel has been a breeze. On the other hand, there are some interoperability clouds on the horizon with potential video interop issues and even alternative APIs.

Time will tell which personality will dominate going forward. Certainly, the standards and implementations are maturing and converging, and this makes our code writing and book writing much easier than it was back in the days of the first edition.

This edition has new content in the form of an enhanced demo application which now shows the use of the data channel for real-time text sent directly between browsers. Also, a full description of the browser media negotiation process including actual SDP session descriptions from Firefox and Chrome. Hints on how to use Wireshark to monitor WebRTC protocols, and example captures are also included. TURN server support for NAT and firewall traversal is also new.

This edition also features a step-by-step introduction to WebRTC, with concepts such as local media, signaling, and the Peer Connection introduced through separate runnable demos. As always, all our code is available for download at http://webrtcbook.com/code3.html and is up and running at http://demo.webrtcbook.com for you to try.

We hope this new edition will be helpful to you in your WebRTC development and integration.

PREFACE TO SECOND EDITION

WebRTC continues to evolve and grow in the handful of months since we published the first edition of WebRTC: APIs and Protocols of the HTML5 Real-Time Web.

There has been real progress in many areas in the IETF and W3C standards, although much work remains. Eventing, stream representation at the protocol level, and even the syntax for some callbacks are all still very much under discussion, while details such as how multiple video tracks within a single MediaStream work and what should happen when a MediaStream attached to an HTML element has tracks added or removed are only now beginning to be considered. Nevertheless, the core APIs are firming up. On the usage side, conferences, meetups, and startups have sprung up and are growing rapidly in size, with the World seeking to understand WebRTC's impact and opportunities.

Other trends have become clear as well. The disagreement about codecs, especially video codecs is escalating from a fight, to a war, to Mutually Assured Patent Destruction. The authors sincerely hope that the standards and industry come to agreement quickly on the mandatory to implement video codec very soon.

While the basic parts of WebRTC are working well in demos and applications today, many of the concerns and issues with WebRTC revolve around security and the signaling channel, which have complete new chapters in this second edition. Additionally, the sample code out there on the Web today is often either too complex or insufficiently explained, motivating the complete running and completely explained example in this new edition. This demo code, running on both Chrome and Firefox, is also on our website at http://demo.webrtcbook.com .

We hope that this new updated edition keeps you excited and informed about WebRTC. Happy reading!

PREFACE TO FIRST EDITION

The Internet and the World Wide Web have changed our world. When the history of this period is written, much will be said about the impact of these technologies on life in the late 20th and early 21st centuries. The web has changed the way we receive information, interact with others, work, and play. Now, the web is about to dramatically change the way we communicate using voice and video. This book gives an up-to-the-minute snapshot of the standards and industry effort known as WebRTC, which is short for Web Real-Time Communications. This technology, along with other advances in HTML5 browsers, has the potential to revolutionize the way we all communicate, in both personal and business spheres.

The authors have been involved in the Internet Communications industry for many years, and have seen the advances and impact of the Internet on voice and video communications. We have worked on signaling protocols such as Session Initiation Protocol (SIP), Session Description Protocol (SDP), and security protocols such as ZRTP for voice and video communication systems that will form the basis of what will inevitably replace the telephone system (called the Public Switched Telephone Network or PSTN). These Internet Communications technologies have brought an amazing wave of disruption, but we believe WebRTC has the potential to create even greater disruption.

This book provides information for web developers and telephony developers who want to catch this new wave while it is still building. The standards and protocols needed for WebRTC are still being developed and invented. Browsers are starting to support WebRTC functionality, little by little. However, the authors have seen the need for a book to explain this still-developing technology. This book will explain the technical goals, architectures, protocols, and Application Programming Interfaces (APIs) of WebRTC. In a publishing experiment, we plan to produce frequent editions of this book, perhaps as often as three per year, and focus on digital delivery and on-demand publishing to keep costs down and for maximum hyper linking usefulness. For information on the latest edition and for a list of updates and changes, visit http://webrtcbook.com .

This book begins with an introduction to WebRTC and discusses what is new about it. The unique aspects of WebRTC peer-to-peer media flows are explored, and Network Address Translation (NAT) traversal explained. We then discuss the working documents and finalized documents that together comprise the WebRTC standards-in-progress in both the World Wide Web Consortium (W3C) and the Internet Engineering Task Force (IETF). Each chapter ends with a references section, listing the various standards documents. References of the form [RFC...] are IETF Request For Comments documents. References of the form [draft-...] are IETF Internet-Drafts, working documents, whose content may have been updated or changed since the publication of this book. The hyperlinks provided will, in most cases, retrieve the most recent version of the document. References to W3C drafts include a link to the latest public working draft, and also a link to the latest editor's draft. For those of you unfamiliar with the standardization processes of W3C and the IETF, we have provided a reference in Appendices A and B. Finally, we discuss the current state of deployment in popular browsers.

If you are a web developer, welcome to the world of Internet Communications! Your users will greatly enjoy the ability to interact with each other using your application's real-time voice and video capabilities. To understand our descriptions of APIs, you will need a working knowledge of HTML and JavaScript, and some experience in web applications. See Appendix D for some useful references for this.

If you are a VoIP or telephony developer, welcome to the web world! Your users will enjoy the capabilities of high quality audio and video communication, and rich, web-powered user interfaces. To understand our descriptions of the on-the-wire protocols for transporting voice, video, and data, you will need a basic understanding of the Internet. Knowledge of another Internet Communication signaling protocol such as SIP or Jingle is also useful. See Appendix D for some additional useful reference reading.

In many ways, WebRTC is a merging of worlds between the web and telephony. To help bridge the gap between the web and telephony world, we have also included a Glossary in Appendix C to briefly explain some common terms and concepts from each world.

The authors look forward to participating in the next wave of disruption and innovation that WebRTC will likely unleash.

We would love to hear from you and interact with you on Twitter (@alanbjohnston and @danielcburnett) or on Google+ (alanbjohnston@gmail.com and danielcburnett@gmail.com).

1 INTRODUCTION TO WEB REAL-TIME COMMUNICATIONS

Web Real-Time Communications (RTC), or WebRTC, adds new functionality to the web browser. For the first time, browsers will interact directly with other browsers, resulting in a number of architectures including a triangle and trapezoid model. The media capabilities of WebRTC are state-of-the-art, with many new features. The underlying standards of WebRTC are being developed by the World Wide Web Consortium (W3C) and the Internet Engineering Task Force (IETF).

1.1 WebRTC Introduction

WebRTC is an industry and standards effort to put real-time communications capabilities into all browsers and make these capabilities accessible to web developers via standard [HTML5] tags and JavaScript APIs (Application Programming Interfaces). For example, consider functionality similar to that offered by Skype™ [SKYPE] but without having to install any software or plug-ins. For a website or web application to work regardless of which browser is used, standards are required. Also, standards are required so that browsers can communicate with non-browsers, including enterprise and service provider telephony and communications equipment.

1.1.1 The Web Browsing Model

The basic model of web applications is shown in Figure 1.1. Transport of information between the browser and the web server is provided by the Hyper-Text Transport Protocol, HTTP (Section 10.2.1), which runs over Transmission Control Protocol, TCP (Section 10.2.9), or in some new

1

implementations, over the WebSocket protocol (see Section 10.2.2). The content or application is carried in Hyper-Text Markup Language, HTML, which typically includes JavaScript and Cascading Style Sheets [CSS]. In the simple case, the browser sends an HTTP request to the web server for content, and the web server sends a response containing the document or image or other information requested. In the more complex case, the server sends JavaScript which runs on the browser, interacting with the browser through APIs and with the user through clicks and selects. The browser exchanges information with the server through an open HTTP or WebSockets channel.

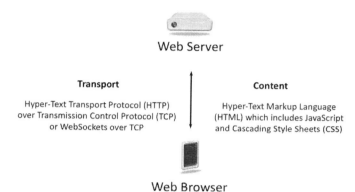

Web Server

Transport	**Content**
Hyper-Text Transport Protocol (HTTP) over Transmission Control Protocol (TCP) or WebSockets over TCP	Hyper-Text Markup Language (HTML) which includes JavaScript and Cascading Style Sheets (CSS)

Web Browser

Figure 1.1 Web Browser Model

In figures in this book, we will show an arrow between the web browser and the web server to indicate the web session between them. Since WebRTC can utilize any web transport, the details of this connection, and whether it is HTTP or WebSockets, is not discussed.

1.1.2 The Real-Time Communication Function in the Browser

Figure 1.2 shows the browser model and the role of the real-time communication function. The lighter block called "Browser RTC Function" is the focus of this book. The unique nature and requirements of real-time communications means that adding and standardizing this block is non-trivial. The RTC function interacts with the web application using standard APIs. It communicates with the Operating System using the browser. A new aspect of WebRTC is the interaction that occurs browser-to-browser, known as a "Peer Connection", where the RTC Function in one browser communicates using on-the-wire standard protocols (not HTTP) with the RTC Function in another browser or Voice over IP (VoIP) or video application. While web traffic uses TCP for transport, the on-the-wire protocol between browsers can use other transport protocols such as

User Datagram Protocol, UDP. Also new is the Signaling Server, which provides the signaling channel between the browser and the other end of the Peer Connection.

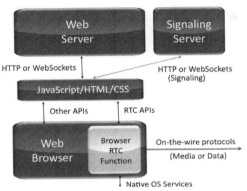

Figure 1.2 Real-Time Communication in the Browser

1.1.3 Elements of a WebRTC System

Figure 1.3 shows a typical set of elements in a WebRTC system. This includes web servers, browsers running various operating systems on various devices including desktop PCs, tablets, and mobile phones, and other servers. Additional elements include gateways to the Public Switched Telephone Network (PSTN) and other Internet communication endpoints such as Session Initiation Protocol (SIP) phones and clients or Jingle clients. WebRTC enables communication among all these devices. The figures in this book will use these icons and elements as examples.

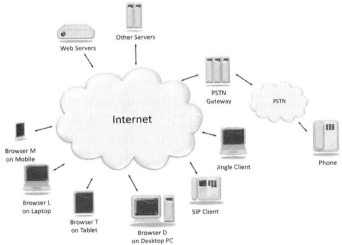

Figure 1.3 Elements in a WebRTC Environment

1.1.4 The WebRTC Triangle

Initially, the most common scenario is likely to be where both browsers are running the same WebRTC web application, downloaded from the same website. This produces the WebRTC "Triangle" shown in Figure 1.4. This arrangement is called a triangle due to the shape of the signaling (sides of triangle) and media or data flows (base of triangle) between the three elements. A Peer Connection establishes the transport for voice and video media and data channel flows directly between the browsers.

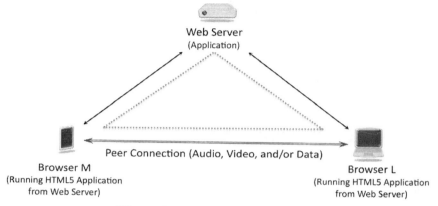

Figure 1.4 The WebRTC Triangle

Note that while we sometimes refer to the connection between the browser and server as signaling, it is not really signaling as used in telephony systems. Signaling is not standardized in WebRTC as it is just considered part of the application. This signaling may run over HTTP or WebSockets to the same web server that serves HTML pages to the browser, or to a completely different web server that just handles the signaling.

1.1.5 The WebRTC Trapezoid

Figure 1.5 shows the WebRTC Trapezoid [draft-ietf-rtcweb-overview], based on the SIP Trapezoid [RFC3261]. The two web servers are shown communicating using a standard signaling protocol such as Session Initiation Protocol (SIP), used by many VoIP and video conferencing systems, or Jingle [XEP-0166], used to add voice and video capability to Jabber [RFC6120] instant messaging and presence systems. Alternatively, a proprietary signaling protocol could be used. Note that in these more complicated cases, the media may not flow directly between the two browsers, but may go through media relays and other elements, as discussed in Chapter 5.

4

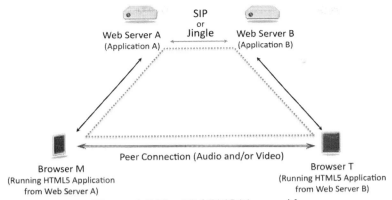

Figure 1.5 The WebRTC Trapezoid

1.1.6 WebRTC and the Session Initiation Protocol (SIP)

Figure 1.6 shows WebRTC interoperating with SIP. The Web Server has a built-in SIP signaling gateway to allow the call setup information to be exchanged between the browser and the SIP client. The resulting media flow is directly between the browser and the SIP client, as the Peer Connection establishes a standard Real-time Transport Protocol (RTP) media session (Section 10.2.3) with the SIP User Agent. Other ways of interoperating with SIP are covered in Section 2.2.6.

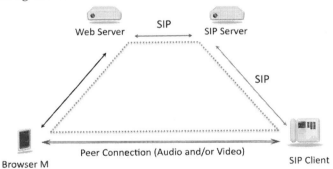

Figure 1.6 WebRTC Interoperating with SIP

1.1.7 WebRTC and Jingle

Figure 1.7 shows how WebRTC can interoperate with Jingle. The Web Server has a built-in Extensible Messaging and Presence Protocol, XMPP [RFC6120], also known as Jabber, server which talks through another XMPP server to a Jingle client.

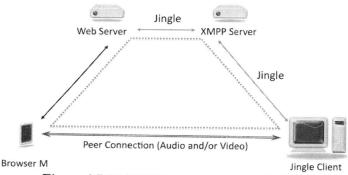

Figure 1.7 WebRTC Interoperating with Jingle

1.1.8 WebRTC and the Public Switched Telephone Network (PSTN)

Figure 1.8 shows how WebRTC can interoperate with the Public Switched Telephone Network (PSTN). The PSTN Gateway terminates the audio-only media stream and connects the PSTN telephone call with the media. Some sort of signaling is needed between the Web Server and the PSTN Gateway. It could be SIP, or a master/slave control protocol.

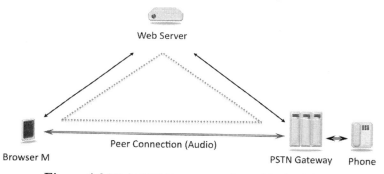

Figure 1.8 WebRTC Interoperating with the PSTN

It is not expected that browsers will be assigned telephone numbers or be part of the PSTN. Instead, an Internet Communication service could assign a telephone number to a user, and that user could use WebRTC to access the service. As a result, a telephone call to that PSTN number would "ring" the browser and an answered call would result in an audio session across the Internet connected to the PSTN caller. Other services could include the ability to "dial" a telephone number in a WebRTC application which would result in the audio path across the Internet to the PSTN.

Note that the phone in Figure 1.8 could be a normal PSTN phone ("landline" or "black phone") or a mobile phone. The fact that it might be running VoLTE (Voice over Long Term Evolution) or other VoIP (Voice

6

over Internet Protocol) protocol doesn't change this picture, as the Peer Connection will terminate with a VoIP gateway.

Another interesting area is the role of WebRTC in providing emergency services. While a WebRTC service could support emergency calling in the same way as VoIP Internet Communication services, there is the potential that the Public Service Answering Point (PSAP) could become a WebRTC application, and answer emergency "calls" directly from other browsers, completely bypassing the PSTN. Of course, this raises all kinds of interesting security, privacy, and jurisdiction issues.

1.2 Multiple Media Streams in WebRTC

Devices today can generate and consume multiple media types and multiple streams of each type. Even in the simple point-to-point example shown in Figure 1.9, a mobile phone and a desktop PC could generate a total of six media streams. For multiparty sessions, this number will be much higher. As a result, WebRTC has built-in capabilities for dealing with multiple media streams and sources.

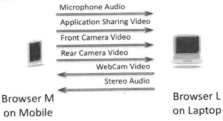

Figure 1.9 Multiple Media Streams in a Point-to-Point WebRTC Session

1.3 Multi-Party Sessions in WebRTC

The preceding examples have been point-to-point sessions between two browsers, or between a browser and another endpoint. WebRTC also supports multi-party or conferencing sessions involving multiple browsers.

One way to do this is to have each browser establish a Peer Connection with the other browsers in the session. This is shown in Figure 1.10. This is sometimes referred to as a "full mesh" or "fully distributed" conferencing architecture. Each browser establishes a full mesh of Peer Connections with the other browsers. For audio media, this might mean mixing the media received from each browser. For video, this might mean rendering the video streams from other browsers to different windows with appropriate labeling. As new browsers join the session, new Peer Connections are established to send and receive the new media streams.

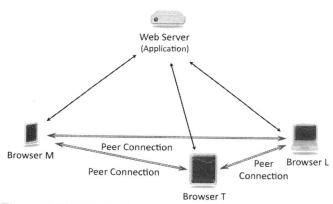

Figure 1.10 Multiple Peer Connections Between Browsers

An alternative architecture to the full-mesh model of Figure 1.10 is also possible with WebRTC. For a multiple browser conference, a centralized media server/mixer/selector can be used; this requires only a single Peer Connection to be established between each browser and the media server. This is shown in Figure 1.11. This is sometimes referred to as a "centrally mixed" conferencing architecture. Each browser sends media to the server, which distributes it to the other browsers, with or without mixing. From the perspective of browser M, media streams from browser L and T are received over a single Peer Connection from the server. As new browsers join the session, no new Peer Connections involving browser M need to be established. Instead, new media streams are received over the existing Peer Connection between browser M and the media server.

The full-mesh architecture of Figure 1.10 has the advantages of no media server infrastructure, and lowest media latency and highest quality. However, this architecture may not be suitable for a large multi-party conference because the bandwidth required at each browser grows with each new participant. The centralized architecture of Figure 1.11 has the advantage of being able to scale to very large sessions while also minimizing the amount of processing needed by each browser when a new participant joins the session, although it is perhaps inefficient when only one or a small number of browsers are involved, such as in peer-to-peer gaming.

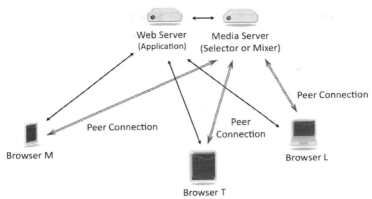

Figure 1.11 Single Peer Connection with Media Server

1.4 WebRTC Standards

The WebRTC standards are currently under joint development by the World Wide Web Consortium (W3C) [W3C] and the Internet Engineering Task Force (IETF) [IETF]. W3C is working on defining the APIs needed for JavaScript web applications to interact with the browser RTC function. These APIs, such as the Peer Connection API, are described in Chapter 8. The IETF is developing the protocols used by the browser RTC function to talk to another browser or Internet Communications endpoint. These protocols, for example, extensions to the Real-time Transport Protocol, are described in Chapter 11.

There are pre-standard implementations of many of the components of WebRTC in some browsers today. See Chapter 14 for details.

Note that there is an important distinction between 'pre-standard' and 'proprietary' implementations. Pre-standard implementations emerge during the development stage of standards, and are critical to gain experience and information before standards are finalized and locked down. Pre-standard implementations often follow an early or draft version of the standards, or partially implement standards as a 'proof of concept'. Once the standard has been finalized, these pre-standard implementations must move towards the standards, or else they risk becoming a proprietary implementation. Proprietary implementations fragment the user and development base, which in an area such as communications can greatly reduce the value of the services.

The W3C work is centered around the WEBRTC Working Group and the IETF work is centered around the RTCWEB (Real-Time

Communications Web) Working Group. The two groups are independent, but closely coordinate together and have many common participants, including the authors.

The projected time frame for core feature stability of the first version of standards in the IETF and W3C is in 2014. However, these dates are most likely overly optimistic. (When do engineers ever realistically estimate level of effort?) Standards-compliant WebRTC browsers are expected to be generally available sometime in late 2014.

1.5 What is New in WebRTC

There are many new and exciting capabilities in WebRTC that are not available even in today's VoIP and video conferencing systems. Some of these features are listed in Table 1.1. The rest of this book will explain how these are achieved using the WebRTC APIs and protocols.

1.6 Important Terminology Notes

In this book, when we refer to the entire effort to add standardized communication capabilities into browsers, we shall use WebRTC. When we are referring to the W3C Working Group, we will use WEBRTC. When we are referring to the IETF Working Group, we will use RTCWEB. Note that WebRTC is also used to describe the Google/Mozilla open source media engine [WEBRTC.ORG], which is an implementation of WebRTC.

In addition, because the main W3C specification is titled "The WebRTC Specification" [WEBRTC 1.0], we use its full title to reference this particular W3C document, which is a key part of WebRTC, but by no means the entire specification.

Also note that the World Wide Consortium refers to itself as "W3C" and not "the W3C". We have adopted this convention throughout this book.

Feature	Provided Using	Why Important
Platform and device independence	Standard APIs from W3C, standard protocols from IETF	Developers can write WebRTC HTML5 code that will run across different OS, browsers, and devices, desktop and mobile.
Secure voice and video	Secure RTP Protocol (SRTP) encryption and authentication	Browsers are used in different environments and over unsecured WiFi networks. Encryption means that others can't listen in or record voice or video.
Advanced voice and video quality	Opus audio codec, VP8 video codec, and others	Having built-in standard codecs ensures interoperability and avoids codec downloads, a way malicious sites install spyware and viruses. New codecs can adapt when congestion is detected.
Reliable session establishment	Hole punching through Network Address Translation (NAT)	Direct media between browsers is noticeably more reliable and better quality than server-relayed media. Also, the load on servers is reduced.
Multiple media streams and media types sent over a single transport	Real-time Transport Protocol (RTP) and Session Description Protocol (SDP) extensions	Establishing direct media using hole punching can take time. Sending all media over a single session is also more efficient and reliable.
Adaptive to network conditions	Multiplexed RTP Control Protocol (RTCP), Secure Audio Video Profile with Feedback (SAVPF)	Feedback on network conditions is essential for video, and will be especially important for the high definition, high bandwidth sessions in WebRTC.
Support for multiple media types and multiple sources of media	APIs and signaling to negotiate size/format of each source individually	The ability to negotiate each individually results in most efficient use of bandwidth and other resources.
Interoperability with VoIP and video communication systems using SIP, Jingle, and PSTN	Standard Secure RTP (SRTP) media, Standard SDP and extensions	Existing VoIP and video systems can work with new WebRTC systems using standard protocols.

Table 1.1 New Features of WebRTC

1.7 References

[HTML5]   http://www.w3.org/TR/html5

[SKYPE]   http://www.skype.com

[CSS]   http://www.w3.org/Style/CSS

[draft-ietf-rtcweb-overview]   http://tools.ietf.org/html/draft-ietf-rtcweb-overview

[RFC3261]   http://tools.ietf.org/html/rfc3261

[XEP-0166]   http://xmpp.org/extensions/xep-0166.html

[RFC6120]   http://tools.ietf.org/html/rfc6120

[W3C]   http://www.w3c.org

[IETF]   http://www.ietf.org

[WEBRTC.ORG]   http://www.webrtc.org

[WEBRTC 1.0]   http://www.w3.org/TR/webrtc

2 HOW TO USE WEBRTC

WebRTC is easy to use, with just a few steps necessary to establish media sessions. A number of messages flow between the browser and the server, while others flow directly between the two browsers, known as peers. WebRTC can even establish sessions with SIP, Jingle, and PSTN endpoints. There are many standards involved in the WebRTC effort – so many that it can be difficult to know where to start when learning about it. Since many readers of this text will likely be developers of WebRTC applications, the following sections give an overview of how to set up a WebRTC session, what can be done while the session is running, and how to close down the session. WebRTC can be used in a number of different architectures. Example pseudo code illustrates the operation of the WebRTC APIs. Later chapters take each of these key pieces and explain them in more detail.

2.1 Setting Up a WebRTC Session

As an application developer, the four main actions to take when setting up a WebRTC session are:

1) Obtain local media,
2) Set up a connection between the browser and the peer (other browser or endpoint),
3) Attach media and data channels to the connection, and
4) Exchange session descriptions

These four steps are shown in Figure 2.1. Note that this figure corresponds with Figure 1.4.

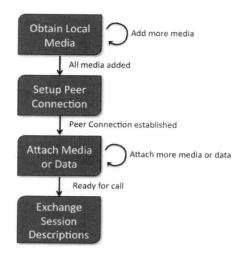

Figure 2.1 WebRTC Session Establishment, API View

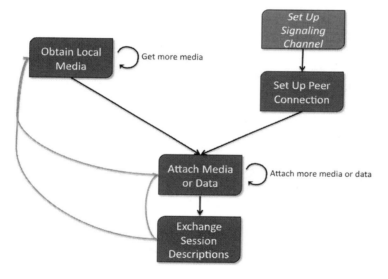

Figure 2.2 WebRTC API View with Signaling

Figure 2.2 shows another view of the steps, this time with signaling steps shown.

The following subsections briefly describe each of these steps, as well as the process for closing down a session when complete.

2.1.1 Obtaining Local Media

There are a variety of ways to obtain media, the complete list of which is out of scope for this book. However, one of the most common ways is defined by the WebRTC effort: getUserMedia() (Section 8.3.2). This method can be used to obtain a single local MediaStream. Once you have one or more media streams, you can piece them together into the streams you want using the MediaStream API (Application Programming Interface). For privacy reasons, a web application's request for access to a user's microphone or camera will only be granted after the browser has obtained permission from the user.

2.1.2 Setting up the Peer Connection

Another important step is to set up the Peer Connection using the API by the same name. The core of WebRTC is the RTCPeerConnection API, which, as its name suggests, sets up a connection between two Peers. In this context, "peers" means two communication endpoints on the World Wide Web, as in the phrase "peer-to-peer file sharing". Instead of requiring communication through a server, the communication is direct between the two entities. In the specific case of WebRTC, a Peer Connection is a direct media connection between two web browsers. This is particularly relevant when a multi-way communication such as a conference call is set up among three or more browsers. Each pair of browsers will require a single Peer Connection to join them, allowing for audio and video media to flow directly between the two, as shown in Figure 1.10. Thus, three browsers communicating would need a total of three connections among them. An application developer will need to set up one Peer Connection per pair of browsers (or a browser and another endpoint such as an existing communications network) being connected. The alternative architecture of Figure 1.11 is also possible.

To establish this connection requires a new RTCPeerConnection object. The only input to the RTCPeerConnection constructor method is a configuration object containing the information that ICE, Interactive Connectivity Establishment (Section 10.2.7), will use to "punch holes" through intervening Network Address Translation (NAT) devices and firewalls.

2.1.3 Exchanging Media or Data

Once the connection is set up, any number of local media streams may be attached to the Peer Connection for sending across the connection to the remote browser. Similarly, any number of remote media streams may also be sent to the local end of the connection, resulting in new media streams at the local end that may be manipulated just like any other local media stream.

It is important to note that every change in media requires a negotiation (or renegotiation) between browsers of how media will be represented on the channel. When a request is made, locally or remotely, to add or remove media, the browser can be asked to generate an appropriate RTCSessionDescription object (a container for a session description – information about how to establish the media session) to represent the complete set of media flowing over the Peer Connection. The RTCPeerConnection API provides a means by which the application author can view and edit (if desired) the session description before it is sent to the remote side. This design allows the browser to handle the "heavy lifting" of proposing codecs and writing Session Description Protocol (SDP), Section 10.2.4, used to represent the session description, while still allowing for minor adjustments by the application as needed. However, it is expected that in the majority of cases, the web developer will not need to modify or inspect RTCSessionDescription objects.

Once the browsers have exchanged RTCSessionDescription objects, the media or data session can be established. Both browsers begin hole punching. Once hole punching completes, key negotiation for the secure media session can begin. Finally, the media or data session can begin. Note that all of this activity, everything after the RTCSessionDescription objects have been exchanged, is done by the browser on behalf of the JavaScript code. The application JavaScript code may add or remove STUN and TURN servers, Sections 10.2.5 and 10.2.6, used for NAT traversal and monitor the process, but the work is done by the browser.

2.1.4 Closing the Connection

Either browser can close the connection. The application calls close() on the RTCPeerConnection object to indicate that it is finished using the connection, perhaps in response to a user clicking a button or closing a tab. This causes ICE processing and media streaming to stop. Similarly, should one browser lose Internet connectivity, or crash, the keep-alives sent in the media or data channel will fail, and the other browser will attempt to restart hole punching, and when that fails close the session. Once the session is over, the browser removes any session-granted permissions to access the microphone and camera of the device, so a new session will require new permission(s) from the user.

2.2 WebRTC Networking and Interworking Examples

The following subsections will show some examples of WebRTC application architectures with call flows. Figure 2.3 shows a protocol view of WebRTC Session Establishment.

The following figures provide more details of the protocol exchanges, using "ladder diagrams", sometimes called call flows.

Protocols such as SRTP, SDP, and ICE are introduced in Chapter 10.

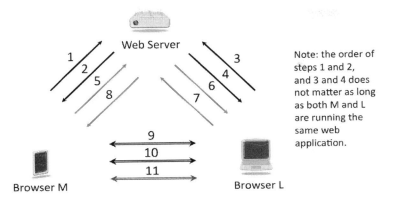

Note: the order of steps 1 and 2, and 3 and 4 does not matter as long as both M and L are running the same web application.

1) Browser M requests web page from web server
2) Web sever provides web pages to M with WebRTC JavaScript
3) Browser L requests web page from web server
4) Web sever provides web pages to L with WebRTC JavaScript
5) M decides to communicate with L, JavaScript on M causes M's session description object (offer) to be sent to the web server
6) Web server sends M's session description object to the JavaScript on L
7) JavaScript on L causes L's session description object (answer) to be sent to web server
8) Web server sends L's session description object to the JavaScript on M
9) M and L begin hole punching to determine the best way to reach the other browser
10) After hole punching completes, M and L begin key negotiation for secure media
11) M and L begin exchanging voice, video, or data

Figure 2.3 WebRTC Session Establishment, Protocol View

2.2.1 Session Establishment in WebRTC Triangle

Basic session establishment with WebRTC is shown in Figure 2.4. Note that this figure corresponds with Figure 2.3.

Browsers M and L are running the same WebRTC enabled JavaScript downloaded from the web server. When one user wishes to communicate with another user, this begins the media negotiation between the browsers, referred to as an offer/answer exchange. This offer answer exchange occurs between the two browsers over a signaling channel established between them. For the remainder of this chapter, the signaling channel is assumed to be over HTTP through the web server. For the details of how this signaling channel works, and alternative signaling channel designs, see Chapter 4.

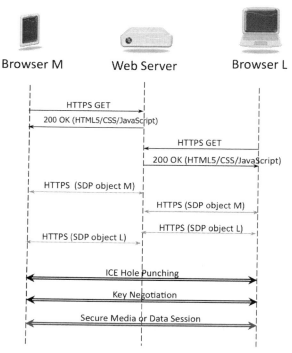

Figure 2.4 WebRTC Triangle Call Flow

Media negotiation is the way in which two parties in a communication session, such as two browsers, communicate and come to agreement on an acceptable media session. Offer/answer is an approach to media negotiation in which one party first sends to the other party what media types and capabilities it supports and would like to establish – this is known as the "offer". The other party then responds indicating which of the offered media types and capabilities are supported and acceptable for this session – this is known as the "answer". This process can be repeated a number of times to setup and modify a session, for example to add new media streams or to change which streams are to be sent. A common question is why this back-and-forth process is needed, rather than, for example, each side merely stating what it intends to do. The primary reason is to ensure that both sides have agreement before media begins flowing. This is crucial for the lower layers in the browser that may not be able to handle media that comes in before the browser is ready for it.

In addition to offers and answers, there is also a "provisional answer" (pranswer). A provisional answer is an answer to an offer, but it is provisional or tentative. It may not be the final answer given in the actual answer, which comes later in the offer/answer exchange. Provisional answers are optional, and in general will only occur when interoperating with the PSTN or some VoIP systems that emulate the "early media" characteristics of the telephone network.

When the user on browser M decides to communicate with the user on browser L, the JavaScript on browser M provides a constraint-based description of the media it wants, requests the media, and gets user permission. It is important that the permission grant is tied to the domain of the web page, and that this permission does not extend to pop-ups and other frames on the web page. The desired media session information is captured in a session description object. This is the offer, which is sent to browser L through the web server. It is important to note that WebRTC does not standardize how browser M sends this offer to browser L. There are a number of ways in which this could be accomplished, such as XML HTTP Request [XHR]. Browser L receives the session description object offer and generates a session description object answer, which is sent back to browser M using the same method. Once the offer/answer exchange is complete, hole punching (and key negotiation) can begin, and eventually the exchange of media packets.

Browser L closes the connection, which causes the Peer Connection to be closed and all permissions for microphone and cameras.

2.2.2 Session Establishment in WebRTC Trapezoid

The call flow for the WebRTC Trapezoid of Figure 1.5 is shown in Figure 2.5 below.

In this scenario, browsers M and L exchange media directly, despite running web applications from different web servers. The session description objects from each browser are mapped to a Jingle [XEP-0166] session-initiate message and session-accept method. Currently, the defined mapping of Jingle to and from Session Description Protocol [XEP-0167] does not include the WebRTC extensions and attributes of SDP, but it could be extended to do so.

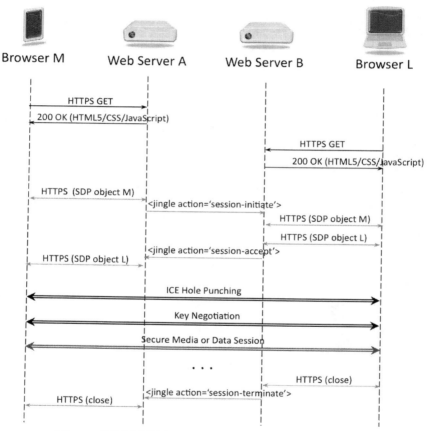

Figure 2.5 WebRTC Trapezoid Call Flow with Jingle

Note that this scenario could alternatively have mapped the session description objects to SDP and used SIP signaling between the browsers. No changes to the SIP protocol are needed to do this.

2.2.3 WebRTC Session Establishment with SIP Endpoint

WebRTC interworking with SIP [RFC3261] is shown in detail in Figure 2.6 below. This corresponds with Figure 1.4. WebRTC defines the mapping of the session description object offers and answers to SIP, which can be carried without modification or extension in normal SIP INVITE and 200 OK messages.

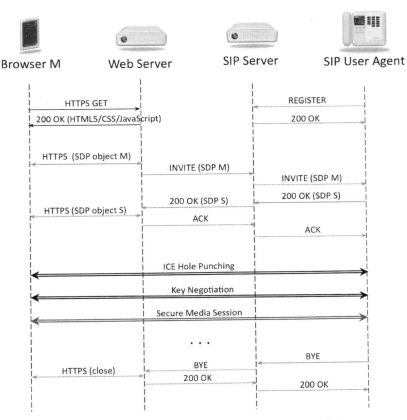

Figure 2.6 WebRTC Interoperating with SIP Call Flow

2.2.4 WebRTC Session Establishment with Jingle Endpoint

Figure 2.7 shows how WebRTC can interoperate with Jingle. This corresponds to Figure 1.4 and works in a similar way to the mapping described in Section 2.2.2. The media can be directly between the browser and the Jingle client provided the Jingle protocol is extended to support WebRTC SDP extensions, and the Jingle client supports the WebRTC media extensions.

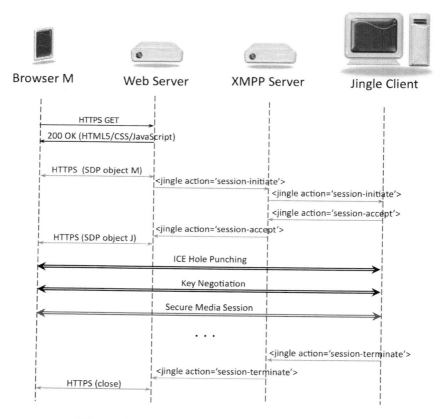

Figure 2.7 WebRTC Interoperating with Jingle

2.2.5 WebRTC Session Establishment with PSTN

Figure 2.8 shows how WebRTC can interoperate with the PSTN. This corresponds to Figure 1.7. The signaling between the Web Server and the PSTN Gateway could utilize any number of signaling or control protocols, or even a SIP trunk [SIP-CONNECT]. The PSTN Gateway terminates the WebRTC media session and connects the audio to a PSTN trunk or line. The G.711 (PCM) codec should be negotiated between the browser and the PSTN Gateway to avoid having to transcode or convert the audio signal.

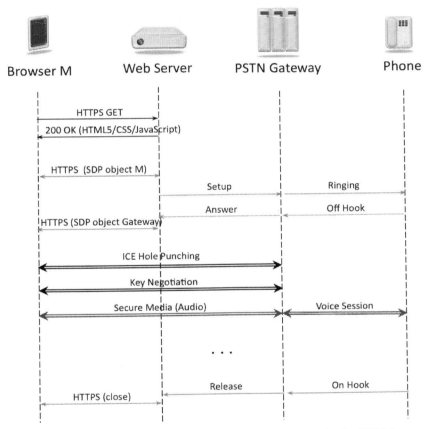

Figure 2.8 WebRTC Session Establishment with the PSTN

2.2.6 WebRTC Session Establishment with SIP and Media Gateway

A slightly different way for WebRTC to interwork with SIP is shown in Figures 2.9 and 2.10. In this example, the media is no longer completely end-to-end. Instead, a Media Gateway is used to terminate the ICE and SRTP, and the media is forwarded to the SIP UA, perhaps even as unencrypted RTP, although this should only be done if the VoIP network utilizes some other security protocol such as IPsec [IPSEC]. This is how VoIP and video endpoints that do not support all the RTP extensions of WebRTC could interwork with WebRTC.

The Media Gateway could also be a border element, known as a Session Border Controller (SBC), used to enable firewall traversal at the edge of a enterprise or service provider network

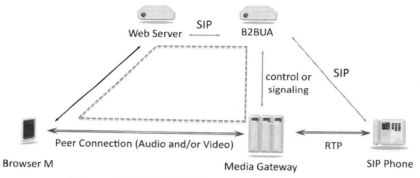

Figure 2.9 WebRTC Alternative SIP Interworking

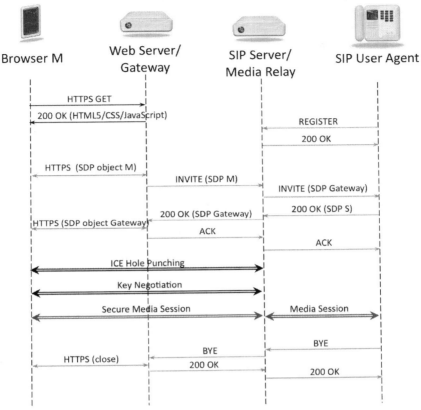

Figure 2.10 Alternative WebRTC Interworking with Media Gateway

2.3 WebRTC Pseudo-Code Example

This section contains a simple example corresponding to the media flows in Figures 1.9 and 5.3 through 5.6. The sample code has been made to look much like real code as one might see when using the WebRTC API; however, to keep the control flow simple to follow it is NOT real code. Additionally, in some places in the code we provide only comments rather than actual code, either because that code is irrelevant and out of scope for WebRTC, or because it has not been defined yet. For that reason we refer to this as pseudo code. You should in particular be aware of the following: no HTML code is shown, although the outputs (display, speakers, etc.) are assumed to have been set up; the media constraints shown have not been defined, although constraints similar to them are under discussion; real code would have error handling, but this has none; and finally, real WebRTC JavaScript code makes use of asynchronous callbacks for many function

25

calls — as a result, pseudo code shown here executing sequentially would not execute properly as JavaScript without waiting for each individual callback to complete. With these caveats, the remaining text of this section describes the examples. (Note that in the next few chapters of the book we will be building up a real, runnable code example that does not have these limitations.)

The WebRTC specification contains an example in section 10 [EXAMPLE] showing code that is intended to run on both the caller and called sites. For easier understanding, to show different media streams in the two directions, and to show different arrangements of when the local media is obtained, the following example is shown in two separate code segments. The first segment is the code running on the mobile device, and it is hard-coded to place a call (as opposed to receiving one). It obtains local media first, then sets up the connection with the remote peer (laptop). It then creates new media streams from the local ones, attaches them to the new RTCPeerConnection, and sends the ids of the media streams to the remote peer so it can distinguish among them. Finally, it starts the call by creating an SDP offer, notifying the browser of the session description via setLocalDescription(), and sending it to the remote peer.

The second segment is the code running on the laptop, and it is hard-coded to receive a call (as opposed to placing one). It is similar in many respects. Unlike the first code segment, though, all of the real work of obtaining local media, attaching streams to the peer connection, and creating and sending an SDP answer all take place only after a message is received on the signaling channel. Until then it waits.

Note in this code snippet that the local media is not obtained until *after* the message is received on the signaling channel. If obtaining the user's permission to access the local devices is a slow process, a real-world application might want to obtain the local media in advance of waiting for a call. Notice also that the call to answer() is not done until we have actually received the offer from the caller. Finally, the code to process incoming messages on the signaling channel needs to expect the stream ids from the caller.

2.3.1 Pseudo Code for Mobile Browser

```
/////////////////////
//  THIS IS PSEUDO CODE.  Yes, it looks just like real code.
//  DON'T BE FOOLED.
//  Don't expect this to run anywhere!
//  The real code is in the next few chapters of the book.
/////////////////////

var pc;
var configuration =
  {"iceServers":[{"url":"stun:198.51.100.9"},
                 {"url":"turn:198.51.100.2",
                  "credential":"myPassword"}]};
var microphone, application, front, rear;
var presentation, presenter, demonstration;
var remote_av, stereo, mono;
var display, left, right;

var signalingChannel = createSignalingChannel();
///////////////////////////////////////////////////////////////
//  Step zero is to set up the signaling channel.  There is no
//  requirement on how this is done.  The identity of the peer
//  is determined during the setup of the signaling channel.
//  As a result, the RTCPeerConnection itself does not
//  have any configuration info indicating the identity of
//  the peer. The preliminary code snippets below assume that
//  this signaling channel has a send() method and an onmessage
//  handler.  The former sends its argument to the peer, where
//  it causes the onmessage handler to execute.
///////////////////////////////////////////////////////////////

//////////////////////////////////////
// These are the four main calls
//////////////////////////////////////

// First, obtain local media
getMedia();

// Next, create the peer connection
createPC();

// Attach media to the peer connection
attachMedia();

// Generate and send SDP offer to peer
call();


/////////////////////
// Below this point are the function and handler definitions
/////////////////////

// Get local media
function getMedia() {
    // get local audio (microphone)
    navigator.getUserMedia({"audio": true }, function (stream) {
      microphone = stream;
    });
```

27

```
    // get local video (application sharing)
    ///// This is outside the scope of this specification.
    ///// Assume that 'application' has been set to this stream.
    //

    // get local video (front-facing camera)
    constraint =
      {"video": {"mandatory": {"facingMode": "environment"}}};
    navigator.getUserMedia(constraint, function (stream) {
      front = stream;
    });

    // get local video (rear-facing camera)
    constraint =
      {"video": {"mandatory": {"facingMode": "user"}}};
    navigator.getUserMedia(constraint, function (stream) {
      rear = stream;
    });
}

// Create a Peer Connection and set callbacks
function createPC() {
    pc = new RTCPeerConnection(configuration);

    // send any ice candidates to the other peer
    pc.onicecandidate = function (evt) {
        signalingChannel.send(
          JSON.stringify({ "candidate": evt.candidate }));
    };

    // process addition of remote streams
    pc.onaddstream =
      function (evt) {handleIncomingStream(evt.stream);};
}

// attach media to PC
function attachMedia() {
    // Create streams to send
    presentation =
      new MediaStream(
        [microphone.getAudioTracks()[0],       // Audio
         application.getVideoTracks()[0]]); // Presentation
    presenter =
      new MediaStream(
        [microphone.getAudioTracks()[0],       // Audio
         front.getVideoTracks()[0]]);          // Presenter
    demonstration =
      new MediaStream(
        [microphone.getAudioTracks()[0],       // Audio
         rear.getVideoTracks()[0]]);           // Demonstration

    // Add streams to Peer Connection
    pc.addStream(presentation);
    pc.addStream(presenter);
    pc.addStream(demonstration);

    // Send stream ids to remote peer as a JSON string
    // **before** SDP negotiation, i.e., before media
```

```
    // begins flowing.
    signalingChannel.send(
      JSON.stringify({ "presentation": presentation.id,
                       "presenter": presenter.id,
                       "demonstration": demonstration.id
      }));
}

// initiate a call by creating and sending an SDP offer
function call() {
    // Note at this point that we have not yet begun the media
    // offer/answer process, so no media is flowing.

    // Create an SDP offer based on the current set of streams
    // and ICE candidates.  gotDescription() will be called with
    // this offer.
    pc.createOffer(gotDescription);

    // This function acts based on an SDP offer just
    // created by the browser.
    function gotDescription(desc) {
        // First, tell the browser that this SDP offer is my
        // local session description.
        pc.setLocalDescription(desc);

        // Send the offer to the peer as a JSON string
        signalingChannel.send(JSON.stringify({ "sdp": desc }));
    }
}

// do something with remote streams as they appear
function handleIncomingStream(s) {
  // save handles for all incoming streams.  For the
  // av_stream, present it.
  if (s.getVideoTracks().length == 1) {
    // then this must be the av_stream
    av_stream = s;
    show_av(av_stream);
  } else if (s.getAudioTracks().length == 2) {
    // then this must be the stereo stream
    stereo = s;
  } else {
    // must be the mono stream
    mono = s;
  }
}

// display/play streams by attaching them to elements
function show_av(s) {
  // display is a video element, while left and right are audio
  // elements
  display.src = URL.createObjectURL(
                new MediaStream(s.getVideoTracks()[0]));
  left.src = URL.createObjectURL(
                new MediaStream(s.getAudioTracks()[0]));
  right.src = URL.createObjectURL(
                new MediaStream(s.getAudioTracks()[1]));
}
```

```
// handle incoming messages from the peer.  They will either be
// SDP or they will be ICE candidates.
signalingChannel.onmessage = function (msg) {
    // first parse the JSON event data back into an object
    var signal = JSON.parse(msg.data);

    if (signal.sdp) {
        // If this is SDP from the peer, tell the browser it is
        // the remote's session description.
        pc.setRemoteDescription(
          new RTCSessionDescription(signal.sdp));
    } else {
        // If not, this must be a candidate from the peer.  Tell
        // the browser that this is a candidate IP address
        // through which the media could possibly reach the
        //  peer.  The browser will then use ICE to try to reach
        // this address.
        pc.addIceCandidate(
          new RTCIceCandidate(signal.candidate));
    }
};
```

2.3.2 Pseudo Code for Laptop Browser

```
///////////////////
//   THIS IS PSEUDO CODE.  Yes, it looks just like real code.
//   DON'T BE FOOLED.
//   Don't expect this to run anywhere!
//   The real code is in the next few chapters of the book.
///////////////////

var pc;
var configuration =
  {"iceServers":[{"url":"stun:198.51.100.9"},
                 {"url":"turn:198.51.100.2",
                  "credential":"myPassword"}]};
var webcam, left, right;
var av, stereo, mono;
var incoming;
var speaker, win1, win2, win3;

var signalingChannel = createSignalingChannel();
//////////////////////////////////////////////////////////////////
//   Step zero is to set up the signaling channel.  There is no
//   requirement on how this is done.  The identity of the peer
//   is determined during the setup of the signaling channel.
//   As a result, the RTCPeerConnection itself does not
//   have any configuration info indicating the identity of
//   the peer. The preliminary code snippets below assume that
//   this signaling channel has a send() method and an onmessage
//   handler.  The former sends its argument to the peer, where
//   it causes the onmessage handler to execute.
//////////////////////////////////////////////////////////////////

// At this end we basically just wait for an SDP offer to come
// our way before we set up the peer connection, obtain local
// media, and attach it.

// There isn't really anything to answer.  This just creates a
// PC and the handlers to deal with incoming streams.  It also
// sets up media.  It is called by the signaling channel's
// onmessage handler.
function prepareForIncomingCall() {
    // First, create the Peer Connection
    createPC();

    // Next, obtain local media
    getMedia();

    // Attach media to the peer connection
    attachMedia();
}

///////////////////
// Below this point are the function and handler definitions
///////////////////

// Create a Peer Connection and set callbacks
function createPC() {
    pc = new RTCPeerConnection(configuration);
```

31

```
    // send any ice candidates to the other peer
    pc.onicecandidate = function (evt) {
        signalingChannel.send(
            JSON.stringify({ "candidate": evt.candidate }));
    };

    // process addition of remote streams
    pc.onaddstream =
            function (evt) {handleIncomingStream(evt.stream);};
}

// Get local media
function getMedia() {

    // get local video (webcam)
    navigator.getUserMedia({"video": true }, function (stream) {
      webcam = stream;
    });

    // get local audio (left stereo channel)
    // note that "direction" has not been defined as
    // a constraint
    constraint =
      {"audio": {"mandatory": {"direction": "left"}}};
    navigator.getUserMedia(constraint, function (stream) {
      left = stream;
    });

    // get local audio (right stereo channel)
    // note that "direction" has not been defined as a
    // constraint
    constraint =
      {"audio": {"mandatory": {"direction": "right"}}};
    navigator.getUserMedia(constraint, function (stream) {
      right = stream;
    });
}

// attach media to PC
function attachMedia() {
    // Create streams to send
    av = new MediaStream(
            [webcam.getVideoTracks()[0],        // Video
             left.getAudioTracks()[0],          // Left audio
             right.getAudioTracks()[0]]);       // Right audio
    stereo = new MediaStream(
                [left.getAudioTracks()[0],      // Left audio
                 right.getAudioTracks()[0]]);   // Right audio

    mono = left;        // Treat the left audio as the mono stream

    // Add streams to Peer Connection
    pc.addStream(av);
    pc.addStream(stereo);
    pc.addStream(mono);

    // Note that here we don't need to inform the remote peer of
    // the stream ids because the streams are uniquely identified
    // by what they contain.
```

```
}

// answer the call by creating and sending an SDP answer
function answer() {
    // Note at this point that we have not begun the media
    // offer/answer process, so no media is flowing.

    // Create an SDP answer based on the remote session
    // description, which the browser already has, and
    // the current set of streams and ICE
    // candidates.  gotDescription() will be called with this
    // answer.
    pc.createAnswer(gotDescription);

    // This function acts based on an SDP answer just
    // created by the browser.
    function gotDescription(desc) {
        // First, tell the browser that this SDP answer is my
        // local session description.
        pc.setLocalDescription(desc);

        // Send the answer to the peer as a JSON string
        signalingChannel.send(JSON.stringify({ "sdp": desc }));
    }
}

// do something with remote streams as they appear
function handleIncomingStream(s) {
    // take audio from only one stream but display all video
    // tracks
    if (s.id === incoming.presentation) {
        // use audio and display presentation screen
        speaker.src = URL.createObjectURL(
                    new MediaStream(s.getAudioTracks()[0]));
        win1.src = URL.createObjectURL(
                    new MediaStream(s.getVideoTracks()[0]));
    } else if (s.id === incoming.presenter) {
        // display presenter
        win2.src = URL.createObjectURL(
                    new MediaStream(s.getVideoTracks()[0]));
    } else {
        // must be demonstration, so display it
        win3.src = URL.createObjectURL(
                    new MediaStream(s.getVideoTracks()[0]));
    }
}

// handle incoming messages from the peer.  They will be
// SDP, ICE candidates, or a structure containing remote
// session ids.
signalingChannel.onmessage = function (msg) {
    // first create a peer connection to answer the call if not
    // already done
    if (!pc) {
        prepareForIncomingCall();
    }
    // now parse the JSON event data back into an object
    var signal = JSON.parse(msg.data);
```

33

```
if (signal.sdp) {
    // If this is SDP from the peer, tell the browser it is
    // the remote's session description and send an SDP
    // answer.
    pc.setRemoteDescription(
      new RTCSessionDescription(signal.sdp));
    answer();
} else if (signal.candidate) {
    // If this is a candidate from the peer, tell
    // the browser that this is a candidate IP address
    // through which the media could possibly reach the
    // peer.  The browser will then use ICE to try to reach
    // this address.
    pc.addIceCandidate(new RTCIceCandidate(signal.candidate));
} else {
    // This must be an object containing the ids of the streams
    // the remote peer will be sending.  Save it for use when
    // the streams appear.
    incoming = signal;
}
};
```

2.4 References

[XHR]   http://www.w3.org/TR/XMLHttpRequest

[XEP-0166]   http://xmpp.org/extensions/xep-0166.html

[XEP-0167]   http://xmpp.org/extensions/xep-0167.html

[RFC3261]   http://tools.ietf.org/html/rfc3261

[SIP-CONNECT] http://www.sipforum.org/sipconnect

[IPSEC] http://tools.ietf.org/html/rfc4301

[EXAMPLE]
    http://dev.w3.org/2011/webrtc/editor/webrtc.html#examples-and-call-flows

3 LOCAL MEDIA

The WebRTC effort involves not only the definition of how media is to be transmitted between two WebRTC peers, but the definition of media itself. This chapter describes the media model for WebRTC, how local media is obtained, and how it can be controlled. Later chapters will describe how the media is transmitted between peers.

3.1 Media in WebRTC

3.1.1 Tracks

The foundational media unit in WebRTC is a `MediaStreamTrack`. This track represents the media of a single type that a single device or recording, called a source, could return. A single stereo source or a 6-channel surround sound audio signal could be treated as a single track, even though both consist of multiple channels of audio. Note that the specification does not define a means to access or manipulate media at the channel level, although it does roughly define channels as having a "well known relationship to each other". From a practical standpoint, the contents of a track are defined in the WebRTC document as "intended to be encoded together for transmission as, for instance, an RTP payload type." In other words, the channels of a track are treated together as a single unit when being transported using a Peer Connection, and even locally with respect to being enabled/disabled or muted.

Every track is associated with a source. We'll get to how this happens in a moment, but for now know that WebRTC does not provide direct access to or control over sources. All control over a source is via a track. The relationship between a `MediaStreamTrack` and its source is undergoing some changes at the moment, but the current direction is towards a track that can be not only the raw media from the source, but perhaps a transformed version provided by the browser. For example, a track might represent a downsampled version of a video that is being recorded by a camera at a higher native resolution.

Different `MediaStreamTrack` objects can represent the same media source, which will be explained more fully in the following section describing `MediaStream` objects. There are two ways in which tracks can have their media suspended: via muting and via disabling. The muting/unmuting of a track is something done by the user and/or browser, indicating that the track's underlying media source is temporarily unable to provide media. This can happen, for example, if the end user has suspended permission to use the media source by clicking a mute button in the browser chrome or toggling a switch on the side of their phone. In general, the application does not have control over when a track is muted. It can, however, check the value of the track's `muted` attribute. When muted, an audio track will have silence and a video track will show blackness. Separately, tracks can be disabled individually by setting the track object's `enabled` attribute to `false`. Both of these attributes are separate from the `readyState` attribute of a track that indicates its status – `new`, `live` or `ended`. A new track is one which has not yet been connected to media, while an ended track is one whose source is not providing and can never again provide more data. This could occur, for example, if a camera in use is then unplugged. A live track is one that could produce media. Since these attributes are independent, as an example one could perhaps have a track that is `live`, `unmuted`, and `disabled`.

3.1.2 Streams

A `MediaStream`, then, is a collection of `MediaStreamTrack` objects. There are two ways to create these `MediaStream` objects – by requesting access to local media by copying tracks from an existing `MediaStream`, or by receiving a new stream using a Peer Connection. Currently the only way to request and access local media is through a `getUserMedia()` call, although in the future there may be other methods, for example, to stream from a local file. One can "copy" the tracks of an existing `MediaStream` object into a new one via the `MediaStream` constructor, which takes as an argument either an existing `MediaStream` object or a list of `MediaStreamTrack` objects. It is also possible to specify no arguments at all, along with the ability to add tracks to (`addTrack()`) and remove tracks from (`removeTrack()`) an existing `MediaStream`, but this is not yet widely supported. The `clone()` method may also be used to duplicate a stream (and all its tracks) for those who find passing a `MediaStream` to a constructor offensive. Note that in a derived media stream (i.e., created from other `MediaStream`s), the elements of the array argument to the `MediaStream` constructor need not all come from the same existing

MediaStream object; mixing and matching is allowed. Tracks may also be of different types, with both audio and video allowed within the same MediaStream object. Regardless of how the MediaStream object is created, a key characteristic is that all of the tracks within the MediaStream object will be synchronized when rendered. However, tracks are not ordered within a stream, and any attempt to add a duplicate track will be silently ignored. Since each track has an id which is preserved across Peer Connections, it is possible to match up tracks in a MediaStream which is sent over a Peer Connection by checking ids after calling getAudioTracks() or getVideoTracks() or even by directly requesting a track via getTrackById(). Similar to the ended status of tracks, a MediaStream has a Boolean ended attribute indicating whether the MediaStream is finished. A MediaStream is considered finished if all of its tracks are ended.

3.2 Capturing Local Media

WebRTC defines a new JavaScript method specifically for requesting access to local media:

```
// request access to audio and video
getUserMedia({"audio":true, "video":true},
             gotUserMedia, didntGetUserMedia);
function gotUserMedia(s) {
  console.log(
    "Should be one audio track: " + s.getAudioTracks().length);
  console.log(
    "Should be one video track: " + s.getVideoTracks().length);
}
function gotUserMedia(s) {
  var myVideoElement = getElementById("myvideoelement");

  // play captured MediaStream via video element
  myVideoElement.srcObject = s;
}
```

In this example we request a media stream containing one audio track and one video track. Note that getUserMedia() itself does not return a value. The user agent is not permitted to return access to a source until it has received user permission (see Figure 3.6), which can take seconds or more. To ensure that the entire JavaScript thread does not halt, the stream is returned via a callback, in this example gotUserMedia. This callback will only be called if the requested media was successfully obtained. Otherwise, the error callback will be called. We'll look at how source selection works in the next section on constraints, but first let's look at what sources are and how they're used. The Media Capture and Streams specification gives a fairly good description of this. A source is only a theoretical entity; the browser makes a source available in whatever way it wishes to based on devices that are available, although in practice there is likely to be a close correlation between physical devices and browser-provided sources. Permissions are tied to sources and each track has its own association to a specific source, although multiple tracks can be associated with the same source.

The example above shows one other new feature provided in WebRTC – the srcObject property added to media elements for use in *direct assignment*. Until recently, the Media Capture and Streams specification defined (and recommended the use of) createObjectURL to create a URL from a MediaStream that could be assigned to the src property of the JavaScript object returned by getElementById(). Unfortunately, there were some problems with the use of a Blob URL that were, ultimately, outside the scope of the specification. Now the specification defines the new srcObject property on all existing media elements such as <audio> and <video>. Any MediaStream object can be assigned directly to this property.

3.3 Media Selection and Control

Although the WebRTC APIs provide no direct control over sources, the selection of sources and control over their properties is provided via constraints. It's easiest to understand how this works if we look first at manipulating an existing track. Let's say you have obtained access to the local video camera:

```
var t;   // will hold the track

// request access to video
getUserMedia({"video":true},
              gotUserMedia, didntGetUserMedia);
function gotUserMedia(s) {
  t = (s.getVideoTracks())[0];

  // get current capabilities
  console.log("Capabilites are\n" +
           JSON.stringify(t.getCapabilities() + "\n");

  // set constraints
  var constraints = {
    "mandatory": {"aspectRatio": 1.3333333333},
    "optional":  [{"width":  {"min": 640}},
                  {"height": {"max": 400}}]
  };
  t.applyConstraints(constraints, successCB, failureCB);
}

function successCB() {
  console.log("Settings are\n" +
           JSON.stringify(t.getSettings() + "\n");
```

```
}
```

This could result in the following printed out on the console:

```
Capabilities are
{"width": {"min": 320, "max": 1800},
 "height": {"min": 240, "max": 1200},
 "aspectRatio": {"min": 1, "max": 1.5},
 "facingMode": ["user", "environment"]
}
Settings are
{"width": 640, "height": 480, "aspectRatio": 1.3333333333,
 "facingMode": "user"}
```

There are two types of constrainable properties: enumerated or range. Enumerated properties can be any value out of a discrete set of string values. Range properties are given as min/max values. A call to `getCapabilities()` returns an object containing all constrainable properties, along with their allowed values – min/max values for ranges and a list of values for enumerated properties. A call to `getSettings()` returns all constrainable properties, along with their current values – one value for each. The interesting part here is the call to `applyConstraints()`. This call is used to affect the settings for the constrainable properties. The use of the word "affect" is intentional here. The goal of the constraint mechanism is to provide a useful middle ground between the desire of application developers to be able to control parameters of sources and the desire of browser (user agent) implementers to be able to "just do the right thing". Think of the constraint mechanism as a sophisticated default-setting system – it allows the application developer to specify only down to the level of detail that matters to the application and letting the browser choose beyond that point. For example, the browser may be able to make rapid changes to codec parameters to deal with varying levels of network congestion, but it is only the application that knows what video resolutions will work for the application. Some applications, for example a remote surgery application, may be able to tolerate a slow refresh rate but only be effective if the resolution of the camera is very high. Other applications, for example the broadcast of a football match, may be able to tolerate a lowering of resolution while the ball is in the air but need to be able to refresh rapidly to make obvious where on the field the ball is going. The constraint mechanism allows the developer to control the parameters that are crucial for their application while allowing flexibility for the browser to act intelligently in other respects.

Here's how constraints work: a constraints structure (called a `Constraints` in the specification) is an object with two optional properties: `mandatory` and `optional`. Either or both may be given values. The value

41

given for the `mandatory` property is a single object containing any of the constrainable properties with values that must be satisfied in order for the success callback to be called. In our example, we are requiring that the `aspectRatio` be set to 1.3333333333. `aspectRatio` is a range property for which `min` and/or `max` values can be set. In this case we are using the allowed shortcut syntax of setting a single value. This is equivalent to setting both `max` and `min` to the same value. The value and interpretation of the optional property in a constraint structure are different. The value is an array (ordered list) of objects, each of which can contain any of the constrainable properties with values that are desired. The browser will attempt to satisfy as many of the objects as possible, but there is no error if any cannot be satisfied. The ordering of these objects is significant, such that if two entries in the array are each individually satisfiable but not jointly satisfiable the one occurring earlier in the array will be satisfied. This actually occurs in the example above. Assuming our example `applyConstraints()` call succeeds, our video track will have the given `aspectRatio`, since it's mandatory. If possible, the track will then have a minimum `width` of 640 pixels. Assuming that constraint is satisfied, the minimum height would then have to be 640/1.3333333333 = 480, which exceeds that requested in the next constraint object in our `optional` list. Thus, if the first optional constraint is satisfied the second cannot be.

Now let's look at initial track selection.

```
var constraints = {
    "mandatory": {"aspectRatio": 1.3333333333},
    "optional":  [{"width":  {"min": 640}},
                  {"height": {"max": 400}}]
};
getUserMedia({"video": constraints}, successCB, failureCB);
```

We have retained the same constraints as in the previous example, but now they are being given to `getUserMedia()`. The primary difference here is that the constraints are used to select a source rather than to control it. The `getUserMedia()` call will only return a `MediaStream` containing tracks pointing to sources that can currently satisfy all given mandatory constraints. When returned, the track will be constrained according to the constraints given. The other thing that is different is that a special syntax is permitted for selection that we used in our first example: `{"video":true, "audio":true}`. This syntax indicates which track types we want returned, but without specifying any constraints.

With any constrained track, it is possible that changes to the source can affect the ability of the source to satisfy all the constraints of all the tracks currently tied to the source. An example is a situation where the user manually changes a switch on the device that selects or prevents certain configurations. In any case, after successful acquisition of a track or successful application of constraints, if the track's constraints can no longer be satisfied, the track is considered to be *overconstrained*. If this happens the track will be muted by the browser and the `overconstrained` event will be thrown. It is highly recommended that applications assign a handler to each track's `onoverconstrained` property to address this case.

The number of constrainable properties currently defined for tracks is fairly small (see Section 8.3.2), but the properties are (or will be, when the specification is done) stored in an IANA registry (see Section 11.4.1) that allows for new properties to be defined as needed.

3.4 Media Streams Example

For the media sources of Figure 1.9, one arrangement of tracks and streams is shown in Figures 3.1 through 3.4. In this example, Figures 3.1 and 3.3 show the media flowing from browser M to browser L, and Figures 3.2 and 3.4 show the reverse. The first thing to notice is that the media flow is not symmetrical, with completely different streams flowing in one direction than in the other.

Beginning with Figure 3.1, four different media sources are available for use on this device: microphone audio, application sharing video, front camera video, and rear camera video. Through four separate calls to `getUserMedia()`, four separate local `MediaStreams` are created. The JavaScript application code then creates three new `MediaStream` objects by mixing and matching. Specifically, the first `MediaStream` contains new audio and video `MediaStreamTracks` pulled from the `MediaStreamTracks` in the local Audio (microphone audio source) and Presentation Video (application sharing video source) `MediaStreams`.

Similarly, the second `MediaStream` contains new `MediaStreamTracks` for the microphone audio and the front camera video derived from the originals in the local `MediaStreams`. Finally, the third `MediaStream` contains new `MediaStreamTracks` for the microphone audio and the rear camera video derived from the originals in the local `MediaStreams`.

Streams from Browser M to Browser L

At this point the application code now has four local `MediaStream` objects and three derived `MediaStream` objects. Notice that the microphone audio track has been duplicated three times. The application then decides to send the three derived `MediaStream` objects to the remote peer (on browser L). Figure 3.3 shows how these streams appear after coming across the Peer Connection from browser M. Notice what the application code on browser L then does with these. It pulls the audio track from the Presentation `MediaStream` and sends it to the speaker, it pulls the video track from the same `MediaStream` and sends it to one window on the display, it pulls the video track from the Presenter `MediaStream` and sends it to another window, and it pulls the video track from the final `MediaStream` and sends it to yet another window. Although not shown, the application can figure out which stream is which because each stream has a unique id that is

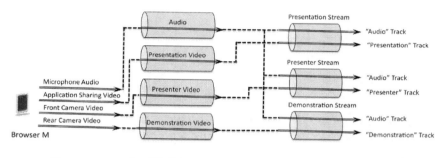

Figure 3.1 Browser M Sending Sources, Streams, and Tracks

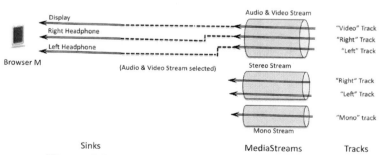

Figure 3.2 Browser M Receiving Tracks, Streams, and Sinks

preserved across the Peer Connection. Of course, Browser L would need to be told which id is the Presentation stream, which the Presenter, etc. The code on Browser M would likely send this information over the signaling channel.

Streams from Browser L to Browser M

A similar process occurs for the streams originating on browser L that are sent to browser M. In Figure 3.4, on the right-hand side, we can see that there are three media sources being used – a webcam video, a left microphone, and a right microphone. As in the other direction, each is obtained through a separate call to `getUserMedia()` resulting in three separate local `MediaStream` objects. These are then mixed into three new derived `MediaStream` objects. The first contains all three tracks, the second contains both audio tracks to make a stereo audio stream, and the third contains only the right audio track to make a mono audio stream. These new `MediaStream` objects are the ones sent over the Peer Connection to browser M.

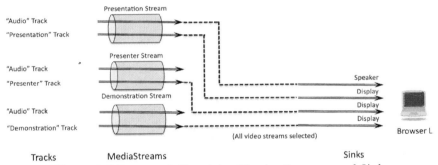

Figure 3.3 Browser L Receiving Tracks, Streams, and Sinks

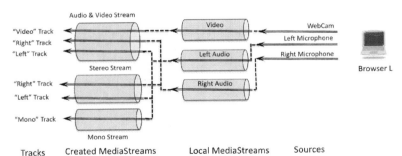

Figure 3.4 Browser L Sending Sources, Streams, and Tracks

Figure 3.2 shows how these streams appear after coming across the Peer Connection from browser L. The JavaScript application code in browser M decides to create two new `MediaStreams` – one containing the video from the only `MediaStream` containing a video track, and one containing the

45

audio from one of the three streams, the choice of which is controlled by a button on the display.

3.5 Local Media Runnable Code Example

Over the course of the next few chapters we will be building up a comprehensive, yet simple, WebRTC example with local media, signaling, peer connections, and data channels. We begin our simple WebRTC demo with a web server and a single HTML page. We include the code for the server for two reasons. First, in coming chapters we will be adding code on the server side to implement our signaling channel, and this provides a baseline so it will be easier to see the changes. Second, many online code examples for WebRTC only work if you sign up for some other online service, and we believe it is useful to provide a complete example, both client and server, that you can experiment with yourself. We often test out ideas on our local machines, without needing any access to the Internet. The next two sections present the web server code and the HTML application. The former is completely generic and is independent of the WebRTC APIs.

3.5.1 Web Server

In their simplest form, WebRTC applications are web applications, meaning that they are accessed from web servers using web browsers. In general the web server provides two useful functions for WebRTC applications: serving the web application itself and acting as a relay (providing a "signaling channel") between two or more browsers that can be used to negotiate the destination, type, and format of media to be communicated between the browsers. Server code for a simple HTTP-based signaling channel will be presented in Section 4.5.

Any modern web server is capable of providing these two functions, although there is an important property of WebRTC application requirements that must be considered. WebRTC applications are *real-time*. Since human beings are waiting on the completion of connection setups, and since they are accustomed to rapid call connections on the PSTN, if the web server is used to provide the signaling channel, then efficient synchronization across requests from browsers intending to communicate is mandatory.

Broadly speaking, web servers fall into one of two categories: a multi-threaded, separate process per request server that makes file retrieval simple but inter-request synchronization complex, or a single-threaded process that makes inter-request synchronization simple but input/output such as file retrieval more complex. The Apache web server is a quintessential example of the former, and Node.js of the latter.

This demo makes use of Node.js (called "Node" from here on) as the server framework because

1) it dramatically simplifies the communication between separate browser requests, and
2) it uses the asynchronous JavaScript programming model with which most web programmers are already familiar.

For more information on Node, please see the Glossary. This demo makes use only of standard built-in Node packages.

We begin by looking at index.js.

3.5.1.1 index.js

```
// Copyright 2013-2014 Digital Codex LLC
// You may use this code for your own education. If you use it
// largely intact, or develop something from it, don't claim
// that your code came first. You are using this code completely
// at your own risk. If you rely on it to work in any particular
// way, you're an idiot and we won't be held responsible.

var server = require("./server");
var log = require("./log").log;
var port = process.argv[2] || 5001;

// returns 404
function fourohfour(info) {
  var res = info.res;
  log("Request handler fourohfour was called.");
  res.writeHead(404, {"Content-Type": "text/plain"});
  res.write("404 Page Not Found");
  res.end();
}

var handle = {};
handle["/"] = fourohfour;

server.serveFilePath("static");
server.start(handle, port);
```

Assuming you already have Node installed, the demo can be run by calling "node index.js 5001".

The code in this file does the following:

1) it loads the server code in "server.js" and the logging code in "log.js",
2) it specifies how certain custom URI paths are to be handled,
3) it specifies the directory containing static files that can be served, and
4) it starts the web server.

Let's next look at the server code in " server.js".

3.5.1.2 server.js

```
// Copyright 2013-2014 Digital Codex LLC
// You may use this code for your own education.  If you use it
// largely intact, or develop something from it, don't claim
// that your code came first.  You are using this code completely
// at your own risk.  If you rely on it to work in any particular
// way, you're an idiot and we won't be held responsible.

var http = require("http");
var url = require("url");
var fs = require('fs');

var log = require("./log").log;
var serveFileDir = "";


// Sets the path to the static files (HTML, JS, etc.)
function setServeFilePath(p) {
  serveFilePath = p;
}
exports.serveFilePath = setServeFilePath;


// Creates a handler to route the
// request based on the path name
function start(handle, port) {
  function onRequest(req, res) {
    var urldata = url.parse(req.url,true),
        pathname = urldata.pathname,
        info = {"res": res};

    log("Request for " + pathname + " received");
    route(handle, pathname, info);
  }

  http.createServer(onRequest).listen(port);

  log("Server started on port " + port);
}

exports.start = start;


// Determines whether requested path is a static file or a custom
// path with its own handler
function route(handle, pathname, info) {
  log("About to route a request for " + pathname);
  // Check if path after leading slash is an existing file that
  // can be served
  var filepath = createFilePath(pathname);
  log("Attempting to locate " + filepath);
  fs.stat(filepath, function(err, stats) {
    if (!err && stats.isFile()) {  // serve file
      serveFile(filepath, info);
    } else {                       // must be custom path
      handleCustom(handle, pathname, info);
    }
  });
```

```
}

// This function adds the serveFilePath to the beginning of the
// given pathname after removing .., ~, and other such
// problematic syntax bits from a security perspective.
// ** There is no claim that this is now secure **
function createFilePath(pathname) {
  var components = pathname.substr(1).split('/');
  var filtered = new Array(),
      temp;

  for(var i=0, len = components.length; i < len; i++) {
    temp = components[i];
    if (temp == "..") continue;    // no updir
    if (temp == "") continue;      // no root
    temp = temp.replace(/~/g,'');  // no userdir
    filtered.push(temp);
  }
  return (serveFilePath + "/" + filtered.join("/"));
}


// Opens, reads, and sends to the client the contents of the
// named file
function serveFile(filepath, info) {
  var res = info.res;

  log("Serving file " + filepath);
  fs.open(filepath, 'r', function(err, fd) {
    if (err) {log(err.message);
              noHandlerErr(filepath, res);
              return;}
    var readBuffer = new Buffer(20480);
    fs.read(fd, readBuffer, 0, 20480, 0,
      function(err, readBytes) {
        if (err) {log(err.message);
                  fs.close(fd);
                  noHandlerErr(filepath, res);
                  return;}
        log('just read ' + readBytes + ' bytes');
        if (readBytes > 0) {
          res.writeHead(200,
                      {"Content-Type": contentType(filepath)});
          res.write(readBuffer.toString('utf8', 0, readBytes));
        }
        res.end();
      });
  });
}


// Determine content type of fetched file
function contentType(filepath) {
  var index = filepath.lastIndexOf('.');

  if (index >= 0) {
    switch (filepath.substr(index+1)) {
      case "html": return ("text/html");
      case "js":   return ("application/javascript");
```

```
      case "css":   return ("text/css");
      case "txt":   return ("text/plain");
      default:      return ("text/html");
    }
  }
  return ("text/html");
}


// Confirm handler for non-file path, then execute it
function handleCustom(handle, pathname, info) {
  if (typeof handle[pathname] == 'function') {
    handle[pathname](info);
  } else {
    noHandlerErr(pathname, info.res);
  }
}


// If no handler is defined for the request, return 404
function noHandlerErr(pathname, res) {
  log("No request handler found for " + pathname);
  res.writeHead(404, {"Content-Type": "text/plain"});
  res.write("404 Page Not Found");
  res.end();
}
```

After loading the Node packages it needs and setting some variables, the code defines the two commands it exports – serveFilePath and start. The first one merely sets an internal variable that will be explained later.

The main method is start(). It uses Node's built-in http server module (http.createServer(onRequest).listen(port)) to start a server that listens on port 5001. The interesting part, though, is the onRequest handler. First, note that Node calls the onRequest handler for every request, sending it the request (the URI) and the res object to hold the response to send.

onRequest() first uses Node's built-in url parsing module to parse the relevant pieces of the request URI, logs receipt of the request, and then calls route().

The primary task of route() is to figure out whether the URI refers to a static file to be served or a custom path that needs its own special handler. It will call serveFile() for the former and handleCustom for the latter. One interesting complication is that file paths can be unsafe unless checked. route() first calls createFilePath before checking for the existence of a file with that (path)name.

createFilePath() checks for some common pathnames that would give access to files outside the official static file directory and removes them. Note that this code is not guaranteed to provide safety of file access. Writing such code, and explaining it, is beyond the scope of this book. However, there are other Node modules such as Express that have had more extensive work to provide security features. You should consider using it.

serveFile(), as mentioned before, asynchronously opens, reads, and responds with the requested file. It uses Node's built-in fs module along with the contentType() helper function.

contentType() examines the file's extension to determine an appropriate value for the Content-Type header in the HTTP response.

handleCustom(), the final piece of code in server.js, simply attempts to locate the custom path in the handle[] array passed into the start() function. If found, it executes the code stored there. Otherwise, it uses noHandlerErr() to return an HTTP 404.

For completeness, let's finish up with the server-side code by looking at the trivial "log.js" module, which makes it easy to enable or disable console logging.

3.5.1.3 log.js

```
// Copyright 2013-2014 Digital Codex LLC
// You may use this code for your own education.  If you use it
// largely intact, or develop something from it, don't claim
// that your code came first.  You are using this code completely
// at your own risk.  If you rely on it to work in any particular
// way, you're an idiot and we won't be held responsible.

var log = console.log;

exports.log = log
```

The explanation here is really simple. Basically, log logs to the console.

3.5.2 Client WebRTC Application

```
<!--
// Copyright 2013-2014 Digital Codex LLC
// You may use this code for your own education.  If you use it
// largely intact, or develop something from it, don't claim that
// your code came first.  You are using this code completely at
// your own risk.  If you rely on it to work in any particular
// way, you're an idiot and we won't be held responsible.
-->

<html>
<head>
  <meta http-equiv="Content-Type"
        content="text/html; charset=UTF-8" />
  <style>
    video {
      width:   320px;
      height:  240px;
      border:  1px solid black;
    }
    div {
      display:  inline-block;
```

```
      }
   </style>
</head>
<body>

<!-- load polyfill, local copy first for local testing -->
<script src="extra/adapter.js" type="text/javascript"></script>
<script
   src="https://webrtc.googlecode.com/svn/trunk/samples/js/base/adapter.js"
   type="text/javascript"></script>

<script>
var myVideoStream, myVideo;

/////////////////////////////
// This is the main routine.
/////////////////////////////

// This kicks off acquisition of local media.
window.onload = function () {

   myVideo = document.getElementById("myVideo");

   getMedia();
};


/////////////////////////////
// This next section is for getting local media
/////////////////////////////

function getMedia() {
   getUserMedia({"audio":true, "video":true},
               gotUserMedia, didntGetUserMedia);
}

function gotUserMedia(stream) {
   myVideoStream = stream;

   // display my local video to me
   attachMediaStream(myVideo, myVideoStream);
}

function didntGetUserMedia() {
   console.log("couldn't get video");
}

</script>

<div id="setup">
   <p>WebRTC Book Demo (local media only)</p>
</div>

<br/>

<div style="width:30%;vertical-align:top">
   <div>
      <video id="myVideo" autoplay="autoplay" controls
            muted="true"/>
```

```
    </div>
  </div>

  </body>
</html>
```

Before we dive into the JavaScript code, let's skip to the end of the file where the HTML markup lives. This initial version of the application is almost trivially simple, showing only a title and a video element. Figure 3.5 shows how this looks on Firefox.

Figure 3.5 Local Media Only in Firefox

Now let's go back up to the top. Skipping the CSS (Cascading Style Sheets) styling, which just sets how the video elements look and the div elements lay out on the screen, we come to two <script> lines. These lines load the adapter.js file that maps the standard API calls to the current non-standard names used by the various versions of Google Chrome and Mozilla Firefox. Only the second line is necessary, since it refers to the online location for this file. This file was created by Mozilla and Google. However, for offline testing it is convenient to copy this file locally. If you do, then the first line will try to load the local copy first.

The next <script> section contains all the JavaScript code that is unique to this simple application.

In this section, we first define all of our common variables. After this the core routine is defined first, as a function that is executed when the page finishes loading. Next, the code calls getMedia() to request access to local media.

The `getMedia()` function is quite simple, calling `getUserMedia` and requesting both audio and video. When it gets the media stream, which requires the user's permission for both the camera and microphone, it calls the `gotUserMedia()` callback with the stream. Figure 3.6 shows the permission request dialog on Firefox.

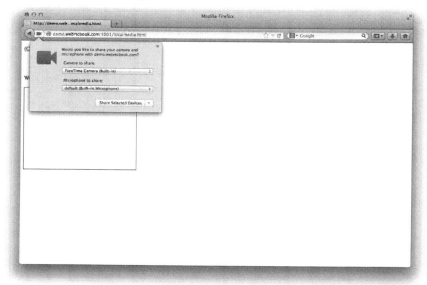

Figure 3.6 Permission Dialog in Firefox

`gotUserMedia()` saves the media stream in the `myVideoStream` variable and calls `attachMediaStream()` to display the new stream in the `myVideo` element. `attachMediaStream()` is a function in adapter.js that displays a stream in a video element. It is needed because Google Chrome and Mozilla Firefox use different syntaxes to accomplish this.

In a full application with good user handling, the `didntGetUserMedia()` callback would notify the user of a problem and offer options to resolve them. In this simple demo, it just logs the inability to get video. In this simple application it's not that big a deal, because the application can be restarted simply by reloading the page in the browser.

In case it isn't obvious, the server code in this example is very simplistic and potentially insecure. Please use good judgment in the development of your own server code!

4 SIGNALING

Signaling plays an important role in WebRTC but is not standardized, allowing the developer to choose. This lack of standardization and multiple options has resulted in some confusion. A number of different signaling approaches have been proposed and used, and an understanding of the differences between the approaches is useful in selecting the right one for a given WebRTC application.

4.1 The Role of Signaling

In real-time communications, signaling has four main roles:
1) Negotiation of media capabilities and settings
2) Identification and authentication of participants in a session
3) Controlling the media session, indicating progress, changing and terminating the session
4) Glare resolution, when both sides of a session try to establish or change a session at the same time.

The next sections will examine these functions in detail, showing how 1) is essential and standardized, while 2), 3), and 4) are optional or are just part of the web application in WebRTC.

4.1.1 Why Signaling is Not Standardized

Signaling is not standardized in WebRTC because it does not need to be standardized to enable interoperability between browsers. Signaling is effectively a matter between the web browser and the web server. The web server can ensure that both browsers utilize the same signaling protocol, using downloaded JavaScript code.

In the web model, only the minimum components are standardized, leaving web developers the freedom to choose and design all other aspects of web pages and applications. In practice, this means that only transport (HTTP), markup (HTML), and media (WebRTC) need to be standardized. As shown in Figure 4.1, the server selects the signaling protocol and ensures that users of the web application or site support the same protocol. Web servers A, B, and C do not need to use the same signaling protocol, but in each case the browsers are able to establish media sessions.

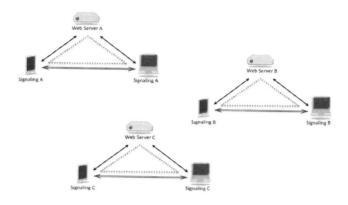

Figure 4.1 Web Server Chooses Signaling Protocol

Compare this situation to the general VoIP or video system where there is no way for a signaling or control server to push signaling code into the end devices. As a result, the only way interoperability can be achieved is for both endpoints to use the same standardized signaling protocol, such as SIP or Jingle, which are introduced in Section 4.3.6 and 4.3.7.

For a federated or trapezoid architecture, such as that shown in Figure 1.5, both web domains need to agree on a signaling protocol in order to interoperate. However, this signaling protocol does not necessarily need to be the same signaling protocol used in each of the browsers. In other words, just because two web domains use SIP to communicate, this doesn't mean that SIP must be used in both browsers.

4.1.2 Media Negotiation

WebRTC specifications include requirements for the "signaling channel." The most important function of signaling is the exchange of information contained in the Session Description Protocol (SDP) objects between the browsers involved in the Peer Connection. SDP contains all the information necessary for the RTP media stack on the browser to configure the media session, including the types of media (audio, video, data), codecs used (Opus, G.711, etc), any parameters or settings for the codecs, and information about the bandwidth. Also, the signaling channel is used to exchange candidate addresses for ICE hole punching. The candidate addresses represent the IP addresses and UDP ports where potentially media packets could be received by the browser. Candidates can also be sent and received outside of SDP in the signaling channel. Keying material for SRTP must also be exchanged in the signaling channel.

ICE hole punching, described in Section 9.2, cannot begin until the candidate addresses have been exchanged over the signaling channel, so without this signaling function, there can be no establishment of a Peer Connection.

4.1.3 Identification and Authentication

When a standard signaling protocol such as SIP or Jingle is used to initiate real-time communication, the signaling channel provides the identity of the participants and also optionally authentication. In WebRTC, there are two non-signaling sources of identity. One is the context provided by the web application. For instance, a user to a WebRTC website might sign on with a particular screen name. When this user wishes to establish a session with another user, the web application presents the screen name to the other user as the identity. A user can only trust the website that this identity is accurate. This is very similar to caller identity in the PSTN (Public Switched Telephone Network). A PSTN user must trust their service provider that the caller ID presented to their telephone is in fact the caller – they have no other way of independently determining it. Or, an identification might be passed in a URL, which could contain a random token. The parties in a WebRTC session established this way would be parties who knew the identification token.

WebRTC defines an alternative approach of identity through the media channel which does not rely on trusting information from the website. The notion of media path identity was first proposed by the ZRTP [RFC6189] media path keying protocol, in which caller identity and authentication was provided in the media path without relying on the signaling channel at all. WebRTC uses DTLS-SRTP [RFC5763] to provide media path identity. This is done using the fingerprint of the public key used during the DTLS handshake. This fingerprint can be authenticated by the use of an Identity Provider, described in Section 13.4. The signaling channel is used to transport the fingerprint and the identity assertion but is not otherwise involved in the generation or validation of the identity assertion.

4.1.4 Controlling the Media Session

A conventional multimedia signaling protocol, such as SIP or Jingle, or some proprietary protocol, can provide call control of the session. The proprietary protocol could be extremely simple, such as the example in the demo application of Section 4.5. However, in WebRTC, while signaling is required to initiate or change a media session, signaling is not needed to indicate status or to terminate a session. Instead, the ICE state machine in the browser can provide this information. For example, as candidate addresses are being checked, this can provide progress information about the session. Once a session is established, if ICE continuing consent checks fail, this is an indication that the session has been terminated.

4.1.5 Glare Resolution

Signaling protocols such as SIP have built-in glare resolution. Glare is when both sides of a communication session attempt to setup or change a session at the same time. It is a race condition that could result in an nondeterministic state for the session. Some of the approaches for using SDP eliminate many glare conditions, and if those approaches are incorporated in WebRTC, the requirements on glare could be greatly reduced. For example, if adding a new media source to a session can be done without a new offer/answer exchange, then this common source of glare can be eliminated.

4.2 Signaling Transport

WebRTC requires a bi-directional signaling channel between the two browsers. First, the transport for signaling messages will be discussed. Three transports are commonly used for WebRTC signaling: HTTP, WebSockets, and the data channel.

4.2.1 HTTP Transport

HTTP can also be used to transport WebRTC signaling. A browser can initiate new HTTP requests to send and receive signaling information from a server. The information can be transported using a GET or POST method, or in responses. If the server used for signaling supports Cross-Origin Resource Sharing (CORS), Section 13.2.3, the signaling server can be at a different IP address than the web server.

Sending information to the server is straightforward, using an XML HTTP Request (XHR) API call in JavaScript. In the other direction, receiving information asynchronously from the server is trickier, and a number of techniques have been developed over the years, known as AJAX (Asynchronous JavaScript And XML) [AJAX]. Some of these approaches are as simple as polling or keeping a GET request continuously open, ready to receive data from the server, such as the signaling approach used in the demo application code of Section 4.5. XHR is often used indirectly via JavaScript libraries such as jQuery [JQUERY]. The demo application of

Section 4.5 uses HTTP transport for the signaling channel.

The use of HTTP transport is shown in Figure 4.2. Note that the use of HTTP for signaling is often referred to as REST (Representational State Transfer) or RESTful signaling.

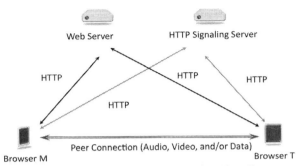

Figure 4.2 HTTP Transport for Signaling

HTTPS is more secure than HTTP, and allows a browser to authenticate the signaling server, as discussed in Section 13.1.2.

4.2.2 WebSocket Transport

WebSocket transport, as introduced in Section 10.2.2, allows a browser to open a bi-directional connection to a server. The connection begins as an HTTP request but then upgrades to a WebSocket. As long as the server supports CORS, the WebSocket server can be at a different IP address than the web server, as shown in Figure 4.3. Although the figure shows a SIP proxy server that supports WebSockets, any signaling can go over the WebSocket transport, including the simple signaling used in the demo in Section 4.5.

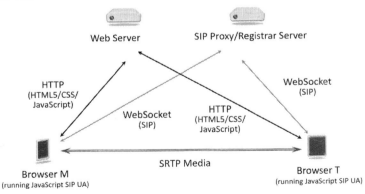

Figure 4.3 Signaling Transport using WebSocket

59

In order for a WebSocket server to be reachable, it must have a public IP address and be running an HTTP server. Note that this means it is not possible to open a WebSocket directly with another browser since browsers implement HTTP user agent functionality and not HTTP server functionality, so the WebSocket server is still needed to relay between two web clients using WebSockets. Even if a computer ran an HTTP server, NAT traversal would prevent end-to-end WebSocket connections between computers on the Internet. A browser uses WebSockets by utilizing the WebSocket API [WS-API].

WebSockets are supported by all major browser vendors. However, some web proxies and firewalls do not fully support WebSockets and can cause problems, especially with authentication.

4.2.3 Data Channel Transport

The data channel, once established between two browsers, provides a direct, low latency connection which makes it suitable for signaling transport. Since the initial establishment of a data channel requires a separate signaling mechanism, the data channel alone cannot be used for all WebRTC signaling. However, it can be used to handle all signaling after it is set up, including all the signaling for the audio and video media over the Peer Connection. This is shown in Figure 4.4 where data channel signaling goes over HTTP to the web server but all other signaling goes over the data channel.

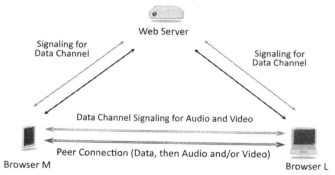

Figure 4.4 Data Channel Signaling Transport

The signaling load on the server to establish just the data channel is much less than handling all signaling for voice and video. The signaling for the data channel could also use a separate server using WebSockets, for example, as shown in Figure 4.5.

An interesting benefit of data channel signaling transport is that it can be used to reduce connection establishment time perceived by users. Before media can be exchanged between browsers, ICE and DTLS-SRTP key management steps must complete. If these steps are started only after the called user accepts the session (i.e. "answers the call"), there can be a perceived delay of perhaps up to a few seconds. With data channel signaling, ICE and DTLS key management is performed in order to establish the data channel, and can happen before the user is alerted or asked to accept a session. When the user accepts the session, adding voice and video can be done comparatively quickly, as the signaling messages go directly to the other browser, and the media streams reuse the Peer Connection so no ICE or DTLS-SRTP processing is performed.

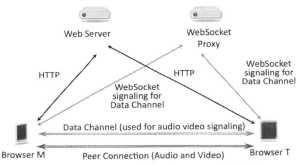

Figure 4.5 Data Channel Signaling Transport with Separate Server

4.3 Signaling Protocol

The choice of signaling protocol for WebRTC is an important one, and not necessarily tied to the choice of signaling transport, discussed in the previous section. A developer may choose to create their own proprietary signaling protocol, use a standard signaling protocol such as SIP or Jingle, or use a library which abstracts away the details of the signaling protocol.

4.3.1 Signaling State Machine

Regardless of the signaling protocol, there will be some sort of "state machine", which could be as simple as Figure 4.6.

Note that not every state in the signaling state machine requires a signaling message be exchanged between the browsers, although some signaling approaches will result in this.

An advantage of using a standard signaling protocol is that the state machine is already fully defined. Also, the signaling message will contain information useful for routing.

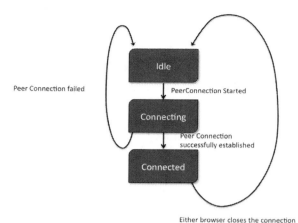

Figure 4.6 A Simple Signaling State Machine.

An advantage of using a proprietary approach is that it can be very simple and only provide the features needed by the application. If the WebRTC Peer Connection is always just between two browsers, and not through an intermediary or to a SIP or Jingle VoIP or video endpoint, this can be a good choice.

An alternative non-signaling approach to identity is to identify the connection rather than the users. For example, a connection identifier could be included in the URL, and knowledge of that identifier could be the only identity and authentication needed to participate in a session.

The following sections will discuss in more detail these different signaling protocol options.

4.3.2 Signaling Identity

In order to implement 2) of Section 4.1, some kind of routing logic will need to be in the server. If a given connection between a browser and the server can be identified by a token, then the signaling message sent to the server could contain the token of the other server to browser connection. The web server code will then proxy or forward the information between the two connections. Two examples of this approach are to use a WebSocket Proxy or use of the Google App Engine Channel API. If a standard signaling protocol is used, the message will contain the identifier of the other browser (user) as the destination. A standard server for the particular signaling protocol can provide this functionality with minimal configuration. For example, if SIP signaling is used, a SIP Proxy Server will perform this function. If Jingle is used, an XMPP Server provides this function.

4.3.3 HTTP Polling

A simple proprietary signaling approach is to use HTTP polling. An example of this is the XHR-based signaling channel shown later in this chapter.

XML HTTP Request (XHR) calls within JavaScript or jQuery allow a JavaScript application to generate a new HTTP request and process HTTP responses to a web server. XHR is a W3C standard API being defined as a Working Draft [XHR] on the way to becoming a standard. Various parts of the XHR JavaScript API functionality are supported in browsers. Despite the name, XHR can be used to send more than XML requests: JSON (JavaScript Object Notation) or plain text can also be sent as well. XHR causes the browser to generate a new HTTP or HTTPS request, such as a GET, POST, PUT, etc. The API call specifies the method to be used and the IP address and port number. The response to the request is returned to the JavaScript.

To use XHR as a signaling channel for WebRTC, the web server needs to run an application which receives the HTTP Request and proxies or forwards the information received from one browser to the other browser over another XHR channel, as shown in Figure 4.7.

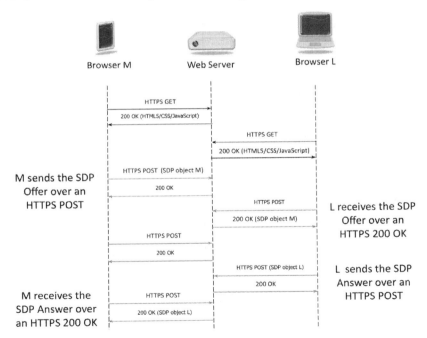

Figure 4.7 Signaling using HTTP Polling of Web Server

To exchange signaling information, the JavaScript running in each browser sends HTTP messages to the signaling server at regular intervals to poll. Signaling information sent by the browser is included in the POST method. Signaling information received from the server is included in the 200 OK response to the POST. Note that in this approach, each message is a new request.

4.3.4 WebSocket Proxy

A WebSocket proxy used for WebRTC signaling would use a server which has a public IP address and is reachable by both browsers establishing the Peer Connection. Each browser opens an independent WebSocket connection with the same server, and the server bridges the connections, proxying information from one to another, as shown in Figure 4.8. Since JavaScript does not support DNS lookups, the WebSocket server will need to be provided by the web server as an IP address and port number.

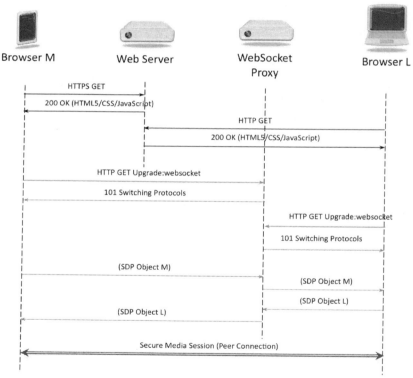

Figure 4.8 Signaling Example: WebSocket Proxy

One example of this is described in [GINGER-TECH]. In this example, a simple WebSocket server is created which listens on a specific port for WebSocket connections. When information is received from a WebSocket, it is broadcast to all open WebSocket connections. For a real WebSocket proxy, the server would not broadcast to all open connections but to one particular connection that has the other browser. Some sort of session ID would be needed for this. Another simple approach would be to allocate one port on the WebSocket proxy for each Peer Connection. The port would be randomly allocated and shared with each browser.

Some signaling pseudo code snippets:

```
// define signaling channel
function createSignalingChannel(msgHandler) {
  var socket = new WebSocket('wss://192.168.0.1:49152/');
  socket.addEventListener("message", msgHandler, false);
  return {"send": socket.send};

}

// open WebSocket
signalingChannel = createSignalingChannel(onMessage);

// send message over WebSocket
signalingChannel.send(message);

// process incoming message over WebSocket
function onMessage(msg) {
    // handle message
}
```

The use of secure WebSockets transport provides encryption between the browser and the WebSocket server.

4.3.5 Google App Engine Channel API

Another common, albeit proprietary approach is to use the Google App Engine Channel API for the signaling channel. This is described in [APPRTC]. The Google App Engine allows a JavaScript client to establish a channel with a server inside the Google cloud. The Channel API uses XHR to send signaling messages from the browser to the Google server. A technique known by the umbrella term Comet is used to forward the message to another browser. Comet uses HTTP long polling techniques, and is also known as Reverse AJAX(Asynchronous JavaScript and XML), AJAX Push, or HTTP Server Push. It typically involves having the client send a request to the server, which is kept open until information is to be sent from the server to the client. (The name Comet was chosen as a pun since it is another brand of cleaner, as is Ajax.) Messages are received from the server via the App Engine channel.

Using unique client IDs, information can be sent to the server to be forwarded to another client. An overview of the Channel API for Java is found here [APP-ENGINE-CHANNEL]. The other browser would be identified by the Client ID.

A call to `goog.appengine.Channel(channelToken)` opens the channel. Event handlers for the following events should be set up: `onopen`, `onmessage`, `onerror`, `onclose`. See the example XHR pseudo code snippets below:

```
function createSignalingChannel(channelToken, msgHandler) {
  var channel = new goog.appengine.Channel(channelToken);
  var handler = {
    'onopen': onChannelOpen,
    'onmessage': msgHandler,
    'onerror': onChannelError,
    'onclose': onChannelClose
  };
  var socket = channel.open(handler);

  function onChannelOpen() {
      // channel open
  }
  function onChannelError() {
      // channel error
  }
  function onChannelClosed() {
      // channel closed
  }

  function XHRSend(msg) {
    var req = new XMLHttpRequest();
    req.open('POST', /* path to service */, true);
    req.send(msg);
  }

  return {'send': XHRSend};
}

// open channel
signalingChannel =
  createSignalingChannel(/* some token here */, onMessage);

// send message over XHR
signalingChannel.send(message);

// process incoming message from App Engine Channel
function onMessage(msg) {
  // handle message
}
```

4.3.6 SIP over WebSockets

SIP over WebSockets is another approach. Session Initiation Protocol [RFC3261] is a signaling protocol commonly used in Voice over IP (VoIP) and video conferencing systems. SIP is a key protocol in service provider

IP Multimedia Subsystems (IMS) and SIP trunking for PSTN replacement. SIP is also used in enterprise communication systems for Unified Communications (UC) and Instant Messaging (IM) and presence. SIP can use UDP, TCP, SCTP, or TLS as transports. A new RFC defines a WebSocket transport for SIP [RFC7118].

In this signaling approach, a browser loads a JavaScript SIP User Agent and then establishes a connection (REGISTER) with a SIP Proxy Server/Registrar which supports WebSockets transport. A browser initiating a WebRTC session would send an INVITE containing the SDP offer from the browser to the Proxy Server. The destination browser would be identified by the SIP URI (e.g. sip:user@webserver.org). The other browser would receive the INVITE and generate appropriate SIP responses, returning the SDP answer in a 200 OK response which would establish the media session.

Table 4.1 lists some open source SIP stacks that currently support SIP over WebSockets. A number of commercial SIP stacks also support SIP over WebSockets.

SIP Stack	Role	URL
JsSIP	JavaScript SIP User Agent	http://jssip.net
sipML5	JavaScript SIP User Agent	http://sipml5.org
WebRTComm	JavaScript SIP User Agent	https://code.google.com/p/webrtcomm
Asterisk	SIP Server supporting WebSockets	http://asterisk.org
OverSIP	SIP Server supporting WebSockets	http://oversip.net
Kamailio	SIP Server supporting WebSockets	http://kamailio.org
OfficeSIP	SIP Server supporting WebSockets	http://officesip.com

Table 4.1 Open Source SIP over WebSockets Implementations

The message flow for SIP over WebSockets signaling for WebRTC is shown in Figure 4.9.

An example SIP over WebSockets message is shown below:

```
INVITE sip:bob@atlanta.com SIP/2.0
Via: SIP/2.0/WS df7jal23ls0d.invalid;branch=z9hG4bK56sdasks
From: sip:alice@atlanta.com;tag=asdyka899
```

```
To: sip:bob@atlanta.com
Call-ID: asidkj3ss
CSeq: 1 INVITE
Max-Forwards: 70
Supported: path, outbound, gruu
Route: <sip:proxy.atlanta.com:443;transport=ws;lr>
Contact: <sip:alice@atlanta.com
  ;gr=urn:uuid:f81-7dec-14a06cf1;ob>
Content-Type: application/sdp

(SDP Offer not shown)
```

Note the host name in the Via header field which is .invalid, making it unroutable, the WS token in the Via, and the transport=ws parameter in the Route header field. SIP over WebSockets uses the SIP Path header field [RFC3327], SIP Outbound [RFC5626], and GRUU [RFC5627].

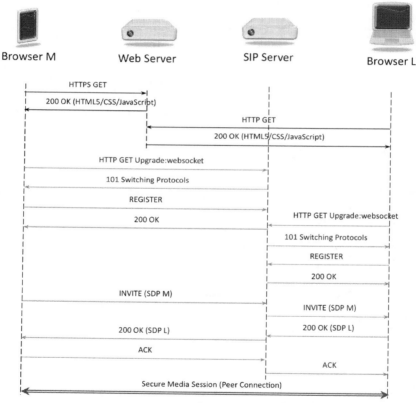

Figure 4.9 SIP over WebSocket Signaling

See the example jsSIP pseudo code snippet below:

```
// initialize SIP UA
var configuration = {
  'outbound_proxy_set': 'ws://sip-ws.example.com',
  'uri': 'sip:alice@example.com',
  'password': '123456'
};

var sipUa = new JsSIP.UA(configuration);

sipUA.call('sip:bob@example.com',useAudio, useVideo, eventHandlers,
views);
```

4.3.7 Jingle over WebSockets

Jingle is an extension of XMPP (extensible Messaging and Presence Protocol), also known as Jabber [RFC6120], that adds media signaling capabilities to XMPP. Jingle provides a way to map SDP session descriptions to an XML format, which can then be transported over TCP or TLS to an XMPP server. Standalone XMPP Jabber clients are commonly used for Instant Messaging and Presence, and is used by GoogleTalk and other enterprise IM services. XMPP has been used embedded in web pages for many years using a variety of techniques including Bidirectional-streams Over Synchronous HTTP (BOSH) [XEP-0124], which can be used as transport for XMPP [XEP-0206]. A new Internet-Draft defines the transport of XMPP over WebSocket [draft-ietf-xmpp-websocket] which promises to offer better performance and interoperability.

To implement a WebRTC signaling channel using Jingle, a Jingle XMPP client written in JavaScript would be downloaded from the web page and run. The client would establish an XMPP connection over WebSockets to an XMPP Server. Clients would then map the SDP offers and answers generated by the browser into Jingle call setup messages and forward them to the other browser. The other browser would be identified by the Jabber ID (JID). The message flows for Jingle signaling in WebRTC are shown in Figure 4.10.

JavaScript XMPP stacks are listed in Table 4.2.

Stack	Role	URL
Strophe	JavaScript XMPP stack using BOSH	http://strophe.im/
node-xmpp	JavaScript XMPP stack using BOSH and WebSocket	https://github.com/astro/node-xmpp
dojox-xmpp	JavaScript XMPP stack using BOSH	http://dojotoolkit.org/api/1.3/dojox
frabjous	JavaScript XMPP stack	https://github.com/theozaurus/frabjous
jQuery-XMPP-plugin	JavaScript XMPP stack	https://github.com/maxpowel/jQuery-XMPP-plugin

Table 4.2 Open Source XMPP Stacks from [XMPP-LIBRARIES].

An example Jingle message is shown below:

```
<iq id="3Tzpd-1650" to=bob@example.com/jitsi-3u1kluu
    from="alice@example.org/jitsi-2rbmomp" type="set">
  <jingle xmlns='urn:xmpp:jingle:1'
        action='session-initiate'
        initiator='alice@example.org/jitsi-2rbmomp'
        sid='3pd4ihhk9t72q'>
    <content creator='initiator' name='audio'>
      <description xmlns='urn:xmpp:jingle:apps:rtp:1'
                media='audio'>
        <payload-type id='96' name='opus' channels='1'
                    clockrate='16000'/>
        <payload-type id='0' name='PCMU' channels='1'
                    clockrate='8000' />
      </description>
      <transport xmlns='urn:xmpp:jingle:transports:ice-udp:1'
              pwd='asd88fgpdd777uzjYhagZg' ufrag='8hhy'>
        <candidate component='1' foundation='1' generation='0'
                id='el0747fg11' ip='10.0.1.1' network='1'
                port='8998' priority='2130706431'
                protocol='udp' type='host'/>
        <candidate component='1' foundation='2' generation='0'
                id='y3s2b30v3r' ip='192.0.2.3' network='1'
                port='45664' priority='1694498815'
                protocol='udp' rel-addr='10.0.1.1'
                rel-port='8998' type='srflx'/>
      </transport>
    </content>
  </jingle>
</iq>
```

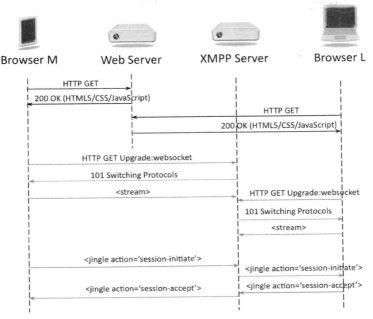

Figure 4.10 Jingle over WebSocket Signaling for WebRTC

4.3.8 Data Channel Proprietary Signaling

Data channel proprietary signaling is shown in Figure 4.11. The nature of the signaling message sent over the data channel can be completely proprietary. Some approaches do not even send SDP objects over the data

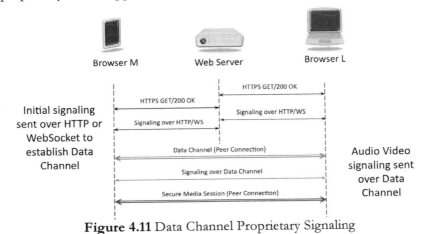

Figure 4.11 Data Channel Proprietary Signaling

channel. Instead, signaling messages are sent over the data channel which are then used to locally generate an SDP object to be passed to the browser.

4.3.9 Data Channel Using an Overlay

An alternative approach to using the data channel for signaling is to build an overlay network using the data channel, and to use that overlay network as the signaling channel. This is a peer-to-peer (P2P) approach that minimizes the need for any types of servers.

An overlay network, as the name suggests, is a network which overlays, or sits on top of another network. The overlay hides the underlying topology and architecture and provides an alternative way to address and message other members of the overlay. For example, one type of overlay network is a ring. Each member of the overlay keeps track of other neighbor nodes in the ring. An example of technology used to implement and utilize an overlay is a Distributed Hash Table or DHT. A DHT provides a way to map information to an overlay. There are a number of overlay routing protocols, such as Chord [CHORD], which define how information can be stored and retrieved and messages routed across an overlay. Some overlay standards such as RELOAD [RELOAD] have been developed in the P2PSIP Working Group in the IETF [PSPSIP-WG].

The data channel can be used to establish an overlay signaling network for WebRTC. The overlay protocol would be written in JavaScript and downloaded to the browser. The web server would act as the bootstrap server and assist the browser in joining the overlay, establishing a few data channel connections with other browsers in the overlay. Once the browser joined the overlay, all future messaging and signaling with the overlay would take place over the data channel. The web server would only become involved again if the browser lost connection to the overlay and required bootstrapping again.

With the overlay established, any member of the overlay could exchange a signaling message with any other member of the overlay, and as a result establish a Peer Connection. For example, the RELOAD protocol could be used, or Open Peer [OPEN-PEER].

The main advantages of a peer-to-peer signaling network are minimal server requirements, self-organizing, self-scaling, and privacy. As an overlay grows in size, the additional signaling load is shared among the new members. The usual peer-to-peer disadvantages also apply. P2P systems do utilize resources of members, so additional bandwidth and processing is required. In addition, P2P systems must deal with malicious members which could try to disrupt the operation of the overlay.

4.4 Summary of Signaling Choices

The various approaches to WebRTC signaling are summarized in Table 4.3.

Approach	Server Requirements	Advantages
WebSocket Proxy	WebSocket server with server code	No signaling infrastructure needed
XML HTTP Request	Web server with server code	No signaling infrastructure needed
SIP	SIP Registrar/Proxy Server which supports SIP WebSocket transport	Easy to interoperate with SIP endpoints or infrastructure, no server code needed
Jingle	XMPP server which supports XMPP WebSocket transport	Easy to interoperate with Jingle endpoints or infrastructure, no server code needed
Data Channel	WebSocket or web server to establish Data Channel	Low latency signaling and signaling privacy

Table 4.3 Comparison of WebRTC Signaling Options

4.5 Signaling Channel Runnable Code Example

In the following subsections we will be adding a two-party-per-key signaling channel to our running example begun in the preceding chapter, allowing two browsers to connect to each other. To set up the call, each browser contacts the web server and provides a key. The first browser to provide that specific key initiates a new two-browser signaling channel, waiting until the next browser connects with the same key, at which point the two now have a signaling channel via the web server. The next browser to connect with that specific key resets the signaling channel for that key and is now again waiting for another browser to connect with that key.

The next three sections describe the web server code, the signaling channel code, and the WebRTC application. Note that the first two are still generic, meaning that they are independent of the WebRTC APIs.

4.5.1 Web Server

In addition to serving up the web application itself, a web server can act as a relay (providing a "signaling channel") between two or more browsers that can be used to negotiate the destination, type, and format of media to be communicated between the browsers. The HTTP polling signaling channel used here is described in Section 4.3.3 and Figure 4.7.

As we mentioned before, WebRTC applications are *real-time* and need a signaling mechanism that is quick and efficient. In the server code we will see how the shared memory space of Node simplifies the communication between separate browser requests from different browsers.

Let's look at what's changed in index.js (the changed text is in bold).

4.5.1.1 index.js

```
// Copyright 2013-2014 Digital Codex LLC
// You may use this code for your own education.  If you use it
// largely intact, or develop something from it, don't claim
// that your code came first.  You are using this code completely
// at your own risk.  If you rely on it to work in any particular
// way, you're an idiot and we won't be held responsible.

var server = require("./server");
var requestHandlers = require("./serverXHRSignalingChannel");
var log = require("./log").log;
var port = process.argv[2] || 5001;

// returns 404
function fourohfour(info) {
  var res = info.res;
  log("Request handler fourohfour was called.");
  res.writeHead(404, {"Content-Type": "text/plain"});
  res.write("404 Page Not Found");
  res.end();
}

var handle = {};
handle["/"] = fourohfour;
handle["/connect"] = requestHandlers.connect;
handle["/send"] = requestHandlers.send;
handle["/get"] = requestHandlers.get;

server.serveFilePath("static");
server.start(handle, port);
```

The first change is that we are loading the signaling channel code from "serverXHRSignalingChannel.js". We then make use of the handlers in that custom library for specific custom URI paths ("/connect", "/send", and "/get"). For example, handle["/connect"] means that a URI of the form "http://webrtcserver.example.com:5001/connect" will be handled via the connect() handler defined in serverXHRSignalingChannel.js.

Before looking at how these handlers are defined and used to make a signaling channel, let's take a quick look at some server code changes needed at this stage.

4.5.1.2 server.js

```
// Copyright 2013-2014 Digital Codex LLC
```

74

```
// You may use this code for your own education.  If you use it
// largely intact, or develop something from it, don't claim
// that your code came first.  You are using this code completely
// at your own risk.  If you rely on it to work in any particular
// way, you're an idiot and we won't be held responsible.

var http = require("http");
var url = require("url");
var fs = require('fs');

var log = require("./log").log;
var serveFileDir = "";


// Sets the path to the static files (HTML, JS, etc.)
function setServeFilePath(p) {
  serveFilePath = p;
}
exports.serveFilePath = setServeFilePath;


// Creates a handler to collect POSTed data and to route the
// request based on the path name
function start(handle, port) {
  function onRequest(req, res) {
    var urldata = url.parse(req.url,true),
        pathname = urldata.pathname,
        info = {"res": res,
                "query": urldata.query,
                "postData":""};

    log("Request for " + pathname + " received");
    req.setEncoding("utf8");
    req.addListener("data", function(postDataChunk) {
      info.postData += postDataChunk;
      log("Received POST data chunk '"+ postDataChunk + "'.");
    });
    req.addListener("end", function() {
      route(handle, pathname, info);
    });
  }

  http.createServer(onRequest).listen(port);

  log("Server started on port " + port);
}

exports.start = start;


// Determines whether requested path is a static file or a custom
// path with its own handler
function route(handle, pathname, info) {
  log("About to route a request for " + pathname);
  // Check if path after leading slash is an existing file that
  // can be served
  var filepath = createFilePath(pathname);
  log("Attempting to locate " + filepath);
  fs.stat(filepath, function(err, stats) {
```

```
      if (!err && stats.isFile()) {  // serve file
        serveFile(filepath, info);
      } else {  // must be custom path
        handleCustom(handle, pathname, info);
      }
    });
}


// This function adds the serveFilePath to the beginning of the
// given pathname after removing .., ~, and other such
// problematic syntax bits from a security perspective.
// ** There is no claim that this is now secure **
function createFilePath(pathname) {
  var components = pathname.substr(1).split('/');
  var filtered = new Array(),
      temp;

  for(var i=0, len = components.length; i < len; i++) {
    temp = components[i];
    if (temp == "..") continue;      // no updir
    if (temp == "") continue;        // no root
    temp = temp.replace(/~/g,'');    // no userdir
    filtered.push(temp);
  }
  return (serveFilePath + "/" + filtered.join("/"));
}



// Opens, reads, and sends to the client the contents of the
// named file
function serveFile(filepath, info) {
  var res = info.res,
      query = info.query;

  log("Serving file " + filepath);
  fs.open(filepath, 'r', function(err, fd) {
    if (err) {log(err.message);
              noHandlerErr(filepath, res);
              return;}
    var readBuffer = new Buffer(20480);
    fs.read(fd, readBuffer, 0, 20480, 0,
      function(err, readBytes) {
        if (err) {log(err.message);
                  fs.close(fd);
                  noHandlerErr(filepath, res);
                  return;}
        log('just read ' + readBytes + ' bytes');
        if (readBytes > 0) {
          res.writeHead(200,
                        {"Content-Type": contentType(filepath)});
          res.write(
            addQuery(readBuffer.toString('utf8', 0, readBytes),
                     query));
        }
        res.end();
      });
  });
}
```

```
// Determine content type of fetched file
function contentType(filepath) {
  var index = filepath.lastIndexOf('.');

  if (index >= 0) {
    switch (filepath.substr(index+1)) {
      case "html":  return ("text/html");
      case "js":  return ("application/javascript");
      case "css":  return ("text/css");
      case "txt":  return ("text/plain");
      default:  return ("text/html");
    }
  }
  return ("text/html");
}


// Intended to be used on an HTML file, this function replaces
// the first empty script block in the file with an object
// representing all query parameters included on the URI of the
// request
function addQuery(str, q) {
  if (q) {
    return str.replace('<script></script>',
                       '<script>var queryparams = ' +
                       JSON.stringify(q) + ';</script>');
  } else {
    return str;
  }
}


// Confirm handler for non-file path, then execute it
function handleCustom(handle, pathname, info) {
  if (typeof handle[pathname] == 'function') {
    handle[pathname](info);
  } else {
    noHandlerErr(pathname, info.res);
  }
}


// If no handler is defined for the request, return 404
function noHandlerErr(pathname, res) {
  log("No request handler found for " + pathname);
  res.writeHead(404, {"Content-Type": "text/plain"});
  res.write("404 Page Not Found");
  res.end();
}
```

The two main features that have been added at this stage are an ability for the server to accept POSTed data and a mechanism to initialize certain variables using URL query parameters. The POST data is addressed in the onRequest() handler by setting handlers to collect up POSTed data as it comes in, only calling route() when all POST data has been collected.

The query parameters are parsed and saved at the head of the `start()` function and made available via the `info` variable, but it is `addQuery()` that handles them.

`addQuery()` is a minor hack to dynamically insert content into a (HTML) file before it is returned. This particular function is intended to take an object representing the query parameters given in the request URI and insert them into the file. For this WebRTC example, this allows a key specified as a query parameter in the request URI to be inserted into the fetched file so it can be used by the browser. The query parameters are converted to a JSON (JavaScript Object Notation) string and inserted into the first empty script block in the file. Do not assume that this code sample is secure. Anytime user input can end up in a rendered file there is a risk of abuse by those with bad intentions, so please be sure you know what you're doing before you include any capability such as this in your own code.

4.5.2 Signaling channel

WebRTC allows for browsers to use any communication method they wish to transmit signaling information, from smoke signals, to tin cans with string, to the faster and more common approaches such as HTTP (XML HTTP Request), WebSockets, and Google App Engine channels. These various approaches were discussed and compared earlier in this chapter. Note in each case, though, that the browser is communicating with the web server and not the other browser. Although there is no restriction against browsers communicating directly, the web model itself assumes that browsers (web clients) only communicate with servers and not directly with other web clients. In fact, unless a web server provides IP addresses to web clients, the clients would have no idea how to reach each other. Thus, in most cases there is a server in the cloud that acts as a relay for the messages from one browser to another.

In general, web server-based signaling approaches fall into one of two categories: polling and session-oriented. With polling approaches such as XML HTTP Request (XHR), all communication is initiated by the browser, and the browser's only means of receiving information from the web server is in the response to its messages. To receive messages *from* the server at all, then, the browser needs to regularly send messages to (poll) the server in case there are messages waiting. With session-oriented approaches such as WebSockets, a virtual connection is established between the browser and the web server, allowing for messages to be sent in either direction.

To simplify application programming, it is convenient to define a signaling channel interface that exposes connect and send methods with an ability to specify handlers for when messages are received. If the application intends to use WebRTC in a peer-to-peer mode (the "triangle" model), the purpose of the virtual signaling channel is to provide a simple connection-oriented model for communicating signaling information to the peer. There are several tricky aspects to creating this illusory connection. The first, and most important, is figuring out how to indicate to the web server what connection to make. Will this truly be a connection to just one peer, or is it intended to be a group "call"? Assuming it is a one-to-one connection, how will the other party be identified? One reasonable approach is to have each browser register with the server and have the server send back the list of registered browsers such that the user can select which one to communicate with. Another approach is to use a key that the other browser also knows and provides. The latter is the approach used in our demo code for this chapter. In this particular demo, the first browser to connect with a given key is registered as the first party and told to wait. When a second client connects with the same key, the signaling channel is established between the two. When another connection attempt is then made using the same key, the existing connection is destroyed and the new party is told to wait. Then, when another browser connections with the same key, the signaling channel is established between these two parties, and so on, toggling between `waiting` and `connected`. Although this approach has the potential disadvantages of requiring both parties to know their keys and a new party destroying an existing connection, it has two very nice properties as well: the key can be included as a parameter in the URI, allowing for the "connection" to be saved merely by bookmarking the URI, and there is very little state to manage when a connection drops because of the browser or network going down. If that happens, both parties just reload their pages and start over.

With that introduction, let's take a look at the code. The signaling channel code in the demo is split across two files — one on the server and one on the client. Let's look first at the server code in serverXHRSignalingChannel.js.

4.5.2.1 serverXHRSignalingChannel.js

```
// Copyright 2013-2014 Digital Codex LLC
// You may use this code for your own education.  If you use it
// largely intact, or develop something from it, don't claim
// that your code came first.  You are using this code completely
// at your own risk.  If you rely on it to work in any particular
// way, you're an idiot and we won't be held responsible.

var log = require("./log").log;

var connections = {},
    partner = {},
    messagesFor = {};


// queue the sending of a json response
function webrtcResponse(response, res) {
```

```
    log("replying with webrtc response " +
        JSON.stringify(response));
    res.writeHead(200, {"Content-Type":"application/json"});
    res.write(JSON.stringify(response));
    res.end();
}


// send an error as the json WebRTC response
function webrtcError(err, res) {
    log("replying with webrtc error:  " + err);
    webrtcResponse({"err": err}, res);
}


// handle XML HTTP Request to connect using a given key
function connect(info) {
    var res = info.res,
        query = info.query,
        thisconnection,
        newID = function() {
            // create large random number unlikely to be repeated
            // soon in server's lifetime
            return Math.floor(Math.random()*1000000000);
        },
        connectFirstParty = function() {
            if (thisconnection.status == "connected") {
                // delete pairing and any stored messages
                delete partner[thisconnection.ids[0]];
                delete partner[thisconnection.ids[1]];
                delete messagesFor[thisconnection.ids[0]];
                delete messagesFor[thisconnection.ids[1]];
            }
            connections[query.key] = {};
            thisconnection = connections[query.key];
            thisconnection.status = "waiting";
            thisconnection.ids = [newID()];
            webrtcResponse({"id":thisconnection.ids[0],
                            "status":thisconnection.status}, res);
        },
        connectSecondParty = function() {
            thisconnection.ids[1] = newID();
            partner[thisconnection.ids[0]] = thisconnection.ids[1];
            partner[thisconnection.ids[1]] = thisconnection.ids[0];
            messagesFor[thisconnection.ids[0]] = [];
            messagesFor[thisconnection.ids[1]] = [];
            thisconnection.status = "connected";
            webrtcResponse({"id":thisconnection.ids[1],
                            "status":thisconnection.status}, res);
        };

    log("Request handler 'connect' was called.");
    if (query && query.key) {
        var thisconnection = connections[query.key] ||
                             {status:"new"};
        if (thisconnection.status == "waiting") { // first half ready
            connectSecondParty(); return;
        } else { // must be new or status of "connected"
            connectFirstParty(); return;
```

```
    }
  } else {
    webrtcError("No recognizable query key", res);
  }
}
exports.connect = connect;


// Queues message in info.postData.message for sending to the
// partner of the id in info.postData.id
function sendMessage(info) {
  log("postData received is ***" + info.postData + "***");
  var postData = JSON.parse(info.postData),
      res = info.res;

  if (typeof postData === "undefined") {
    webrtcError("No posted data in JSON format!", res);
    return;
  }
  if (typeof (postData.message) === "undefined") {
    webrtcError("No message received", res);
    return;
  }
  if (typeof (postData.id) === "undefined") {
    webrtcError("No id received with message", res);
    return;
  }
  if (typeof (partner[postData.id]) === "undefined") {
    webrtcError("Invalid id " + postData.id, res);
    return;
  }
  if (typeof (messagesFor[partner[postData.id]]) ===
                "undefined") {
    webrtcError("Invalid id " + postData.id, res);
    return;
  }
  messagesFor[partner[postData.id]].push(postData.message);
  log("Saving message ***" + postData.message +
      "*** for delivery to id " + partner[postData.id]);
  webrtcResponse("Saving message ***" + postData.message +
                "*** for delivery to id " +
                partner[postData.id], res);
}
exports.send = sendMessage;


// Returns all messages queued for info.postData.id
function getMessages(info) {
  var postData = JSON.parse(info.postData),
      res = info.res;

  if (typeof postData === "undefined") {
    webrtcError("No posted data in JSON format!", res);
    return;
  }
  if (typeof (postData.id) === "undefined") {
    webrtcError("No id received on get", res);
    return;
  }
```

```
if (typeof (messagesFor[postData.id]) === "undefined") {
  webrtcError("Invalid id " + postData.id, res);
  return;
}

log("Sending messages ***" +
    JSON.stringify(messagesFor[postData.id]) + "*** to id " +
    postData.id);
webrtcResponse({'msgs':messagesFor[postData.id]}, res);
messagesFor[postData.id] = [];
}
exports.get = getMessages;
```

The code begins by requiring the logging framework and establishing variables to hold a) the list of connections, b) a simple array to map between peers, and c) an array to hold the messages intended for a client. Before the meat of the code (defining how to connect, send messages, and retrieve messages), we define two heavily-used functions for handling replies to the HTTP request: webrtcResponse(), which turns any passed in object into a JSON string and returns it, and webrtcError(), which returns a given object (possibly a string) as the value of the "err" property using webrtcResponse().

The three main handlers are connect(), sendMessage(), and getMessages(). Aside from fetching files, connect() is the first interaction a browser will have with the WebRTC server. The original request and any query parameters are passed in as properties of the info object. It's easiest to follow the code if we first look at the end of this function, after all the function definitions. After logging that the connect handler was called, the code confirms that the URI contained a key, e.g., "http://webrtc.example.org:5001/connect&key=1234". It finds the connection if it already exists in the connections[] array or creates a new one if not. It then calls either connectFirstParty() if the connection is new or already connected, or connectSecondParty() if the status is waiting. Now take a look at connectFirstParty(), and you'll see that the first thing we do is to delete any existing connection using that key, along with the corresponding entries in the partner[] and messagesFor[] arrays that will be explained later. Yes, if this occurs during a live connected call this will remove the "signaling channel" for that call, preventing any further signaling. Of course, if we had any media flowing directly between the parties it would keep flowing, because that's what peer-to-peer media means! Although this code sample doesn't, it could check for the loss of the signaling channel and take a useful action, such as trying again. Getting back to the code, after deleting any existing connection using that key, a new connections[] entry is created for the key. Its status is set to waiting, and a new ids[] array property is created containing a newly-generated id for this browser client. Finally, a response to the connect request is generated that contains the new id and the status.

`connectSecondParty()` behaves similarly to `connectFirstParty()`, but in this case, we

1) don't delete the existing (`waiting`) connection,
2) create a second id to add to the connection, and
3) set up the ancillary arrays that link the two partners (peers) by id and that store the messages from each side for the other.

This shows one of the key benefits of using Node – there is a shared memory space used by all requests to the server, and there is only one thread of control, so it is safe for all requests to access the same connection arrays. As we'll see shortly, all messages are simply stored as values in these shared arrays (in a single memory space).

`sendMessage()` is the handler for a URI of the form `"http://webrtc.example.org:5001/send"`. Note that all information from the client is assumed to be encoded as POST data. After the various error checks for missing POST data, no message, no id, or lack of a connection (meaning no entry in the `partner[]` or `messagesFor[]` arrays), we push the message onto the end of the `messagesFor` entry for the partner of this client. Then we send a status message back to the client.

Finally, `getMessages()` is the handler for a URI of the form `"http://webrtc.example.org:5001/get"`. As with `sendMessage()`, all info from the client is assumed to be encoded as POST data. Again, we make sure that there *is* POST data, an id, and an entry in the `messagesFor[]` array for this client id, and then we send back the messages array as the value of the `msgs` property. Oh, and we reset the `messagesFor[]` entry for this id so we don't get the same messages over and over again.

There is one subtlety about when the response is sent back that is due to using Node and asynchronous JavaScript. Because there is only one thread of control, the response is only sent after our code finishes. To keep this clear, the code largely sets the response as the last thing it does before returning, for every path through the code.

Now let's look at the signaling code on the client side, in clientXHRSignalingChannel.js.

4.5.2.2 clientXHRSignalingChannel.js

```
// Copyright 2013-2014 Digital Codex LLC
// You may use this code for your own education.  If you use it
// largely intact, or develop something from it, don't claim
// that your code came first.  You are using this code completely
// at your own risk.  If you rely on it to work in any particular
// way, you're an idiot and we won't be held responsible.

// This code creates the client-side commands for an XML HTTP
// Request-based signaling channel for WebRTC.
```

```javascript
// The signaling channel assumes a 2-person connection via a
// shared key.  Every connection attempt toggles the state
// between "waiting" and "connected", meaning that if 2 browsers
// are connected and another tries to connect the existing
// connection will be severed and the new browser will be
// "waiting".

var createSignalingChannel = function(key, handlers) {


var id, status, doNothing = function(){},
  handlers = handlers || {},
  initHandler = function(h) {
    return ((typeof h === 'function') && h) || doNothing;
  },
  waitingHandler = initHandler(handlers.onWaiting),
  connectedHandler = initHandler(handlers.onConnected),
  messageHandler = initHandler(handlers.onMessage);


// Set up connection with signaling server
function connect(failureCB) {
  var failureCB = (typeof failureCB === 'function') ||
                  function() {};

  // Handle connection response, which should be error or status
  //  of "connected" or "waiting"
  function handler() {
    if(this.readyState == this.DONE) {
      if(this.status == 200 && this.response != null) {
        var res = JSON.parse(this.response);
        if (res.err) {
          failureCB("error:  " + res.err);
          return;
        }

        // if no error, save status and server-generated id,
        // then start asynchronous polling for messages
        id = res.id;
        status = res.status;
        poll();

        // run user-provided handlers for waiting and connected
        // states
        if (status === "waiting") {
          waitingHandler();
        } else {
      connectedHandler();
        }
        return;
      } else {
        failureCB("HTTP error:  " + this.status);
        return;
      }
    }
  }

  // open XHR and send the connection request with the key
  var client = new XMLHttpRequest();
```

```
  client.onreadystatechange = handler;
  client.open("GET", "/connect?key=" + key);
  client.send();
}

// poll() waits n ms between gets to the server.  n is at 10 ms
// for 10 tries, then 100 ms for 10 tries, then 1000 ms from then
// on. n is reset to 10 ms if a message is actually received.
function poll() {
  var msgs;
  var pollWaitDelay = (function() {
    var delay = 10, counter = 1;

    function reset() {
      delay = 10;
      counter = 1;
    }

    function increase() {
      counter += 1;
      if (counter > 20) {
        delay = 1000;
      } else if (counter > 10) {
        delay = 100;
      }                              // else leave delay at 10
    }

    function value() {
      return delay;
    }

    return {reset: reset, increase: increase, value: value};
  }());

  // getLoop is defined and used immediately here.  It retrieves
  // messages from the server and then schedules itself to run
  // again after pollWaitDelay.value() milliseconds.
  (function getLoop() {
    get(function (response) {
      var i, msgs = (response && response.msgs) || [];

      // if messages property exists, then we are connected
      if (response.msgs && (status !== "connected")) {
        // switch status to connected since it is now!
        status = "connected";
        connectedHandler();
      }
      if (msgs.length > 0) {              // we got messages
        pollWaitDelay.reset();
        for (i=0; i<msgs.length; i+=1) {
          handleMessage(msgs[i]);
        }
      } else {                           // didn't get any messages
        pollWaitDelay.increase();
      }

      // now set timer to check again
      setTimeout(getLoop, pollWaitDelay.value());
    });
```

```
    }());
}


// This function is part of the polling setup to check for
// messages from the other browser.  It is called by getLoop()
// inside poll().
function get(getResponseHandler) {

  // response should either be error or a JSON object.  If the
  // latter, send it to the user-provided handler.
  function handler() {
    if(this.readyState == this.DONE) {
      if(this.status == 200 && this.response != null) {
        var res = JSON.parse(this.response);
        if (res.err) {
          getResponseHandler("error:  " + res.err);
          return;
        }
        getResponseHandler(res);
        return res;
      } else {
        getResponseHandler("HTTP error:  " + this.status);
        return;
      }
    }
  }

  // open XHR and request messages for my id
  var client = new XMLHttpRequest();
  client.onreadystatechange = handler;
  client.open("POST", "/get");
  client.send(JSON.stringify({"id":id}));
}


// Schedule incoming messages for asynchronous handling.
// This is used by getLoop() in poll().
function handleMessage(msg) {    // process message asynchronously
  setTimeout(function () {messageHandler(msg);}, 0);
}


// Send a message to the other browser on the signaling channel
function send(msg, responseHandler) {
  var reponseHandler = responseHandler || function() {};

  // parse response and send to handler
  function handler() {
    if(this.readyState == this.DONE) {
      if(this.status == 200 && this.response != null) {
        var res = JSON.parse(this.response);
        if (res.err) {
          responseHandler("error:  " + res.err);
          return;
        }
        responseHandler(res);
        return;
      } else {
```

```
        responseHandler("HTTP error:  " + this.status);
        return;
      }
    }
  }

  // open XHR and send my id and message as JSON string
  var client = new XMLHttpRequest();
  client.onreadystatechange = handler;
  client.open("POST", "/send");
  var sendData = {"id":id, "message":msg};
  client.send(JSON.stringify(sendData));
}


return {
  connect:  connect,
  send:   send
};

};
```

`createSignalingChannel()` takes the shared key and a set of handlers
and returns (at the end of the file) an object containing `connect()` and
`send()` methods. The code first initializes some variables, including
handlers for a status of `waiting`, a status of `connected`, and receipt of a
message.

  `connect()` takes a callback for the case of a problem with the
connection request. Let's look at the end of the routine first. A new
`XMLHttpRequest()` is created for the connection request. After setting the
handler that will be discussed shortly, the GET (as opposed to POST) request
is made to the "/connect" URI at the web server, with the key attached as
a query parameter. In looking at the handler, first note that there are a
variety of events from `XMLHttpRequest()` that can trigger execution of the
handler. In this code the only case we care about is that the result is
complete and parsed, i.e., has a `readyState` of DONE. The code then
confirms that there was a successful HTTP response (status of 200), calling
the `failureCB()` if not. The next line of the handler points out an
interesting fact about `XMLHttpRequest()` – it actually can receive arbitrary
data in any format, not just XML. In our case, we parse the response as
JSON and first check to see whether the returned object contains an error
response. If it does, we call the `failureCB()` callback with the error.
Otherwise, we parse out the id generated by the server for this browser
client and the status (`waiting` or `connected`), and then start
asynchronously polling for messages (discussed in a moment). Then, we
finish up handling the response by calling the appropriate handler for the
status returned.

  `poll()` is the most complex section of code in this file, and its sole
purpose is to check frequently for new messages from the peer (via the

server). Code such as this is necessary when using a signaling channel approach that is not session-oriented. The first part in this routine is the definition of a counter object, `pollWaitDelay`. When `reset()` it has a value of 10, but otherwise each call to `increase()` increments a counter. At a count of 11 after the reset the value becomes 100, and at a count of 21 after the reset the value becomes 1000. This value will be used as the number of milliseconds until the next get request. The point of all this is to rapidly check for messages after receiving some and then fall back to less frequent checks if no new messages are forthcoming, in an attempt to be responsive when messages are sent but not flood the server when messages aren't being exchanged.

`getLoop()` is the routine that schedules get requests. It calls `get()`, which requests any waiting messages from the server, and passes the response from the server to the handler given as the argument. The handler, defined inline in `getLoop()`, first creates a `msgs` array and fills it with messages from the server, if any. Since the server only sends back a response with a `msgs` property if the client browser is connected to another, if there is such a property and the browser didn't already know it was connected, it can now be marked as connected and the `connectedHandler()` can be run. This will happen if the browser is the first to connect, meaning that it is waiting for another to connect. Receipt of the response with a `msgs` property is the indication that the connection has been completed, even if no actual messages were available. What happens next depends upon whether any messages were returned. If there were, two things would happen: first, the timing counter would be reset, and second, the messages would be sent to the message handler for asynchronous handling. The timing counter is reset to ensure that any rapidly-following messages from the other browser will be picked up quickly. In either case, `getLoop()` is scheduled to run again after `pollWaitDelay.value()` milliseconds.

`get()` actually does the message fetch, sending the response to the handler given as input. The main part of this code is at the end of the routine and looks much like `connect()` does — a new XMLHttpRequest to the server. In this case, though, the URI is to `"/get"` and we send along this client browser's id (assigned to the browser in the `connect()` call), encoded as a JSON string. As with `connect()`, the response handler

1) confirms a `readyState` of `DONE`, meaning we have the final response,
2) confirms that the HTTP request succeeded (status of `200` and non-null response), and
3) confirms that the response does not contain an `err` property.

Assuming nothing went wrong, the entire response is sent to the response handler passed in as argument to the `get()` method.

`handleMessage()`, the next piece of code, is called from within `getLoop()` inside `poll()` for each received message. All it does is to schedule the signaling channel's `messageHandler()` callback to be run asynchronously on the message.

The final piece of client signaling code is the definition of `send()`, the routine that sends a message on the signaling channel to the peer. The main code at the end of this method looks much like `connect()` and `get()` did – a new XMLHttpRequest to the server. In this case, though, the URI is to `"/send"` and we send along this client browser's id (assigned to the browser in the `connect()` call) and message (provided as a parameter to `send()`). Again, these two are encoded as a JSON string, and as with `connect()` and `get()`, the routine's response handler

1) confirms a `readyState` of DONE, meaning we have the final response,
2) confirms that the HTTP request succeeded (status of 200 and non-null response), and
3) confirms that the response did not contain an `err` property.

As with `get()`, we merely pass the entire response to the response handler passed in as argument to the `send()` method. Unlike for `connect()` and `get()`, note that for `send()` we don't expect any real info in the response – it's there mainly for passing errors and, perhaps, status messages that can be logged.

4.5.3 Client WebRTC Application

Once again, we are building onto our existing demo, this time adding a signaling channel. Here's the code, then the explanation.

```html
<!--
// Copyright 2013-2014 Digital Codex LLC
// You may use this code for your own education.  If you use it
// largely intact, or develop something from it, don't claim that
// your code came first.  You are using this code completely at
// your own risk.  If you rely on it to work in any particular
// way, you're an idiot and we won't be held responsible.
-->

<html>
<head>
  <meta http-equiv="Content-Type"
        content="text/html; charset=UTF-8" />
  <style>
    video {
      width:   320px;
      height:  240px;
      border:  1px solid black;
    }
    div {
      display:  inline-block;
```

```
    }
  </style>
</head>
<body>

<!-- blank script section is placeholder for query params -->
<script></script>

<!-- load polyfill, local copy first for local testing -->
<script src="extra/adapter.js" type="text/javascript"></script>
<script
  src="https://webrtc.googlecode.com/svn/trunk/samples/js/base/adapter.js"
  type="text/javascript"></script>

<!-- load XHR-based signaling channel that direct connects based
     on a key -->
<script src="clientXHRSignalingChannel.js"
        type="text/javascript"></script>

<script>
var signalingChannel, key, id,
    haveLocalMedia = false,
    connected = false,
    myVideoStream, myVideo;

////////////////////////////
// This is the main routine.
////////////////////////////

// This kicks off acquisition of local media.  Also, it can
// automatically start the signaling channel.
window.onload = function () {

  // auto-connect signaling channel if key provided in URI
  if (queryparams && queryparams['key']) {
    document.getElementById("key").value = queryparams['key'];
    connect();
  }

  myVideo = document.getElementById("myVideo");

  getMedia();
};


//////////////////////
// This next section is for setting up the signaling channel.
//////////////////////

// This routine connects to the web server and sets up the
// signaling channel.  It is called either automatically on doc
// load or when the user clicks on the "Connect" button.
function connect() {
  var errorCB, scHandlers, handleMsg;

  // First, get the key used to connect
  key = document.getElementById("key").value;

  // This is the handler for all messages received on the
```

```
  // signaling channel.
  handleMsg = function (msg) {
    // Post the message on-screen
    var msgE = document.getElementById("inmessages");
    var msgString = JSON.stringify(msg);
    msgE.value = msgString + "\n" + msgE.value;
  };

  // handlers for signaling channel
  scHandlers = {
    'onWaiting' : function () {
      setStatus("Waiting");
    },
    'onConnected': function () {
      connected = true;
      setStatus("Connected");
      // wait for local media to be ready
      verifySetupDone();
    },
    'onMessage': handleMsg
  };

  // Finally, create signaling channel
  signalingChannel = createSignalingChannel(key, scHandlers);
  errorCB = function (msg) {
    document.getElementById("response").innerHTML = msg;
  };

  // and connect.
  signalingChannel.connect(errorCB);
}


// This routine sends a message on the signaling channel, either
// by explicit call or by the user clicking on the Send button.
function send(msg) {
  var handler = function (res) {
    document.getElementById("response").innerHTML = res;
    return;
  },

  // Get message if not passed in
  msg = msg || document.getElementById("message").value;

  // Post it on-screen
  msgE = document.getElementById("outmessages");
  var msgString = JSON.stringify(msg);
  msgE.value = msgString + "\n" + msgE.value;

  // and send on signaling channel
  signalingChannel.send(msg, handler);
}


/////////////////////////////
// This next section is for getting local media
/////////////////////////////

function getMedia() {
```

```
    getUserMedia({"audio":true, "video":true},
               gotUserMedia, didntGetUserMedia);
}

function gotUserMedia(stream) {
  myVideoStream = stream;
  haveLocalMedia = true;

  // display my local video to me
  attachMediaStream(myVideo, myVideoStream);
  // wait for signaling channel to be set up
  verifySetupDone();
}

function didntGetUserMedia() {
  console.log("couldn't get video");
}


// This guard routine effectively synchronizes completion of two
// async activities:  the creation of the signaling channel and
// acquisition of local media.
function verifySetupDone() {
  // If signaling channel is ready and we have local media,
  // proceed.
  if (connected && haveLocalMedia) {setStatus('Set up');}
}


//////////////////////////////////
// This section is for changing the UI based on application
// progress.
//////////////////////////////////

// This function hides, displays, and fills various UI elements
// to give the user some idea of how the browser is progressing
// at setting up the signaling channel and getting local media.
function setStatus(str) {
  var statuslineE = document.getElementById("statusline"),
      statusE = document.getElementById("status"),
      sendE = document.getElementById("send"),
      connectE = document.getElementById("connect"),
      scMessageE = document.getElementById("scMessage");

  switch (str) {
    case 'Waiting':
      statuslineE.style.display = "inline";
      statusE.innerHTML =
        "Waiting for peer signaling connection";
      sendE.style.display = "none";
      break;
    case 'Connected':
      statuslineE.style.display = "inline";
      statusE.innerHTML =
        "Peer signaling connected, waiting for local media";
      sendE.style.display = "inline";
      scMessageE.style.display = "inline-block";
      break;
    case 'Set up':
      statusE.innerHTML =
        "Peer signaling connected and local media obtained";
```

```
        break;
     default:
   }
}

</script>

<div id="setup">
  <p>WebRTC Book Demo (local media and signaling only)</p>
  <p>Key:
    <input type="text" name="key" id="key"
           onkeyup="if (event.keyCode == 13) {
                      connect(); return false;}"/>
    <button id="connect" onclick="connect()">Connect</button>
    <span id="statusline" style="display:none">Status:
      <span id="status">Disconnected</span>
    </span>
  </p>
</div>

<div id="scMessage" style="float:right;display:none">
  <p>Signaling channel message:
    <input type="text" width="100%" name="message" id="message"
           onkeyup="if (event.keyCode == 13) {
                      send(); return false;}"/>
    <button id="send" style="display:none"
            onclick="send()">Send</button>
  </p>

  <p>Response:  <span id="response"></span></p>
</div>

<br/>

<div style="width:30%;vertical-align:top">
  <div>
    <video id="myVideo" autoplay="autoplay" controls
           muted="true"/>
  </div>
  <p><b>Outgoing Messages</b>
    <br/>
    <textarea id="outmessages" rows="100"
              style="width:100%"></textarea>
  </p>
</div>

<div style="width:30%;vertical-align:top">
  <div>
    <video id="placeholder" autoplay="autoplay" controls />
  </div>
  <p><b>Incoming Messages</b>
    <br/>
    <textarea id="inmessages" rows="100"
              style="width:100%"></textarea>
  </p>
</div>

</body>
</html>
```

As before, we'll begin our explanation at the end of the file where the HTML markup lives. There are now three main sections: the upper left app control area, the upper right status and signaling message section (hidden by default via "display:none"), and the lower video/messages section. Figure 4.12 shows how this looks on Firefox.

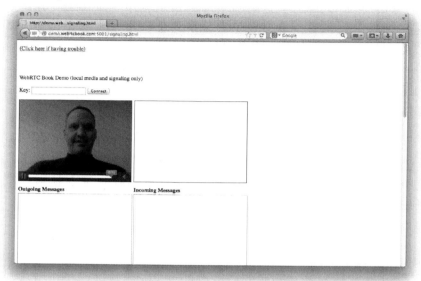

Figure 4.12 Signaling Demo Before Connection

The upper left app control area initially shows a field for entering a key and a Connect button that, when clicked, calls the connect() function that contacts the server with the key to set up the signaling channel. We'll get to that code in a moment. It also contains a status line that is initially hidden ("display:none"). Figure 4.13 shows the field with the key entered, but before clicking the Connect button. Note that the status line is not visible yet.

The upper right status and signaling message area will be explained when we get to the code that activates it, but for now know that it will contain an information area to hold responses to the various XMLHttpRequests, with an ability to manually send a message on the signaling channel. This section is largely for testing purposes, but it can be used as a primitive chat capability over the signaling channel. It is also not yet visible in Figure 4.13.

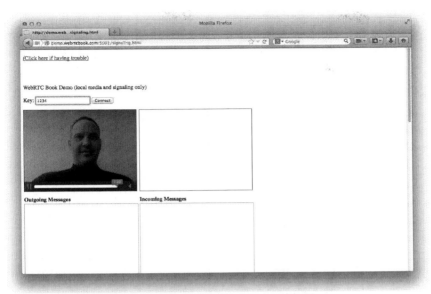

Figure 4.13 Signaling Demo with Key

The final section consists of two side-by-side video elements, one for this browser's video and one which will be used in a later version of the code to hold the peer's video, with a section under each showing the messages sent by that browser over the signaling channel. This is where all signaling channel messages will appear, most recent at the top. Note that we begin with the audio from our side muted in the video element. It's not necessary to play our own audio, and muting it reduces problems with feedback.

Let's look next at the `setStatus()` function right above the HTML. It simplifies display of the various HTML components into a single status setting. Screen shots of the various states are shown in Figures 4.14 through 4.19.

Now let's go back up to the top. We have added a new `<script></script>` block before we load adapter.js. Yes, it's empty! Remember our server code? `addQuery()` in server.js will insert into this block any query parameters included in the URI requesting this file. They will be inserted as properties on a new local `queryparams` variable. We now also load the clientXHRSignalingChannel.js library that we just covered.

In the main script section we have added a bunch of variables that will be used in setting up and working with the signaling channel. Although their use will likely be obvious later in the code, the two most interesting variables here are `haveLocalMedia` and `connected`. The first one is used

95

to track whether we have yet succeeded in capturing the local media, and the second is used to track whether we are yet connected to the other browser via the signaling channel (our server). It is only when both of these values are `true` that we know our application is completely set up. By tracking both of these independently, we can allow both processes to proceed in parallel – contacting the signaling server and waiting for the user to give permission to use the camera and microphone. We'll discuss the code that does this in a moment.

We have also added something quite useful to the page's `onload` handler. If the key is given as a query parameter on the URI, for example `"http://www.example.org:5001/signaling.html?key=1234"`, the key field on the screen is filled in with this value and then `connect()` is called automatically to connect to the server for setting up the signaling channel.

`connect()` is next, the routine that sets up the signaling channel. It can be activated by the user clicking the Connect button or automatically (in `window.onload` that we just reviewed) if the key is provided as a query parameter in the URI for this file request. The first action is to get the key from the key input field on the screen. We then define the handlers that will be used by the signaling channel. The `onWaiting` and `onConnected` handlers are defined in-line later, but the code for the `onMessage` handler will grow substantially later on when we add peer media negotiation, so we define it separately here as the `handleMsg()` function. At this stage all we do is to prepend the message to the messages list under the remote video (since it was sent by the remote browser).

Look at the handlers defined next for `onWaiting` and `onConnected`. When connected we set our status to `connected` and wait for local media to be set up. Figure 4.14 shows how it looks if we manage to connect before local media is obtained. Note that if we happen to be the first browser to connect with the given key, the `onWaiting` handler will be called, in which case we set the status to `waiting` so the user can be informed, and we record that we were the one who waited. (See Figure 4.15.)

Now that the handlers for the signaling channel have all been set, we can call `createSignalingChannel()` with the key and handlers and then call its `connect()` method to connect. Figure 4.16 shows how things look when everything is set up – both local media and the signaling channel.

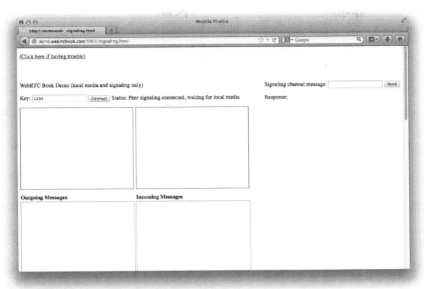

Figure 4.14 Waiting for Local Media

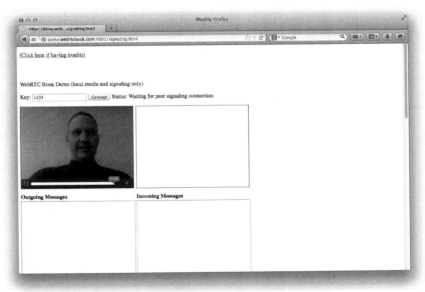

Figure 4.15 Waiting for Peer to Connect

Figure 4.16 Signaling Channel Established

send() is used to send a message on the signaling channel to the other browser. If the message is passed as a parameter it will be sent; otherwise, the message will be pulled from the message field on-screen. The user can call send() explicitly by clicking on the Send button in the upper right portion of the screen. In either case, the message is prepended to the message list under this browser's video, since it's an outgoing message. The final step is to send it on the signaling channel. Figure 4.17 shows an incoming message, and Figure 4.18 shows a message ready to be sent on the signaling channel.

Figure 4.17 Incoming Signaling Message

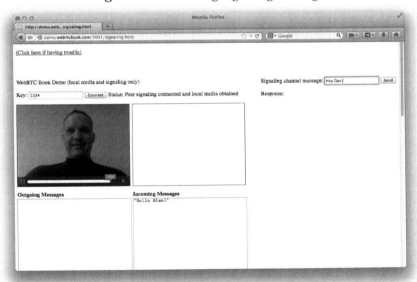

Figure 4.18 Outgoing Signaling Message

The only other change is in `gotUserMedia()`, which now records that we actually have received local media (`haveLocalMedia = true`) and finishes up by calling `verifySetupDone()` to check whether the signaling channel has finished being set up.

99

Note that, in this code example, there is no authentication or authorization in the use of the server's signaling channel capabilities. You will most likely want to have both in any real application you write!

4.6 References

[RFC6189] http://tools.ietf.org/html/rfc6189

[RFC5763] http://tools.ietf.org/html/rfc5763

[AJAX]   http://en.wikipedia.org/wiki/Ajax_(programming)

[JQUERY]   http://jquery.com

[WS-API] http://www.w3.org/TR/websockets/

[XHR] http://www.w3.org/TR/XMLHttpRequest/

[GINGER-TECH]   http://blog.gingertech.net/2012/06/04/video-conferencing-in-html5-webrtc-via-web-sockets/

[APPRTC] https://apprtc.appspot.com/

[APP-ENGINE-CHANNEL]
https://developers.google.com/appengine/docs/java/channel/overview

[RFC3261]   http://tools.ietf.org/html/rfc3261

[RFC7118]   http://tools.ietf.org/html/rfc7118

[RFC3327]   http://tools.ietf.org/html/rfc3327

[RFC5627]   http://tools.ietf.org/html/rfc5627

[RFC5626]   http://tools.ietf.org/html/rfc5626

[RFC6120]   http://tools.ietf.org/html/rfc6120

[XEP-0124] http://xmpp.org/extensions/xep-0124.html

[XEP-0206] http://xmpp.org/extensions/xep-0206.html

[draft-ietf-xmpp-websocket]   http://tools.ietf.org/html/draft-ietf-xmpp-websocket

[XMPP-LIBRARIES] http://xmpp.org/xmpp-software/libraries/

[CHORD]   Stoica, I., Morris, R., Liben-Nowell, D., Karger, D., Kaashoek, M., Dabek, F., and H. Balakrishnan, "Chord: A Scalable Peer-to-peer Lookup Protocol for Internet Applications", IEEE/ACM Transactions on Networking Volume 11, Issue 1, 17-32, Feb 2003, 2001

[RELOAD]   http://tools.ietf.org/html/draft-ietf-p2psip-base

[P2PSIP] http://tools.ietf.org/wg/p2psip/

[OPEN-PEER]   http://openpeer.org

5 PEER-TO-PEER MEDIA

WebRTC uses unique peer-to-peer media flows, where voice, video, and data connections are established directly between browsers. Unfortunately, Network Address Translation (NAT) and firewalls make this difficult and require special protocols and procedures to work. STUN and TURN servers, introduced in this chapter, are used to help establish peer-to-peer media.

5.1 WebRTC Media Flows

For the media flows between browsers discussed in this chapter, the four browsers in Figure 5.1 will be used as a reference to illustrate the concepts.

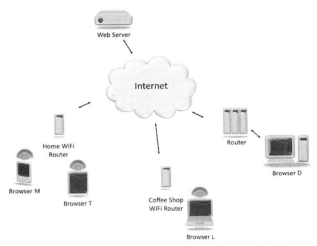

Figure 5.1 WebRTC Browsers Connecting to the Internet

The mobile and the tablet access the Internet through the home WiFi router. The laptop connects through a WiFi router at a coffee shop. The PC connects to the Internet through a corporate router.

5.1.1 Media Flows without WebRTC

Without WebRTC or a plugin, a browser could establish media flows. However, these media flows must follow the same path as the web browsing traffic. In other words, the media packets will flow from one browser to the web server, then to the other browser. This is shown in Figure 5.2 below. The web server needs to handle the extra traffic as a result. High definition video streams can use considerable bandwidth. This limits the scalability of this architecture.

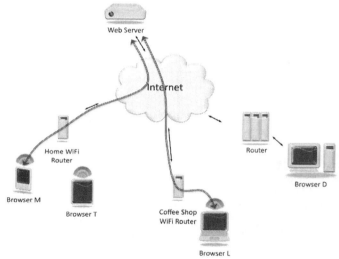

Figure 5.2 Media Flows without WebRTC

5.1.2 Media Flows with WebRTC

The goal of the `RTCPeerConnection` API in WebRTC is to enable the establishment of direct peer-to-peer media connections between browsers. This flow would look like Figure 5.3.

This path for the media can have few Internet hops, take less time (lower latency), and have a lower chance of packet loss. As a result, these types of peer-to-peer media flows can result in much better quality connections. It reduces the bandwidth used by the web server. It also makes the geographic proximity of the web server to the browsers a non-issue. For example, if the two browsers were located, for instance, in Japan, but the web server was located in Europe, the media flow of Figure 5.2 would be very problematic, but the peer-to-peer flow of Figure 5.3 would be much better. These peer-to-peer media flows dramatically reduce the costs of offering a real-time communications service.

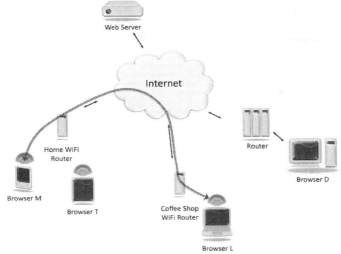

Figure 5.3 Peer-to-Peer Media Flow with WebRTC

However, establishing this media flow is actually quite complicated, as most Internet devices connect to the Internet through a Network Address Translation (NAT) function, as will be discussed in the next section.

5.2 WebRTC and Network Address Translation (NAT)

It is extremely common for browsers to be behind NATs – Network Address Translation devices. A more realistic connection of the browsers is shown in Figure 5.4 with every browser behind a NAT.

NAT is a function often built into Internet routers or hubs that map one IP address space to another space. Usually, NATs are used to allow a number of devices to share an IP address, such as in a residential router or hub. NATs are also used by enterprises or service providers to segment IP networks, simplifying control and administration. Each network behind a NAT is effectively an island, and hosts on that network rely completely on the NAT device providing access. Note that NATs are actually NAPTs – Network Address and Port Translators. Mostly, the term NAT is used even for devices that change transport port numbers in addition to transport addresses.

Many Internet protocols, especially those using a client/server architecture (for instance normal web browsing, email, etc.), have no difficulty traversing NATs. However, end-to-end or peer-to-peer protocols and services can have major difficulties. Unfortunately, WebRTC is one

105

such service.

In Figure 5.4, the laptop is connected to the Internet through a WiFi router that has built in NAT. The mobile browser and tablet browser connect to the Internet through a WiFi hub that has built in NAT and share a single IP address. The PC connects using an enterprise router with NAT.

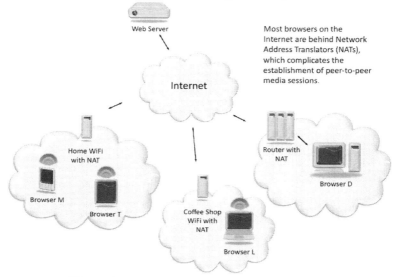

Figure 5.4 WebRTC Browsers Behind NAT

The next sections will discuss the types of media flows that can be established with WebRTC. Some are peer-to-peer across multiple NATs, peer-to-peer behind the same NAT, or relayed through dedicated TURN servers.

5.2.1 Peer-to-Peer Media Flow through Multiple NATs

Figure 5.5 shows a peer to peer media flow that can be established using WebRTC, using the hole punching techniques described in Chapter 9. The media flow can bypass the web server and flow directly between the two browsers, through the NATs.

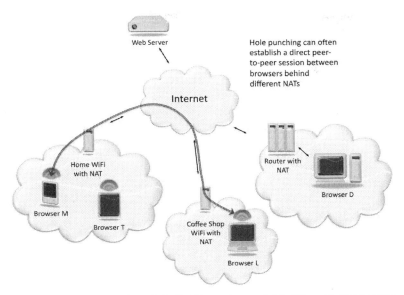

Figure 5.5 Peer-to-Peer Media Flow through NATs with WebRTC

5.2.2 Peer-to-Peer Media Flow through a Common NAT

Figure 5.6 shows the case where a media session is established between two browsers behind the same NAT. In this case, the

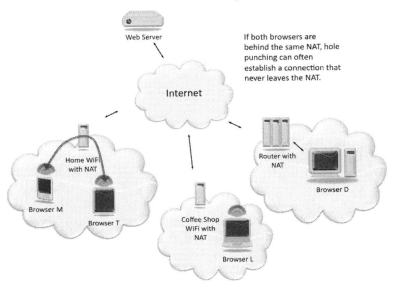

Figure 5.6 Media Flow when Browsers are Behind the Same NAT

optimal media path is to stay on the local area network and never go up to the Internet, as shown. This case also has very desirable quality, bandwidth, and security properties. As in the previous case, hole punching is needed to achieve this media flow.

5.2.3 Private and Public Addresses

Common NAT terminology uses the terms "private address" and "public address". The IP addresses behind a NAT (or "inside" the NAT) are "private" IP addresses (used inside each of the NAT clouds in the figures). The IP address (or possibly multiple addresses) assigned to the NAT, and used whenever the NAT forwards packets from the inside to the outside, is the "public" IP addresses (used "outside" the NAT). This is shown for the home WiFi network in Figure 5.7.

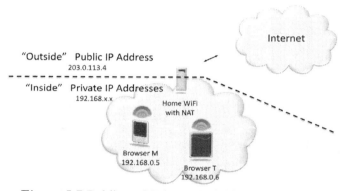

Figure 5.7 Public and Private IP Addresses and NAT

In this example, the home Wifi NAT has been assigned (by the Internet Service Provider of the house) the IP address 203.0.113.4 – this is the outside public IP address of the NAT, and all hosts that connect to the Internet through this NAT will share this IP address. The mobile device and the tablet each have an IP address that has been assigned by the NAT, which is a private IP address.

Note that these addresses are public in the same sense as we call the telephone network the Public Switched Telephone Network. Public IP addresses are usable (routable) anywhere on the Internet. Public IP addresses have to be unique on the Internet, and they are managed in central registries for the Internet and assigned by Internet Service Providers. They are analogous to a full mailing address including the country name, or a telephone number that includes the country code. Private IP addresses, on the other hand, do not have any special privacy features or capabilities. Rather, they are private as in private property – they are only valid within the network hosted by the NAT. There are specific IP address ranges (e.g. 192.168.x.x, 10.x.x.x, and 172.16.x.x-172.31.x.x) that anyone may use inside their own network. They do not need to be unique as they are only valid inside that network. They are analogous to a campus box or intra-company mail address, or a telephone number that is an extension, and only valid inside that building or campus.

A NAT maintains tables of mapping between inside IP (private) addresses and port numbers, and outside (public) IP address and port numbers. In addition to this mapping, NATs also maintain filter rules about which IP addresses and port numbers in the public Internet are permitted to use the mappings that have been created. There are a number of different categories of NATs depending on the rules they apply in generating the NAT mappings and filter rules.

5.3 STUN Servers

One type of server used to help traverse NATs is known as a STUN (Session Traversal Utilities for NAT) Server, described in Section 10.2.5. Each browser queries the STUN Server by sending a STUN packet. The STUN Server responds indicating the IP address that it observes in the test packet as shown in Figure 5.8. That is, it responds with the mapped address from the NAT (actually the outermost NAT if there are multiple levels of NAT). This IP address learned from the STUN server is shared with the other browser and becomes a potential "candidate" address.

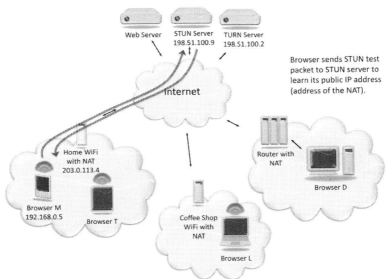

Figure 5.8 Browser use of STUN Server.

The private IP address is obtained through the operating system from the network interface cards, NICs. These addresses could be IPv4 or IPv6, or a combination of both. In addition, a Virtual Private Network or VPN connection could provide an additional address. Other NAT traversal protocols such as Universal Plug and Play (UPnP) could be used, although these are uncommon.

5.4 TURN Servers

Another server used to help traverse NATs is a TURN (Traversal Using Relay around NAT) Server, described in Section 10.2.6. A browser queries a TURN Server to obtain a media relay address. The media relay address is a public IP address that will forward packets received to and from the browser. A relayed address will work in cases where a direct peer-to-peer media session is simply not possible due to the types of NATs between the peers.

While this media flow is not ideal, at least the media is not being relayed through the Web Server as it was in Figure 5.2. Also, this will only occur in a limited number of scenarios where there is no alternative – all direct media paths have failed, as shown in Figure 5.9.

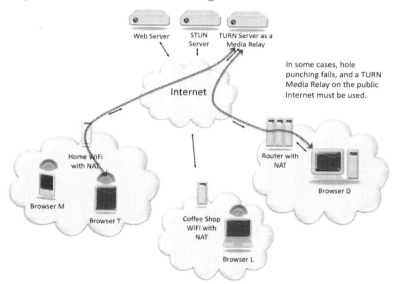

Figure 5.9 Media Relayed Through TURN Server

5.5 Candidates

Hole punching, described in Chapter 9, relies on each peer in the to-be-established session to gather a set of potential ways in which they might be reachable over the Internet. These sets of IP addresses and ports are known as address candidates, or simply as candidates. With the help of a STUN server, a browser can learn if it is behind a NAT, and the IP address of that NAT – this is known as a reflexive candidate. Using a TURN server, a browser can acquire a relayed address – an IP address and port on the public Internet that will forward traffic to the browser. This is known as a relayed candidate. In JavaScript, these are held in the `candidate` property of the `RTCIceCandidates` object.

The protocol used to implement hole punching, known as ICE, Interactive Connectivity Establishment, is discussed in Chapter 9.

6 PEER CONNECTION AND OFFER/ANSWER NEGOTIATION

The WebRTC standard defines two main batches of functionality: media capture, described in Chapter 3, and Media transmission, covered in this chapter. At the heart of establishing WebRTC peer-to-peer media and data is the notion of a Peer Connection along with an offer/answer negotiation. This chapter looks at these two key pieces – Peer Connections and offer/answer negotiation – in detail.

6.1 Peer Connections

The RTCPeerConnection interface is the primary API of the WebRTC effort. The function of this API is to set up media and data connection paths between two browsers. Although the API is strongly tied to the JavaScript Session Establishment Protocol (JSEP, described in Section 11.3.8) for media negotiation, most of the details for JSEP are handled by the browser.

The definition of a Peer Connection in the WebRTC specification can be a bit confusing. The RTCPeerConnection interface defines how to create a Peer Connection, which as we'll see in a moment is trivial. However, several other APIs are defined as part of the RTCPeerConnection interface as well: data channel creation, DTMF enabling and control, a connection statistics API, and controls for (human) peer identity establishment and verification. In this chapter we will only be discussing Peer Connections and media negotiation.

A WebRTC Peer Connection is, oddly enough, not a connection, at least not in the same way that TCP is. It is a set of path establishment processes (ICE) and a negotiation machine that can figure out what media and data paths should be established.

The constructor for the RTCPeerConnection object takes a

configuration object containing several properties, the most important of which, iceServers, is a list of the addresses of servers that assist in establishing sessions through NATs and firewalls (STUN and TURN servers, described in Section 10.2.5 and 10.2.6):

```
// create Peer Connection
pc = new RTCPeerConnection(
      {iceServers:[{"url":"stun:stun.1.google.com:19302"},
                   {"url":"turn:user@turn.myserver.com",
                    "credential":"test"}]});
```

The next step in getting your local MediaStream to the other browser is to tell your browser about it. The method for doing that is addStream():

```
// get local audio and video
getUserMedia({"audio":true, "video":true}, successCB, failureCB);

function successCB(myStream) {
  // tell my browser I want to send the MediaStream
  pc.addStream(myStream);
}
```

As you can see, "adding" a MediaStream to a Peer Connection is very simple. The surprise here is that no media flows as a result of doing this. All addStream() actually does is to tell the browser that you want it to negotiate with the peer about sending the MediaStream. There is a corresponding removeStream() method, but there are ongoing discussions about potentially removing that method since it is rare to remove a stream without also intending to remove the entire Peer Connection.

So, how do we get media flowing? Before we can look at the methods to set that up, we need to review offer/answer negotiation.

6.2 Offer/Answer Negotiation

In order to establish a media session between two parties, the session must be negotiated between them. A negotiation is necessary because the two parties need to determine a common set of capabilities and features for the session. This set is not known in advance, as it depends on the particular version of the browser used by each side, the JavaScript running on that browser, and the choices of each user. The approach used in WebRTC is known as "offer/answer," which is a single pass negotiation mechanism. One party initiates the media session by creating a description of the type of media session they would like to establish – this is known as the "offer." The first party sends the offer to the other party using the signaling channel. The other party then replies with a reply known as the "answer." The answer will list the capabilities and features of the session proposed by the first party that the other party is able or willing to support or use for this session. The answer is sent back to the first party again over the signaling channel. The whole exchange, from the generation of the offer to the receipt of the answer, is known as the offer/answer exchange or the offer/answer negotiation.

The offer/answer exchange ensures that both parties know what type of media to send and receive and how to decode and process that media properly. This includes information such as the codec or codecs to be used, parameters of those codecs, keying information for the media encryption and authentication. In addition, the exchange also allows both parties to agree on which media types (audio, video, or data channel) are to be established, and how many of each type will be multiplexed over the same transport addresses. Identifying information about the media flows is also exchanged, such as media stream IDs (MSIDs) which tie the JavaScript operations to the received media. Note that in practice it is possible that more than one offer/answer exchange may be needed in order to get everything negotiated properly. For example, if multiple `MediaStreamTracks` are to be multiplexed and sent together over a single port, it may take more than one offer/answer exchange to arrange that.

WebRTC uses an `RTCSessionDescription` object, which is a container for a session description, to represent offers and answers. Each browser will generate an `RTCSessionDescription` object and also receive one from the other browser through the signaling channel. The details about how the Session Description Protocol is used in an `RTCSessionDescription` are covered in Section 12.2.1. The next section discusses how JavaScript generates and uses `RTCSessionDescription` objects.

6.3 JavaScript Offer/Answer Control

There are several coding steps involved in arranging this offer/answer negotiation. Really, all your local browser cares about is two particular calls:

```
// tell my browser what my session description is
pc.setLocalDescription(mySessionDescription);

// tell my browser what the peer's session description is
pc.setRemoteDescription(yourSessionDescription);
```

In this code, `mySessionDescription` is an object that describes the media flow *from my browser's perspective*. In other words, this particular session description may well describe not only what I want to send, but what I want to receive. In contrast, `yourSessionDescription` is an object that describes the media flow from the *other browser's* perspective. It may also describe not only what it wants to send, but what it wants to receive as well. If these two are compatible according to SDP negotiation rules (see the examples of actual browser SDP offers and answers in Sections 12.2.2.1

and 12.2.2.2), then we have a successful negotiation and the media can begin flowing. Note that one of these will be an offer and the other an answer, but either one can be our local description and the other one the remote description. Successful negotiation with only one offer and one answer, then, depends on having them be compatible, with one set as the local description and the other set as the remote description. Since the syntax for these offer and answer RTCSessionDescription objects can be quite complex, and since WebRTC tries to hide as much complexity as possible from the web developer, WebRTC provides special methods for the developer that will have the browser generate the offers and answers for you:

```
// generate an offer
pc.createOffer(gotOffer, didntGetOffer);
function gotOffer(aSessionDescription) {
    // life is good.
    setLocalDescription(aSessionDescription);
    // Now send the session description (the offer) to the peer so
    // it can a) pass the offer to setRemoteDescription and b) call
    // createAnswer as shown below.
}

///////// OR /////////

// generate an answer (requires setRemoteDescription to have been
// called already with the offer)
pc.createAnswer(gotAnswer, didntGetAnswer);
function gotAnswer(aSessionDescription) {
    // life is really good.
    setLocalDescription(aSessionDescription);
    // Now send the session description (the answer) to the peer so
    // it can pass the answer to setRemoteDescription.
}

// Note that for a given negotiation, you will only generate *one*
// of these!  Whoever generates the offer is starting the
// negotiation.  Whoever receives the offer from the other must
// then generate an answer and send it back.
```

Whew! The code above looks complex for two reasons:
1. it shows both the calling and answering code, and
2. it shows the parallel steps that have to be taken of a) creating offers or answers and b) setting the local **and** remote descriptions.

This will all make more sense when you can see the code in context in the example in the next section, but before looking at that there are a few other points to cover. It's easy to know when to generate an answer – when you have received an offer from the peer. But when do you generate an offer? Ultimately only the browser knows when a new offer/answer negotiation needs to occur, and WebRTC provides the negotiationneeded event and associated onnegotiationneeded handler that can be defined to generate an offer, etc. It will execute this handler anytime it realizes that something has changed that would require media negotiation. This could happen because your application called addStream(), it could happen because the remote peer changed a stream, and it could even happen because of some media failure that the browser realized it could fix with a new negotiation. In short, your code should set the onnegotiationneeded handler in order to be robust to calls for new media negotiation. For simplicity of explanation, the sample code in this book never does that. Instead, one side generates an offer just as soon as the media has been added via addStream() and there is a signaling channel over which the offer and answer can be exchanged.

Another important point to note here is that there are no standardized methods for exchanging the offers and answers. That is the job of your code, your *signaling channel code* to be precise. If you don't know what that is, you must have skipped Chapter 4, so go back and read it!

Finally, there are a large number of handlers and status attributes that will eventually be usable for tracking the state of the offer/answer exchange, something you may wish to use to increase the user-friendliness of your application when the simple offer/answer negotiation fails for some reason. Chapter 8 briefly lists many of these handlers and attributes, but be aware that the specific names and particularly allowed values for many of these are still in flux at this time.

6.4 Runnable Code Example: Peer Connection and Offer/Answer Negotiation

We continue building on our example from the signaling chapter by adding peer connections and negotiation of media using the offer/answer capabilities of WebRTC. Media connections are negotiated between the two browsers by sending SDP offers and answers across the signaling channel between the two parties. Then, the browsers send media as directly as possible between themselves.

This time, the only differences are in the HTML file. That is what will be presented in the next section.

6.4.1 Client WebRTC Application

```
<!--
// Copyright 2013-2014 Digital Codex LLC
// You may use this code for your own education. If you use it
// largely intact, or develop something from it, don't claim that
// your code came first. You are using this code completely at
// your own risk. If you rely on it to work in any particular
// way, you're an idiot and we won't be held responsible.
-->
```

```html
<html>
<head>
  <meta http-equiv="Content-Type"
        content="text/html; charset=UTF-8" />
  <style>
    video {
      width:   320px;
      height:  240px;
      border:  1px solid black;
    }
    div {
      display:  inline-block;
    }
  </style>
</head>
<body>

<!-- blank script section is placeholder for query params -->
<script></script>

<!-- load polyfill, local copy first for local testing -->
<script src="extra/adapter.js" type="text/javascript"></script>
<script
  src="https://webrtc.googlecode.com/svn/trunk/samples/js/base/adapter.js"
  type="text/javascript"></script>

<!-- load XHR-based signaling channel that direct connects based
     on a key -->
<script src="clientXHRSignalingChannel.js"
        type="text/javascript"></script>

<script>
var signalingChannel, key, id,
    haveLocalMedia = false,
    weWaited = false,
    myVideoStream, myVideo,
    yourVideoStream, yourVideo,
    doNothing = function() {},
    pc,
    constraints = {mandatory: {
                    OfferToReceiveAudio: true,
                    OfferToReceiveVideo: true}};

////////////////////////////
// This is the main routine.
////////////////////////////

// This kicks off acquisition of local media.  Also, it can
// automatically start the signaling channel.
window.onload = function () {

  // auto-connect signaling channel if key provided in URI
  if (queryparams && queryparams['key']) {
    document.getElementById("key").value = queryparams['key'];
    connect();
  }

  myVideo = document.getElementById("myVideo");
```

```
yourVideo = document.getElementById("yourVideo");

getMedia();

// connect() calls createPC() when connected.
// attachMedia() is called when both createPC() and getMedia()
// have succeeded.
};


///////////////////////
// This next section is for setting up the signaling channel.
///////////////////////

// This routine connects to the web server and sets up the
// signaling channel.  It is called either automatically on doc
// load or when the user clicks on the "Connect" button.
function connect() {
  var errorCB, scHandlers, handleMsg;

  // First, get the key used to connect
  key = document.getElementById("key").value;

  // This is the handler for all messages received on the
  // signaling channel.
  handleMsg = function (msg) {
    // First, we clean up the message and post it on-screen
    var msgE = document.getElementById("inmessages");
    var msgString = JSON.stringify(msg).replace(/\\r\\n/g,'\n');
    msgE.value = msgString + "\n" + msgE.value;

    // Then, we take action based on the kind of message
    if (msg.type === "offer") {
      pc.setRemoteDescription(new RTCSessionDescription(msg));
      answer();
    } else if (msg.type === "answer") {
      pc.setRemoteDescription(new RTCSessionDescription(msg));
    } else if (msg.type === "candidate") {
      pc.addIceCandidate(
        new RTCIceCandidate({sdpMLineIndex:msg.mlineindex,
                             candidate:msg.candidate}));
    }
  };

  // handlers for signaling channel
  scHandlers = {
    'onWaiting' : function () {
      setStatus("Waiting");
      // weWaited will be used later for auto-call
      weWaited = true;
    },
    'onConnected': function () {
      setStatus("Connected");
      // set up the RTC Peer Connection since we're connected
      createPC();
    },
    'onMessage': handleMsg
  };
```

```
  // Finally, create signaling channel
  signalingChannel = createSignalingChannel(key, scHandlers);
  errorCB = function (msg) {
    document.getElementById("response").innerHTML = msg;
  };

  // and connect.
  signalingChannel.connect(errorCB);
}


// This routine sends a message on the signaling channel, either
// by explicit call or by the user clicking on the Send button.
function send(msg) {
  var handler = function (res) {
    document.getElementById("response").innerHTML = res;
    return;
  },

  // Get message if not passed in
  msg = msg || document.getElementById("message").value;

  // Clean it up and post it on-screen
  msgE = document.getElementById("outmessages");
  var msgString = JSON.stringify(msg).replace(/\\r\\n/g,'\n');
  msgE.value = msgString + "\n" + msgE.value;

  // and send on signaling channel
  signalingChannel.send(msg, handler);
}


/////////////////////////////
// This next section is for getting local media
/////////////////////////////

function getMedia() {
  getUserMedia({"audio":true, "video":true},
               gotUserMedia, didntGetUserMedia);
}

function gotUserMedia(stream) {
  myVideoStream = stream;
  haveLocalMedia = true;

  // display my local video to me
  attachMediaStream(myVideo, myVideoStream);
  // wait for RTCPeerConnection to be created
  attachMediaIfReady();
}

function didntGetUserMedia() {
  console.log("couldn't get video");
}


/////////////////////////////
// This next section is for setting up the RTC Peer Connection
/////////////////////////////
```

```
function createPC() {
  var stunuri = true,
      turnuri = false,
      myfalse = function(v) {
                  return ((v==="0")||(v==="false")||(!v)); },
      config = new Array();

  // adjust config string based on any query params
  if (queryparams) {
    if ('stunuri' in queryparams) {
      stunuri = !myfalse(queryparams['stunuri']);
    }
    if ('turnuri' in queryparams) {
      turnuri = !myfalse(queryparams['turnuri']);
    };
  };

if (stunuri) {
    // this is one of Google's public STUN servers
    config.push({"url":"stun:stun.l.google.com:19302"});
  }
  if (turnuri) {
    if (stunuri) {
      // can't use TURN-only TURN server in this case because of
      // bug in Chrome that causes STUN server responses to be
      // ignored, so we use TURN server that also does STUN
      config.push({"url":"turn:user@turn.webrtcbook.com",
                   "credential":"test"});
    } else {
      // this is our TURN-only TURN server
      config.push({"url":"turn:user@turn-only.webrtcbook.com",
                   "credential":"test"});
    }
  }
  console.log("config = " + JSON.stringify(config));

  pc = new RTCPeerConnection({iceServers:config});
  pc.onicecandidate = onIceCandidate;
  pc.onaddstream = onRemoteStreamAdded;
  pc.onremovestream = onRemoteStreamRemoved;

  // wait for local media to be ready
  attachMediaIfReady();
}

// When our browser has another candidate, send it to the peer
function onIceCandidate(e) {
  if (e.candidate) {
    send({type:  'candidate',
          mlineindex:  e.candidate.sdpMLineIndex,
          candidate:  e.candidate.candidate});
  }
}

// When our browser detects that the other side has added the
// media stream, show it on screen
function onRemoteStreamAdded(e) {
  yourVideoStream = e.stream;
  attachMediaStream(yourVideo, yourVideoStream);
```

```
      setStatus("On call");
    }

    // Yes, we do nothing if the remote side removes the stream.
    // This is a *simple* demo, after all.
    function onRemoteStreamRemoved(e) {}


    ///////////////////////////////////
    // This next section is for attaching local media to the Peer
    // Connection.
    ///////////////////////////////////

    // This guard routine effectively synchronizes completion of two
    // async activities:  the creation of the Peer Connection and
    // acquisition of local media.
    function attachMediaIfReady() {
      // If RTCPeerConnection is ready and we have local media,
      // proceed.
      if (pc && haveLocalMedia) {attachMedia();}
    }

    // This routine adds our local media stream to the Peer
    // Connection.  Note that this does not cause any media to flow.
    // All it does is to let the browser know to include this stream
    // in its next SDP description.
    function attachMedia() {
      pc.addStream(myVideoStream);
      setStatus("Ready for call");

      // auto-call if truthy value for call param in URI
      // but also make sure we were the last to connect (to increase
      // chances that everything is set up properly at both ends)
      if (queryparams && queryparams['call'] && !weWaited) {
        call();
      }

    }


    /////////////////////////////
    // This next section is for calling and answering
    /////////////////////////////

    // This generates the session description for an offer
    function call() {
      pc.createOffer(gotDescription, doNothing, constraints);
    }

    // and this generates it for an answer.
    function answer() {
      pc.createAnswer(gotDescription, doNothing, constraints);
    }

    // In either case, once we get the session description we tell
    // our browser to use it as our local description and then send
    // it to the other browser.  It is the setting of the local
    // description that allows the browser to send media and prepare
    // to receive from the other side.
```

```
function gotDescription(localDesc) {
  pc.setLocalDescription(localDesc);
  send(localDesc);
}


//////////////////////////////////////
// This section is for changing the UI based on application
// progress.
//////////////////////////////////////

// This function hides, displays, and fills various UI elements
// to give the user some idea of how the browser is progressing
// at setting up the signaling channel, getting local media,
// creating the peer connection, and actually connecting
// media (calling).
function setStatus(str) {
  var statuslineE = document.getElementById("statusline"),
      statusE = document.getElementById("status"),
      sendE = document.getElementById("send"),
      connectE = document.getElementById("connect"),
      callE = document.getElementById("call"),
      scMessageE = document.getElementById("scMessage");

  switch (str) {
    case 'Waiting':
      statuslineE.style.display = "inline";
      statusE.innerHTML =
        "Waiting for peer signaling connection";
      sendE.style.display = "none";
      connectE.style.display = "none";
      break;
    case 'Connected':
      statuslineE.style.display = "inline";
      statusE.innerHTML =
        "Peer signaling connected, waiting for local media";
      sendE.style.display = "inline";
      connectE.style.display = "none";
      scMessageE.style.display = "inline-block";
      break;
    case 'Ready for call':
      statusE.innerHTML = "Ready for call";
      callE.style.display = "inline";
      break;
    case 'On call':
      statusE.innerHTML = "On call";
      callE.style.display = "none";
      break;
    default:
  }
}

</script>

<div id="setup">
  <p>WebRTC Book Demo (local media, signaling, and peer connection
only)</p>
  <p>Key:
    <input type="text" name="key" id="key"
```

```
                onkeyup="if (event.keyCode == 13) {
                        connect(); return false;}"/>
     <button id="connect" onclick="connect()">Connect</button>
     <span id="statusline" style="display:none">Status:
       <span id="status">Disconnected</span>
     </span>
     <button id="call" style="display:none"
             onclick = "call()">Call</button>
  </p>
</div>

<div id="scMessage" style="float:right;display:none">
  <p>Signaling channel message:
     <input type="text" width="100%" name="message" id="message"
            onkeyup="if (event.keyCode == 13) {
                        send(); return false;}"/>
     <button id="send" style="display:none"
             onclick="send()">Send</button>
  </p>

  <p>Response:   <span id="response"></span></p>
</div>

<br/>

<div style="width:30%;vertical-align:top">
  <div>
     <video id="myVideo" autoplay="autoplay" controls
            muted="true"/>
  </div>
  <p><b>Outgoing Messages</b>
     <br/>
     <textarea id="outmessages" rows="100"
               style="width:100%"></textarea>
  </p>
</div>

<div style="width:30%;vertical-align:top">
  <div>
     <video id="yourVideo" autoplay="autoplay" controls />
  </div>
  <p><b>Incoming Messages</b>
     <br/>
     <textarea id="inmessages" rows="100"
               style="width:100%"></textarea>
  </p>
</div>

</body>
</html>
```

Starting with the HTML markup at the end again, the only addition is a Call button that is hidden until everything is ready for the call to take place. Figure 6.1 shows that this version looks similar to our previous iteration before connecting, but in Figure 6.2 you can see how it looks now with the new Call button after setting up the signaling connection. Note now that the signaling message windows below the video elements are where the

SDP messages will appear, most recent at the top. In the description for the signaling code we noted that the audio from our side was muted in the video element. Even with our own audio muted it is still helpful to have headphones so the audio from the peer doesn't get fed back into the microphone on the device, something that happens easily on laptops.

Figure 6.1 Peer Connection Demo

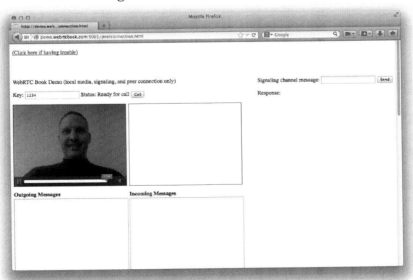

Figure 6.2 Ready for Call

Before going to the top of the file, take a quick look at the changes to the `setStatus()` function right above the HTML. We have done away with the "Set up" state and replaced it with the "Ready for call" state that enables the "Call" button. There is also a new "On call" state that is activated when the Peer Connection has been created and media offer/answer negotiation is complete.

Now we're ready to go to the top of the HTML file. The first change you'll notice is that there are several new variables. The only one worth noting at this point is `pc`, the variable which will hold the `RTCPeerConnection` object. It effectively replaces the `connected` variable since, as we will see in a moment, the Peer Connection is created as soon as we are connected. Thus, this variable having a defined value serves the purpose that `connected === true` did in our earlier code iteration.

Although the page's `onload` handler only adds a line that stores a reference to the video element for the remote video, there are now some important comments there as well. In the pseudo code we called `getMedia()` and `createPC()`, then `attachMedia()` to attach the local media to the newly-created Peer Connection. As mentioned above, in this real code it is `connect()` that calls `createPC()` when the signaling connection is established between the two browsers (still via the web server, of course), and `attachMedia()` is only called when both `createPC()` and `getMedia()` have succeeded, since you need both a Peer Connection and media to attach media to a Peer Connection! This will be clearer when we reach the code that does that.

Although we described in the signaling chapter how the basic `connect()` routine works, we have now added some code specific to the offer/answer messages we will be relaying over the signaling channel. The first new thing is the `replace(...)` code, whose sole purpose is to improve the visual display of SDP in the messaging windows. This is not something you would need to do in most WebRTC applications, since the end user will normally never see the SDP. Now that the signaling channel is being used for WebRTC, the next bit of new code takes appropriate WebRTC action based on the type of message we received. This is very similar to what's in the pseudo code, where for either an offer or an answer we set the remote session description to the value received. If what we received was an offer, then we need to generate and send an answer by calling `answer()`. The only other type of WebRTC message we send in this demo is an ICE candidate, so if we receive one from the other side we need to tell our browser about it by calling `addIceCandidate`. Note that by the time we handle a message we have already set up the Peer Connection, so all of these methods should be defined. How do we know that's the case? If you look at the handlers defined next for `onWaiting` and `onConnected`, you'll see that when connected we set our status to `connected` and call `createPC()` to set up the Peer Connection. Since we can't process a message until we are connected, and since messages are scheduled to be processed after the `onConnected` handler completes, we should be safe. In the `onWaiting` handler, the new `weWaited` variable gives us a hint as to the real reason that we are monitoring who connected first. We'll see later how this variable is used to determine which browser sends the offer if the `"call=1"` query parameter and value are set on the URI to indicate that the call should happen automatically.

In `send()`, we have also added the `replace(...)` code to help format the outgoing SDP messages. The next important change, though, is in the `gotUserMedia()` callback. We have replaced `verifySetupDone()` with the call that really matters — the guard function `attachMediaIfReady()`. The pseudo code immediately called `attachMedia()` to attach the media to the Peer Connection, but in this real code we need to make sure that we both have local media and have created the Peer Connection. Since both are asynchronous and can take significant time, `attachMediaIfReady()` is a check function that is called both after getting local media and after the Peer Connection is set up, so that once both are ready we can call `attachMedia()`.

`createPC()` here is very similar to the pseudo code. We create a new connection and set the various handlers for it. As with `getMedia()`, we finish by calling the `attachMediaIfReady()` check function. It's worth saying a few words here about the code that includes the STUN and TURN server URIs in the configuration for the call to new `RTCPeerConnection()`. The first bit of code checks to see if the `stunuri` and/or `turnuri` query parameters have been set. The `myfalse()` routine deals with JavaScript truthy values such as the string `"0"`, converting them to false so the query params will behave as expected. Next we use our `stunuri` and `turnuri` flags in the code to determine whether we will configure the Peer Connection with STUN and TURN servers. This code should be much simpler, but Google Chrome's WebRTC implementation has a bug that when you give a TURN URI for a TURN server that only supports TURN (and not STUN, as many do) it then ignores all STUN responses from all STUN servers, even ones provided in the servers list. Anyway, the code adds a STUN server if requested (the default), then adds a TURN server if requested, choosing a TURN-only or a TURN server with STUN support, depending on whether a STUN server was requested as well.

Next are the three handlers. First, `onIceCandidate()` will be called when our browser determines it has a new candidate address at which it might be reachable. So, to inform the other browser the code calls `send()` with the new candidate in the format the other browser expects for `addIceCandidate()`.

`onRemoteStreamAdded()` is called by the Peer Connection when the remote browser adds a new stream (via an offer or answer). The handler saves the media stream, displays it in the `yourVideo` element, and sets the status to "On Call" since our media streams are now set up.

Finally, `onRemoteStreamRemoved()` does absolutely nothing. It should do something, but that's a topic for a more advanced demo.

We have replaced `verifySetupDone()` with `attachMediaIfReady()`, the guard function that confirms that we have both a Peer Connection and local media, at which point it calls `attachMedia()`. `attachMedia()` is similar to how it appears in the pseudo code, calling `addStream()` with our local video so it can be included in the next offer or answer. At this point our Peer Connection is ready to negotiate media, so we are ready for the call. We set the status accordingly and then add a new automatic capability that will trigger if the `call` query parameter is given on the URI for this page with a value that will be interpreted by JavaScript as true – initiation of the `call()`, the offer/answer exchange the Peer Connection will do to negotiate media. Of course, there is a risk that both browsers will reach this point at the same time and both send offers. We can avoid this by picking one of the browsers to be the one that initiates the offer/answer exchange. Since all requests to our Node server are naturally serialized, one browser will have been the first to connect, receiving a status of `waiting` from the server. Hopefully that browser will already have set up both the Peer Connection and local media, so when the second browser, the one that wasn't waiting, has attached its media to the Peer Connection it should be ready to call. In short, we don't guarantee but do increase the chances that everything is set up on both sides by having the browser that didn't wait be the one to `call()`. The neat thing now about the key and call query parameters is that two users can just load a URI like `"http://www.example.org:5001/start.html?key=1234&call=1"`, the same URI for both, and the two apps should just connect up automatically – first the signaling channel and then the Peer Connection/media. A URI such as this could even be bookmarked with the person's name, or stored in an address book entry for that person's name.

Moving on, the final section of new code handles the calling and answering (offer and answer). `call()` calls `createOffer()` and `answer()` calls `createAnswer()`. In both cases, when the session description is ready it is given to the `gotDescription` callback, which sets it as our local description and then sends it to the other browser. Once both the local and remote descriptions have been set the two browsers can initiate the media and the "call" is set up! (See Figure 6.3.)

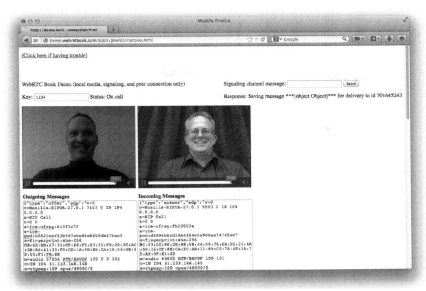

Figure 6.3 Call Established

Note that this code example only provides a single offer and a single answer. A real application should make use of `negotiationneeded` to handle the case where media needs to be renegotiated.

7 DATA CHANNEL

The WebRTC data channel is a non-media peer-to-peer connection established between browsers. It provides a flexible and configurable channel for web developers to exchange data directly, bypassing servers. While passing small amounts of data through a server using a WebSocket connection or HTTP message might be adequate for some applications, a data channel supports high volume and low latency connections with flexibility in the reliability. This chapter explains the data channel, the JavaScript APIs, and the underlying protocols.

7.1 Introduction to the Data Channel

Although advertisements for WebRTC primarily focus on its support for peer-to-peer media, the original designers always intended it to support real-time data as well.

The data channel is modeled on WebSockets, with a simple `send` method and an `onmessage` handler that can be set. Creation is simple and will be covered in the next section. Unlike with media, though, multiple data channels in a single Peer Connection all use the same underlying stream. Practically this means that only one offer/answer negotiation is needed to set up the first data channel, and after that all new data channels are negotiated automatically in the protocols used for the data channel, so there is no need for additional offer/answer exchanges at the JavaScript level to add more data channels.

One of the intended use cases for data channels was to provide real-time game status updates. With discussion, it became clear that there was a need for both guaranteed (reliable) delivery, even if it delayed the message, and unreliable but fast delivery. The former is useful for critical events such as "you shot me", while the latter could be useful for something like position updates which arrive at regular intervals.

The underlying protocol details about the Stream Control Transport Protocol (SCTP) that provides this functionality for the data channel are covered in Sections 10.2.12, 11.3.6, and 11.3.7.

7.2 Using Data Channels

The data channel API is part of the Peer Connection API, so a data channel can only be created once an RTCPeerConnection instance has been created.

```
pc = new RTCPeerConnection();
dc = pc.createDataChannel("dc1");
```

This is the simplest way to create a data channel. In this example, the new data channel will have a label of dc1. As mentioned earlier, only the first such data channel will require application-level offer/answer negotiation. With the simple syntax shown above, creating the data channel will cause the peer to receive an RTCDataChannelEvent which can be handled at the peer by setting the ondatachannel handler for the Peer Connection:

```
pc = new RTCPeerConnection();
pc.ondatachannel = function(e) {
  dc = e.channel;
};
```

At this point there is a bidirectional data channel between the peers. Whether created via createDataChannel() or returned via ondatachannel, you can now use it via the send() method and the onmessage handler:

```
dc.send("I can send a text string");
dc.send(new Blob(["I can send blobs"], {type:
"text/plain"}));
dc.send(new arrayBuffer(32));       // arrayBuffer also
dc.send(new uInt8Array([1,2,3])); // and arrayBufferViews
dc.onmessage = function(e) {
  console.log("Received message" + e.data);
}
```

A variety of configuration options exists for the data channel. These may only be used at the time the channel is created since they are negotiated between the peers. All are included as properties of an RTCDataChannelInit object. The properties you will likely use fall into two categories: reliability and creation style. By default, data channels are created to be *reliable*, meaning that any losses of data packets will be covered up automatically by the underlying transport through the use of retransmissions. Of course, if the connection is bad enough that no packets are getting through, then that means you don't have a connection at all. Assuming you do have a connection and most packets are getting through, you can control the level of retransmissions via two configuration parameters:

```
// Limit the number of times the channel will retransmit
// the data if it fails the first time
dc = pc.createDataChannel("", {maxRetransmits: 3});

// Limit the number of milliseconds the channel will
// permit for retries to occur
dc = pc.createDataChannel("", {maxRetransmitTime: 30});

// NOTE:  THESE ARE MUTUALLY EXCLUSIVE PROPERTIES
```

Although you can specify either configuration option, you may not specify both for the same data channel – they are mutually exclusive. When might you want to reduce the reliability of your data channel? When your need for speed is more important, and when lost data is not critical, perhaps because successive sends replace prior values.

Since each send occurs independently over the network, it is possible for different messages to take different paths and thus arrive in a different order than that in which they were sent. By default, WebRTC data channels will wait as long as necessary for messages to be assembled in order. For example, if message 1 fails and requires several retries, its successful retry might arrive after message 2 arrives. In the default case, the user agent will wait for a successful receipt of message 1 before releasing messages 1 and 2 to the onmessage handler. There is a configuration property to control this as well:

```
// Allow messages to be received as they arrive, even if
// out of order
dc = pc.createDataChannel("", {ordered: false});
```

Again, this may result in faster delivery to your application, which could be useful if messages are independent enough that order does not matter.

Since the remote peer does not create the data channel, but merely receives notification that one has been created, at this point you may be wondering how the remote peer could establish different values for the above settings than the initiating peer. Of course the remote peer could also call createDataChannel() and create yet another bidirectional channel with different properties, but that seems wasteful. Luckily, there are configuration options that allow you to create a different style of data channels, where each direction is configured independently:

```
// Local peer:  create first half of data channel
properties = {negotiated: true, id: 1, maxRetransmits: 3});
dc = pc.createDataChannel("", properties);

// Remote peer:  create second half of data channel
properties = {negotiated: true, id: 1, maxRetransmits: 6});
dc = pc.createDataChannel("", properties);
```

We have now created a bidirectional data channel which allows 3 retransmits from our local browser to the remote one, and 6 retransmits from the remote one to us. The key parts here are the `negotiated` property, which must be set to `true`, and the `id` property, which must be set to the same value at both peers in order for the two unidirectional data channels to be associated. Note that if the `id` property is left unset the browser will choose a value. Thus, for the creation of the first half of the channel the application could let the browser choose the `id`, send the `id` to the peer over the signaling channel, and then have the peer use that `id` in creating its data channel.

For more details on the various properties that can be set and checked, see Section 8.3.1.2.

7.3 Data Channel Runnable Code Example

We are now ready to add the final piece to the code example we've been building throughout the book – the data channel. Again, the server and signaling code are unchanged. The only new bits are in the JavaScript in the HTML application. The next section shows the complete code, again with the new bits highlighted, and then explains them. You may be surprised at how little new code is necessary.

7.3.1 Client WebRTC Application

```
<!--
// Copyright 2013-2014 Digital Codex LLC
// You may use this code for your own education. If you use it
// largely intact, or develop something from it, don't claim that
// your code came first. You are using this code completely at
// your own risk. If you rely on it to work in any particular
// way, you're an idiot and we won't be held responsible.
-->

<html>
<head>
  <meta http-equiv="Content-Type"
        content="text/html; charset=UTF-8" />
  <style>
    video {
      width:   320px;
      height:  240px;
```

134

```
      border:  1px solid black;
    }
    div {
      display:  inline-block;
    }
  </style>
</head>
<body>

<!-- blank script section is placeholder for query params -->
<script></script>

<!-- load polyfill, local copy first for local testing -->
<script src="extra/adapter.js" type="text/javascript"></script>
<script
  src="https://webrtc.googlecode.com/svn/trunk/samples/js/base/adapter.js"
  type="text/javascript"></script>

<!-- load XHR-based signaling channel that direct connects based
     on a key -->
<script src="clientXHRSignalingChannel.js"
        type="text/javascript"></script>

<script>
var signalingChannel, key, id,
    haveLocalMedia = false,
    weWaited = false,
    myVideoStream, myVideo,
    yourVideoStream, yourVideo,
    doNothing = function() {},
    pc, dc, data = {},
    constraints = {mandatory: {
                   OfferToReceiveAudio: true,
                   OfferToReceiveVideo: true}};

/////////////////////////////
// This is the main routine.
/////////////////////////////

// This kicks off acquisition of local media.  Also, it can
// automatically start the signaling channel.
window.onload = function () {

  // auto-connect signaling channel if key provided in URI
  if (queryparams && queryparams['key']) {
    document.getElementById("key").value = queryparams['key'];
    connect();
  }

  myVideo = document.getElementById("myVideo");
  yourVideo = document.getElementById("yourVideo");

  getMedia();

  //  connect() calls createPC() when connected.
  //  attachMedia() is called when both createPC() and getMedia()
  //  have succeeded.
};
```

135

```
//////////////////////
// This next section is for setting up the signaling channel.
//////////////////////

// This routine connects to the web server and sets up the
// signaling channel.  It is called either automatically on doc
// load or when the user clicks on the "Connect" button.
function connect() {
  var errorCB, scHandlers, handleMsg;

  // First, get the key used to connect
  key = document.getElementById("key").value;

  // This is the handler for all messages received on the
  // signaling channel.
  handleMsg = function (msg) {
    // First, we clean up the message and post it on-screen
    var msgE = document.getElementById("inmessages");
    var msgString = JSON.stringify(msg).replace(/\\r\\n/g,'\n');
    msgE.value = msgString + "\n" + msgE.value;

    // Then, we take action based on the kind of message
    if (msg.type === "offer") {
      pc.setRemoteDescription(new RTCSessionDescription(msg));
      answer();
    } else if (msg.type === "answer") {
      pc.setRemoteDescription(new RTCSessionDescription(msg));
    } else if (msg.type === "candidate") {
      pc.addIceCandidate(
        new RTCIceCandidate({sdpMLineIndex:msg.mlineindex,
                             candidate:msg.candidate}));
    }
  };

  // handlers for signaling channel
  scHandlers = {
    'onWaiting' : function () {
      setStatus("Waiting");
      // weWaited will be used later for auto-call
      weWaited = true;
    },
    'onConnected': function () {
      setStatus("Connected");
      // set up the RTC Peer Connection since we're connected
      createPC();
    },
    'onMessage': handleMsg
  };

  // Finally, create signaling channel
  signalingChannel = createSignalingChannel(key, scHandlers);
  errorCB = function (msg) {
    document.getElementById("response").innerHTML = msg;
  };

  // and connect.
  signalingChannel.connect(errorCB);
}
```

```
// This routine sends a message on the signaling channel, either
// by explicit call or by the user clicking on the Send button.
function send(msg) {
  var handler = function (res) {
    document.getElementById("response").innerHTML = res;
    return;
  },

  // Get message if not passed in
  msg = msg || document.getElementById("message").value;

  // Clean it up and post it on-screen
  msgE = document.getElementById("outmessages");
  var msgString = JSON.stringify(msg).replace(/\\r\\n/g,'\n');
  msgE.value = msgString + "\n" + msgE.value;

  // and send on signaling channel
  signalingChannel.send(msg, handler);
}

/////////////////////////////
// This next section is for getting local media
/////////////////////////////

function getMedia() {
  getUserMedia({"audio":true, "video":true},
               gotUserMedia, didntGetUserMedia);
}

function gotUserMedia(stream) {
  myVideoStream = stream;
  haveLocalMedia = true;

  // display my local video to me
  attachMediaStream(myVideo, myVideoStream);
  // wait for RTCPeerConnection to be created
  attachMediaIfReady();
}

function didntGetUserMedia() {
  console.log("couldn't get video");
}

/////////////////////////////
// This next section is for setting up the RTC Peer Connection
/////////////////////////////

function createPC() {
  var stunuri = true,
      turnuri = false,
      myfalse = function(v) {
                 return ((v==="0")||(v==="false")||(!v)); },
      config = new Array();

  // adjust config string based on any query params
  if (queryparams) {
    if ('stunuri' in queryparams) {
```

```
      stunuri = !myfalse(queryparams['stunuri']);
    }
    if ('turnuri' in queryparams) {
      turnuri = !myfalse(queryparams['turnuri']);
    };
  };

  if (stunuri) {
    // this is one of Google's public STUN servers
    config.push({"url":"stun:stun.1.google.com:19302"});
  }
  if (turnuri) {
    if (stunuri) {
      // can't use TURN-only TURN server in this case because of
      // bug in Chrome that causes STUN server responses to be
      // ignored, so we use TURN server that also does STUN
      config.push({"url":"turn:user@turn.webrtcbook.com",
                   "credential":"test"});
    } else {
      // this is our TURN-only TURN server
      config.push({"url":"turn:user@turn-only.webrtcbook.com",
                   "credential":"test"});
    }
  }
  console.log("config = " + JSON.stringify(config));

  pc = new RTCPeerConnection({iceServers:config});
  pc.onicecandidate = onIceCandidate;
  pc.onaddstream = onRemoteStreamAdded;
  pc.onremovestream = onRemoteStreamRemoved;
  pc.ondatachannel = onDataChannelAdded;

  // wait for local media to be ready
  attachMediaIfReady();
}

// When our browser has another candidate, send it to the peer
function onIceCandidate(e) {
  if (e.candidate) {
    send({type: 'candidate',
          mlineindex:  e.candidate.sdpMLineIndex,
          candidate:  e.candidate.candidate});
  }
}

// When our browser detects that the other side has added the
// media stream, show it on screen
function onRemoteStreamAdded(e) {
  yourVideoStream = e.stream;
  attachMediaStream(yourVideo, yourVideoStream);
  setStatus("On call");
}

// Yes, we do nothing if the remote side removes the stream.
// This is a *simple* demo, after all.
function onRemoteStreamRemoved(e) {}

// When our browser detects that the other side has added the
// data channel, save it, set up handlers, and send welcome
```

```
// message
function onDataChannelAdded(e) {
  dc = e.channel;
  setupDataHandlers();
  sendChat("hello");
}


// Set up the data channel message handler
function setupDataHandlers() {
  data.send = function(msg) {
    msg = JSON.stringify(msg);
    console.log("sending " + msg + " over data channel");
    dc.send(msg);
  }
  dc.onmessage = function(e) {
    var msg = JSON.parse(e.data),
        cb = document.getElementById("chatbox"),
        rtt = document.getElementById("rtt");

    if (msg.rtt) {
      // if real-time-text (per keypress) message, display in
      // real-time window
      console.log("received rtt of '" + msg.rtt + "'");
      rtt.value = msg.rtt;
      msg = msg.rtt;
    } else if (msg.chat) {
      // if full message, display in chat window,
      // reset real-time window,
      // and force chat window to last line
      console.log("received chat of '" + msg.chat + "'");
      cb.value += "<- " + msg.chat + "\n";
      rtt.value = "";
      cb.scrollTop = cb.scrollHeight;
      msg = msg.chat;
    } else {
      console.log("received " + msg + "on data channel");
    }
  };
}

// Send real-time text.  Basically for every keyup event we send
// the entire string so far as a real-time message so it can be
// displayed at each keyup.
function sendRtt() {
  var msg = document.getElementById("chat").value;
  data.send({'rtt':msg});
}


// Send normal chat message.  This happens when there is an enter
// keyup event, meaning that the remote user has finished typing
// a line.  This is also used to send our initial hello message.
function sendChat(msg) {
  var cb = document.getElementById("chatbox"),
      c = document.getElementById("chat");

  // display message locally, send it, and force chat window to
  // last line
  msg = msg || c.value;
  console.log("sendChat(" + msg + ")");
```

```
    cb.value += "-> " + msg + "\n";
    data.send({'chat':msg});
    c.value = '';
    cb.scrollTop = cb.scrollHeight;
}


//////////////////////////////////////
// This next section is for attaching local media to the Peer
// Connection.
//////////////////////////////////////

// This guard routine effectively synchronizes completion of two
// async activities:  the creation of the Peer Connection and
// acquisition of local media.
function attachMediaIfReady() {
  // If RTCPeerConnection is ready and we have local media,
  // proceed.
  if (pc && haveLocalMedia) {attachMedia();}
}

// This routine adds our local media stream to the Peer
// Connection.  Note that this does not cause any media to flow.
// All it does is to let the browser know to include this stream
// in its next SDP description.
function attachMedia() {
  pc.addStream(myVideoStream);
  setStatus("Ready for call");

  // auto-call if truthy value for call param in URI
  // but also make sure we were the last to connect (to increase
  // chances that everything is set up properly at both ends)
  if (queryparams && queryparams['call'] && !weWaited) {
    call();
  }

}

////////////////////////////////
// This next section is for calling and answering
////////////////////////////////

// This creates a data channel and generates the
// session description for an offer
function call() {
  dc = pc.createDataChannel('chat');
  setupDataHandlers();

  pc.createOffer(gotDescription, doNothing, constraints);
}

// and this generates it for an answer.
function answer() {
  pc.createAnswer(gotDescription, doNothing, constraints);
}

// In either case, once we get the session description we tell
// our browser to use it as our local description and then send
// it to the other browser.  It is the setting of the local
```

140

```
// description that allows the browser to send media and prepare
// to receive from the other side.
function gotDescription(localDesc) {
  pc.setLocalDescription(localDesc);
  send(localDesc);
}


/////////////////////////////////////
// This section is for changing the UI based on application
// progress.
/////////////////////////////////////

// This function hides, displays, and fills various UI elements
// to give the user some idea of how the browser is progressing
// at setting up the signaling channel, getting local media,
// creating the peer connection, and actually connecting
// media (calling).
function setStatus(str) {
  var statuslineE = document.getElementById("statusline"),
      statusE = document.getElementById("status"),
      sendE = document.getElementById("send"),
      connectE = document.getElementById("connect"),
      callE = document.getElementById("call"),
      scMessageE = document.getElementById("scMessage");

  switch (str) {
    case 'Waiting':
      statuslineE.style.display = "inline";
      statusE.innerHTML =
        "Waiting for peer signaling connection";
      sendE.style.display = "none";
      connectE.style.display = "none";
      break;
    case 'Connected':
      statuslineE.style.display = "inline";
      statusE.innerHTML =
        "Peer signaling connected, waiting for local media";
      sendE.style.display = "inline";
      connectE.style.display = "none";
      scMessageE.style.display = "inline-block";
      break;
    case 'Ready for call':
      statusE.innerHTML = "Ready for call";
      callE.style.display = "inline";
      break;
    case 'On call':
      statusE.innerHTML = "On call";
      callE.style.display = "none";
      break;
    default:
  }
}

</script>

<div id="setup">
  <p>WebRTC Book Demo (local media, signaling, peer connection, and
data channel)</p>
  <p>Key:
```

```
    <input type="text" name="key" id="key"
           onkeyup="if (event.keyCode == 13) {
                        connect(); return false;}"/>
    <button id="connect" onclick="connect()">Connect</button>
    <span id="statusline" style="display:none">Status:
      <span id="status">Disconnected</span>
    </span>
    <button id="call" style="display:none"
           onclick = "call()">Call</button>
  </p>
</div>

<div id="scMessage" style="float:right;display:none">
  <p>Signaling channel message:
    <input type="text" width="100%" name="message" id="message"
           onkeyup="if (event.keyCode == 13) {
                        send(); return false;}"/>
    <button id="send" style="display:none"
           onclick="send()">Send</button>
  </p>

  <p>Response:  <span id="response"></span></p>
</div>

<br/>

<div style="width:30%;vertical-align:top">
  <div>
    <video id="myVideo" autoplay="autoplay" controls
           muted="true"/>
  </div>
  <p><b>Outgoing Messages</b>
     <br/>
     <textarea id="outmessages" rows="100"
               style="width:100%"></textarea>
  </p>
</div>

<div style="width:30%;vertical-align:top">
  <textarea id="chatbox" rows="10" style="width:100%"></textarea>
  <p style="width:100%"><b>Real-time:</b>
    <textarea id="rtt" rows="2" style="width:100%"></textarea>
  </p>
  <p style="width:100%"><b>Chat message:</b>
    <input type="text" style="width:100%" name="chat" id="chat"
           onkeyup="sendRtt();
                    if (event.keyCode == 13) {
                      sendChat(); return false;}"/>
  </p>
</div>

<div style="width:30%;vertical-align:top">
  <div>
    <video id="yourVideo" autoplay="autoplay" controls />
  </div>
  <p><b>Incoming Messages</b>
     <br/>
     <textarea id="inmessages" rows="100"
               style="width:100%"></textarea>
```

142

```
    </p>
  </div>

  </body>
</html>
```

At the end of the file, there is now a new section of the user interface specifically for the data channel. (See Figure 7.1.) It contains the chat history window, a real-time text window, and an input field for messages. The input field is where you type messages to be sent to the other browser. As you type, each character is sent to the other browser for display in its real-time text window. (Actually, what is sent is slightly different, but we'll cover that shortly). When you press the enter key, the entire message is sent to the other browser for display in its top chat history window. As we'll see, the majority of the new JavaScript code is for display and formatting, since use of the data channel itself is fairly simple.

Figure 7.1 Data Channel Demo

Let's walk through the JavaScript code now. The first bit of new JavaScript is the declaration of two new variables: dc, which will hold the pointer to the actual data channel, and data, which wraps the data channel's methods with functions that format messages for sending and display. The next new line of code, that sets the ondatachannel handler, is needed in case the data channel is created by the peer. Its definition is a bit further down. It saves the channel created by the peer into the dc variable, sets up handlers for the data channel, and then sends a first message to the peer.

`setupDataHandlers()` next sets up the `send()` method on the `data` variable. This takes any message object, converts it to JSON, and sends it. Conveniently, this trivially supports both simple strings and arbitrary data objects. We take advantage of this in sending different kinds of messages over the data channel. Let's skip over the `dc.onmessage` handler for the moment so we can look at how `data.send()` is used. The most common message is the one sent via `sendRtt()`. Each time there is a keyup event in the chat input field, we capture the entire string in the input field and send it over the data channel as the value of the `rtt` property of a new object. Although sending the entire string adds a few extra bytes of data to send, it simplifies the programming since we don't need to track character positions, deletes, etc. It also is self-correcting in the event that one of the real-time messages is lost.

The other kind of message we send is the regular chat message, via `sendChat()`. This routine will use the `msg` passed in, if it exists, and otherwise the value of the input field. After writing to the console it appends the message to the chat history window with an arrow that indicates it's an outgoing message from us, then it sends the message on the data channel as the `chat` property of a new object, then it clears the chat input field, and finally it forces the chat window to scroll to the last line to ensure that we can see the message. An example of the real-time text and chat history is shown in Figure 7.2.

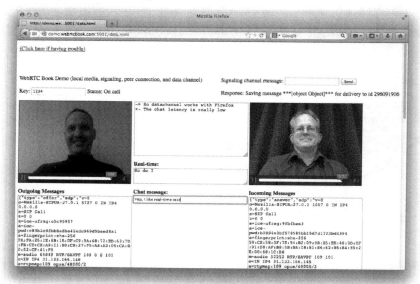

Figure 7.2 Chat and Real-Time Text over the Data Channel

Now let's go back up and look at the `onmessage` handler for the data channel. We first parse the JSON string back into an object. The handler checks for both the `rtt` and `chat` properties. If the former is present, we log the message and save it into the real-time window. If the latter is present, we log the message, append it to the chat history window with an arrow indicating it's an incoming message, clear the real-time window, and force the chat window to scroll to the last line as for outgoing messages. If neither `rtt` nor `chat` was present, then we assume this is a simple string and log it.

The only remaining bit of new code is for creating the data channel. If you'll remember, the only code we've seen so far that initiates `setupDataHandlers()` is the one that activated when the peer created the data channel. The code we're discussing now does that. It's extremely simple, merely a call to `createDataChannel()`.

Well, that's the last expansion we'll be doing to our example. Notice how easy the data channel setup is. In fact, the creation and use of the data channel itself was almost trivial; most of the new code was needed for formatting, parsing, or taking action based on messages received. Given how simple the setup is, and the fact that a data channel message may reach the remote peer faster than one relayed over the signaling channel, in a real application it might make sense to establish the data channel first and then, as described in Section 4.3.8, to use the data channel as the signaling channel for all remaining setup.

Although this application is now fairly complete in terms of functionality, it is far from complete in terms of both user interface and error handling. The former is outside the scope of this book, and the latter is, well, still being worked on by the standards groups!

As mentioned in Chapter 3, the complete code for this example, including all the other html files described in the past few chapters (localmedia.html, signaling.html, peerconnection.html, and data.html), is available online at http://webrtcbook.com/code3.html. Note that the file start.html is the same as data.html, our final complete html file.

8 W3C DOCUMENTS

WebRTC is defined by the APIs, many of which are still-being-written. The following sections describe the W3C WebRTC standards documents. Links to both the public working draft and the editor's drafts are provided for reference. Appendix A describes the W3C standards process.

8.1 WebRTC API Reference

Tables 8.1 through 8.11 list the WebRTC APIs and provide a summary of their use. Those documents are described in the next two sections. In the tables, the Reference column (Ref) indicates in which W3C document the API is defined, and contains the value "PC" for Peer Connection [1], described in Section 8.3.1, or "gUM" for getUserMedia [2] described in Section 8.3.2.

Interface and Description	Ref
`AudioMediaStreamTrack` Subclass of `MediaStreamTrack` that can only hold media of sourceType "audio".	gUM
`MediaStream` Represents a collection of `MediaStreamTrack`s, currently only audio and video.	gUM
`MediaStreamEvent` Returns the `MediaStream` added or removed by the remote peer. Handled by `onaddstream` or `onremovestream`.	PC
`MediaStreamTrack` Represents a single track of a media source. Note that a track can consist of multiple channels, as with a 6-channel surround sound source encoded into a single track. Also, a track may only contain one kind of media regardless of how many channels it has.	gUM
`MediaStreamTrackEvent` Returns a `MediaStreamTrack` when a track is added or removed. Handled by `onaddtrack` or `onremovetrack`.	gUM
`NavigatorUserMedia` Pre-existing interface in all web browsers.	gUM
`Constrainable` Adds methods and attributes for manipulating constraints, capabilities, and settings. Implemented by `MediaStreamTrack`.	PC
`MediaError` Represents an error returned from a call to `NavigatorUserMedia.getUserMedia()`.	gUM
`MediaErrorEvent` Returns a `MediaError` object containing the error name and message, along with the unsatisfied mandatory constraint if the error name is "CONSTRAINT_NOT_SATISFIED". The latter situation can be handled by `onoverconstrained`.	gUM

Interface and Description	Ref
RTCDataChannel Represents a channel over an RTCPeerConnection that can carry arbitrary application data.	PC
RTCDataChannelEvent Returns an RTCDataChannel when one is created by the remote	PC
RTCIceCandidate Container for an ICE candidate.	PC
RTCPeerConnection Represents a WebRTC connection between two peers.	PC
RTCPeerConnectionIceEvent Returns an RTCIceCandidate when one is identified by the browser. Handled by onicecandidate.	PC
RTCSessionDescription Container for SDP offer, answer, or pranswer (provisional answer).	PC
RTCSDPError Contains the SDP line number of the first error when setLocalDescription() or setRemoteDescription() fails because of a problem with the RTCSessionDescription given.	PC
RTCDTMFSender Container and control object for inserting DTMF into an audio track.	PC
RTCDTMFToneChangeEvent Returns the DTMF tone that has just begun to be sent. Handled by ontonechange.	PC

Table 8.1 WebRTC API Interface Summary
(PC=Peer Connection [1], gUM=getUserMedia [2])

149

RTCPeerConnection API and Description	Type	Ref
`RTCPeerConnection` Represents a WebRTC connection between two peers.	Interface	PC
`new RTCPeerConnection(configuration)` Creates a new `RTCPeerConnection` object using the given STUN and TURN server information. The configuration parameter is of type `RTCConfiguration`.	Constructor	PC
`RTCPeerConnection.close()` Closes the `RTCPeerConnection`, effectively removing all attached streams and closing all attached `RTCDataChannels`.	Method	PC
`RTCPeerConnectionErrorCallback` Application-settable to a function/method that takes a `DOMString` of error information as a parameter. Used by `RTCPeerConnection.createOffer()`, `RTCPeerConnection.createAnswer()`, `RTCPeerConnection.setLocalDescription()`, `RTCPeerConnection.setRemoteDescription()`, and `RTCPeerConnection.getStats()`.	Callback	PC

Table 8.2 WebRTC RTCPeerConnection APIs
(PC=Peer Connection [1], gUM=getUserMedia [2])

SDP Processing APIs and Description	Type	Ref
RTCSessionDescription Container for SDP offer, answer, or pranswer (provisional answer).	Interface	PC
new RTCSessionDescription(descriptionInitDict) Creates a new RTCSessionDescription object. The descriptionInitDict parameter is of type RTCSessionDescriptionInit.	Constructor	PC
RTCSessionDescription.**type** Indicates whether the session description is an offer, an answer, or a pranswer.	Attribute	PC
RTCSessionDescription.**sdp** A string representation of the SDP for the session description.	Attribute	PC
RTCSessionDescriptionInit Container for a session description to initialize an RTCSessionDescription object.	Dictionary	PC
RTCSessionDescriptionInit.**type** Indicates whether the session description is an offer, an answer, or a pranswer.	Attribute	PC
RTCSessionDescriptionInit.**sdp** A string representation of the SDP for the session description.	Attribute	PC
RTCSessionDescriptionCallback Application-settable to a function/method that accepts an RTCSessionDescription as a parameter. Used by RTCPeerConnection.createOffer() and RTCPeerConnection.createAnswer().	Callback	PC

SDP Processing APIs and Description	Type	Ref
`RTCSDPError` Contains the SDP line number of the first error when `setLocalDescription()` or `setRemoteDescription()` fails because of a problem with the `RTCSessionDescription` given.	Interface	PC
`RTCSDPError.sdpLineNumber` The SDP line number of the first error when `setLocalDescription()` or `setRemoteDescription()` fails because of a problem with the `RTCSessionDescription` given.	Attribute	PC
`RTCIceCandidate.sdpMid` Media stream identifier for the m-line associated with this candidate.	Attribute	PC
`RTCIceCandidate.sdpMLineIndex` Zero-based index of the m-line associated with this candidate.	Attribute	PC
`RTCPeerConnection.createOffer()` Creates an `RTCSessionDescription` for an offer with SDP representing the complete set of available local media streams, codec options, ICE candidates, etc.	Method	PC
`RTCPeerConnection.createAnswer()` Creates an `RTCSessionDescription` for an answer with SDP representing an appropriate set of available local media streams, codec options, ICE candidates, etc.	Method	PC
`RTCPeerConnection.setLocalDescription()` Records the given `RTCSessionDescription` object as the current local description. If the object is a final answer, media will then change/begin flowing.	Method	PC
`RTCPeerConnection.setRemoteDescription()` Records the given `RTCSessionDescription` object as the current remote description.	Method	PC
`RTCPeerConnection.localDescription` The `RTCSessionDescription` representing the currently active local description (SDP).	Attribute	PC

SDP Processing APIs and Description	Type	Ref
RTCPeerConnection.**remoteDescription** The RTCSessionDescription representing the currently active remote description (SDP).	Attribute	PC
RTCPeerConnection.**signalingState** Holds the status of SDP exchanges over the RTCPeerConnection: stable, have-local-offer, have-remote-offer, have-local-pranswer, have-remote-pranswer, closed.	Attribute	PC
RTCPeerConnection.**onnegotiationneeded** Application-settable to a function/method that will be called whenever local or remote changes to the RTCPeerConnection will result in SDP changes that will require renegotiation.	Attribute	PC
RTCPeerConnection.**onsignalingstatechange** Application-settable to a function/method that will be called whenever RTCPeerConnection.signalingState changes.	Attribute	PC

Table 8.3 WebRTC SDP Processing APIs
(PC=Peer Connection [1], gUM=getUserMedia [2])

ICE Processing APIs and Description	Type	Ref
RTCIceCandidate Container for an ICE candidate.	Interface	PC
new RTCIceCandidate(candidateInitDict) Creates a new RTCIceCandidate object from the input parameter. This parameter is of type RTCIceCandidateInit.	Constructor	PC
RTCIceCandidate.candidate A string representing the ICE candidate.	Attribute	PC
RTCIceCandidate.sdpMid Media stream identifier for the m-line associated with this candidate.	Attribute	PC
RTCIceCandidate.sdpMLineIndex Zero-based index of the m-line associated with this candidate.	Attribute	PC
RTCIceCandidateInit Container for an ICE server URL for initializing an RTCIceCandidate object.	Dictionary	PC
RTCIceCandidateInit.candidate A string representing the ICE candidate.	Attribute	PC
RTCIceCandidateInit.sdpMid Media stream identifier for the m-line associated with this candidate.	Attribute	PC
RTCIceCandidateInit.sdpMLineIndex Zero-based index of the m-line associated with this candidate.	Attribute	PC
RTCIceServer Container for an ICE server URL.	Dictionary	PC
RTCIceServer.urls One or more URLs of STUN and/or TURN servers.	Attribute	PC

ICE Processing APIs and Description	Type	Ref
RTCIceServer.**username** The username to use if the RTCIceServer.urls are the URLs of TURN servers.	Attribute	PC
RTCIceServer.**credential** The credential (e.g., password) to use if the RTCIceServer.urls are the URLs of TURN servers.	Attribute	PC
RTCConfiguration Contains an array of ICE server objects.	Dictionary	PC
RTCConfiguration.**iceServers** An array of RTCIceServer objects.	Attribute	PC
RTCConfiguration.**iceTransports** Indicates which ICE transports to use: none (no ICE processing), relay (TURN services only), or all (STUN and TURN acceptable). The default is all.	Attribute	PC
RTCPeerConnection.**updateIce()** Causes the browser ICE Agent to restart or update its collection of local candidates and remote candidates, depending on the parameters given.	Method	PC
RTCPeerConnection.**addIceCandidate()** Provides a remote candidate to the browser ICE Agent.	Method	PC
RTCPeerConnection.**getConfiguration()** Returns the current RTCConfiguration.	Method	PC
RTCPeerConnection.**iceGatheringState** Holds the ICE Agent's current state with regard to gathering candidate addresses: new, gathering, complete.	Attribute	PC
RTCPeerConnection.**iceConnectionState** Holds the ICE Agent's current state with respect to connecting the two peers: new, checking, connected, completed, failed, disconnected, closed.	Attribute	PC

ICE Processing APIs and Description	Type	Ref
RTCPeerConnection.**onicecandidate** Application-settable to a function/method that will be called whenever a new ICE candidate is available to be sent to the remote peer. This is useful for "trickle ICE."	Attribute	PC
RTCPeerConnection.**oniceconnectionstatechange** Application-settable to a function/method that will be called whenever RTCPeerConnection.RTCIceConnectionState changes.	Attribute	PC
RTCPeerConnectionIceEvent Returns an RTCIceCandidate when one is identified by the browser. Handled by onicecandidate.	Event	PC
RTCPeerConnectionIceEvent.**candidate** The RTCIceCandidate identified by the browser.	Attribute	PC

Table 8.4 WebRTC ICE Processing APIs
(PC=Peer Connection [1], gUM=getUserMedia [2])

Data Channel APIs and Description	Type	Ref
RTCPeerConnection.**createDataChannel**() Creates a new data channel over the RTCPeerConnection.	Method	PC
RTCPeerConnection.**ondatachannel** Application-settable to a function/method that will be called whenever a RTCDataChannel is created.	Attribute	PC
RTCDataChannelInit Contains parameters configuring the creation of a data channel.	Dictionary	PC
RTCDataChannel Represents a channel over an RTCPeerConnection that can carry arbitrary application data.	Interface	PC
RTCDataChannel.**label** A string label for this data channel set by the application when the data channel is created.	Attribute	PC
RTCDataChannel.**ordered** A Boolean value, set by the application when this data channel was created, indicating whether messages must be delivered in order. Delivering messages in order may require delaying some messages.	Attribute	PC
RTCDataChannel.**maxRetransmitTime** For unreliable data channels, this attribute holds the number of milliseconds for which the browser will continue attempting to retransmit data. This value is configured by the application when the data channel is first created. Note that setting both this and RTCDataChannel.maxRetransmits will result in an error.	Attribute	PC

Data Channel APIs and Description	Type	Ref
RTCDataChannel.**maxRetransmits** For unreliable data channels, this attribute holds the maximum number of times the browser will attempt to retransmit data. This value is configured by the application when the data channel is first created. Note that setting both this and RTCDataChannel.maxRetransmitTime will result in an error.	Attribute	PC
RTCDataChannel.**protocol** The specification is not clear on this. Don't use it.	Attribute	PC
RTCDataChannel.**negotiated** A Boolean value indicating whether this data channel was automatically negotiated (i.e., not in explicit SDP exchanges). It reflects the value configured by the application when the data channel was created.	Attribute	PC
RTCDataChannel.**id** A numeric value for the channel established when the channel was created. It is determined automatically by the browser unless the application provides the value as part of the configuration when the channel is created.	Attribute	PC
RTCDataChannel.**readyState** The state of the RTCDataChannel. It will have one of the following values: connecting, open, closing,	Attribute	PC
RTCDataChannel.**bufferedAmount** The number of bytes queued for sending (by RTCDataChannel.send()) that have not yet been transmitted.	Attribute	PC
RTCDataChannel.**onopen** Application-settable to a function/method that will be called when the data channel is ready to transmit data.	Attribute	PC

Data Channel APIs and Description	Type	Ref
RTCDataChannel.onerror Application-settable to a function/method that will be called whenever an error occurs in the functioning of the data channel.	Attribute	PC
RTCDataChannel.onclose Application-settable to a function/method that will be called when the data channel is closed.	Attribute	PC
RTCDataChannel.close() Closes the data channel.	Method	PC
RTCDataChannel.onmessage Application-settable to a function/method that will be called when a message (data) is received on the data channel.	Attribute	PC
RTCDataChannel.binaryType A string indicating how binary data is to be exposed to the application. Its default value is "blob".	Attribute	PC
RTCDataChannel.send() Sends the argument over the data channel to the remote end. There are a variety of formats the argument can take, but the two most common are a string and a blob.	Method	PC
RTCDataChannelEvent Returns an RTCDataChannel when one is created by the remote peer. Handled by ondatachannel.	Event	PC
RTCDataChannelEvent.channel The RTCDataChannel created by the remote peer.	Attribute	PC

Table 8.5 WebRTC Data Channel APIs
(PC=Peer Connection [1], gUM=getUserMedia [2])

DTMF Processing APIs and Description	Type	Ref
RTCPeerConnection.**createDTMFSender()** For the MediaStreamTrack given as input, this method creates an RTCDTMFSender object whose purpose is to inject DTMF tones into the RTCPeerConnection's representation of the track.	Method	PC
RTCDTMFSender Container and control object for inserting DTMF into an audio track.	Interface	PC
RTCDTMFSender.**canInsertDTMF** This Boolean value indicates whether the associated track is able to insert DTMF. Normally true, this value can become false if there is a problem with the track or the Peer Connection.	Attribute	PC
RTCDTMFSender.**insertDTMF()** Inserts the given DTMF string into the associated track. Note that this call replaces any to-be-played-out tones remaining in the toneBuffer.	Method	PC
RTCDTMFSender.**track** The MediaStreamTrack associated with this object.	Attribute	PC
RTCDTMFSender.**ontonechange** Application-settable to a function/method that will be called when a message (data) is received on the data channel.	Attribute	PC
RTCDTMFSender.**toneBuffer** Contains the tones remaining to be played out.	Attribute	PC
RTCDTMFSender.**duration** The number of milliseconds for which each tone should be played. The default value is 100 ms.	Attribute	PC
RTCDTMFSender.**interToneGap** The number of milliseconds between the end of a tone and the start of the next one. The default value is 50 ms.	Attribute	PC

DTMF Processing APIs and Description	Type	Ref
RTCDTMFSenderToneChangeEvent Returns the DTMF tone that has just begun to be sent. Handled by `ontonechange`.	Event	PC
RTCDTMFSenderToneChangeEvent.**tone** The DTMF tone that has just begun to be sent.	Attribute	PC

Table 8.6 WebRTC DTMF Processing APIs
(PC=Peer Connection [1], gUM=getUserMedia [2])

Statistics Processing APIs and Description	Type	Ref
RTCPeerConnection.**getStats**() For the MediaStreamTrack given as input, this method collects and returns transmission statistics about the track via the RTCStatsCallback handler.	Method	PC
RTCStatsCallback Application-settable to a function/method that takes an RTCStatsReport as a parameter. Used by RTCPeerConnection.getStats().	Callback	PC
RTCStatsReport Contains one or more RTCStats objects for the track passed as input to getStats(). Since a track may be transmitted over a Peer Connection using one or multiple SSRCs, this report returns an RTCStats object for each such SSRC.	Interface	PC
RTCStats Base class for an object containing statistics for a single RTP object type. This base class contains a timestamp, and id, and the type. RTCRTPStreamStats inherits from this class.	Dictionary	PC
RTCRTPStreamStats Parent class for an object containing statistics for a single RTP stream. This class contains the id of the other end of the stream (so its statistics can be checked) and the SSRC for this RTP stream. This class inherits from RTCStats. RTCInboundRTPStreamStats and RTCOutboundRTPStreamStats inherit from this class.	Dictionary	PC
RTCInboundRTPStreamStats Object containing the following statistics for a single inbound RTP stream: the total number of packets received and the total number of bytes received, since transmission began over the Peer Connection. This object inherits from RTCRTPStreamStats.	Dictionary	PC

Statistics Processing APIs and Description	Type	Ref
`RTCOutboundRTPStreamStats` Object containing the following statistics for a single outbound RTP stream: the total number of packets sent and the total number of bytes sent, since transmission began over the Peer Connection. This object inherits from `RTCRTPStreamStats`.	Dictionary	PC

Table 8.7 WebRTC Statistics Processing APIs
(PC=Peer Connection [1], gUM=getUserMedia [2])

Identity Processing APIs and Description	Type	Ref
RTCConfiguration.`requestIdentity` Indicates whether the browser is to verify the identity of the remote party. Possible values are `yes` (an identity must be requested, `no` (no identity is to be requested), and `ifconfigured` (identity will be requested if the user has configured an identity in the browser or if `setIdentityProvider()` has been called.) The default is `ifconfigured`.	Attribute	PC
RTCPeerConnection.`setIdentityProvider()` Allows the application to specify an identity provider, protocol, and claimed username (identity) for this Peer Connection. This may be unnecessary if the browser already has this information configured.	Method	PC
RTCPeerConnection.`getIdentityAssertion()` Begins the Identity Provider process (of obtaining an identity assertion). Use of this method is optional but may speed up the application by starting this process before an offer or answer is generated.	Method	PC
RTCPeerConnection.`peerIdentity` This is an RTCIdentityAssertion for the remote peer. It is set only if the peer's identity has been verified.	Attribute	PC
RTCPeerConnection.`onidentityresult` Application-settable to a function/method that will be called when an attempt to verify identity either succeeds or fails.	Attribute	PC
RTCIdentityAssertion Contains the verified identity provider and identity (name) for the peer.	Dictionary	PC

Table 8.8 WebRTC Identity Processing APIs
(PC=Peer Connection [1], gUM=getUserMedia [2])

Stream Processing APIs and Description	Type	Ref
`MediaStream` Represents a collection of `MediaStreamTracks`, currently only audio and video.	Interface	gUM
`new MediaStream(MediaStream or MediaStreamTrackSequence)` Creates a new `MediaStream` consisting of tracks of audio and video from other `MediaStream` objects. The input parameter is either a single `MediaStream` or a `MediaStreamTrackSequence`, which is an array of `MediaStreamTracks`.	Constructor	gUM
`MediaStream.id` A unique, browser-generated identifier string for this `Media Stream` defined in the "Media Capture and Streams" document. The "WebRTC 1.0" document explains how remote-originated stream labels are created.	Attribute	gUM and PC
`MediaStream.getAudioTracks()` Returns an array of all of the `AudioMediaStreamTracks` in this `MediaStream`.	Method	gUM
`MediaStream.getVideoTracks()` Returns an array of all of the `VideoMediaStreamTracks` in this `MediaStream`.	Method	gUM
`MediaStream.clone()` Returns a clone of the `MediaStream` that has a different id and clones of all tracks in the `MediaStream`.	Method	gUM
`MediaStream.ended` Set by the browser, this attribute has the value `true` if and only if the stream has finished.	Attribute	gUM
`MediaStream.onended` Application-settable to a function/method that will be called when the `MediaStream` finishes.	Attribute	gUM

Stream Processing APIs and Description	Type	Ref
`MediaStreamEvent` Returns the `MediaStream` added or removed by the remote peer. Handled by `onaddstream` or `onremovestream`.	Event	PC
`MediaStreamEvent.`**`stream`** The `MediaStream` added or removed by the remote peer.	Attribute	PC
`URL` Pre-existing interface in all web browsers.	Interface	gUM
`URL.`**`createObjectURL`** Creates and returns a "blob" URL for the `MediaStream` given as the parameter. The URL will be suitable for passing to the `<audio>` element if the stream contains audio and for passing to the `<video>` element if the stream contains video.	Method	gUM
`RTCPeerConnection.`**`addStream()`** Adds an existing media stream to an `RTCPeerConnection` for sending to the remote peer.	Method	PC
`RTCPeerConnection.`**`removeStream()`** Removes one of the `RTCPeerConnection`'s streams from the `RTCPeerConnection`, which will ultimately result in the stream not being sent anymore.	Method	PC
`RTCPeerConnection.`**`getLocalStreams()`** Returns an array containing all of the locally-originated `MediaStream` values.	Method	PC
`RTCPeerConnection.`**`getRemoteStreams()`** Returns an array containing all of the remotely-originated `MediaStream` values.	Method	PC
`RTCPeerConnection.`**`getStreamById()`** Returns the `MediaStream` in the Peer Connection with the given id, or null if there isn't one.	Method	PC

Stream Processing APIs and Description	Type	Ref
RTCPeerConnection.`onaddstream` Application-settable to a function/method that will be called whenever a remote stream is added.	Attribute	PC
RTCPeerConnection.`onremovestream` Application-settable to a function/method that will be called whenever a remote stream is removed.	Attribute	PC
NavigatorUserMedia Pre-existing interface in all web browsers.	Interface	gUM
NavigatorUserMedia.`getUserMedia()` Returns a `MediaStream` containing one or more media tracks that satisfy the constraints (see `MediaStreamConstraints`) given as input.	Method	gUM
NavigatorUserMediaSuccessCallback Application-settable to a function/method that accepts a `MediaStream` as a parameter. Used by `NavigatorUserMedia.getUserMedia()`.	Callback	gUM
MediaError Represents an error returned from a call to `NavigatorUserMedia.getUserMedia()`.	Interface	gUM
MediaError.`name` The error that occurred in calling `NavigatorUserMedia.getUserMedia()`. Must be either "PERMISSION_DENIED", indicating that the user denied permission for the page to use the local device(s), or "CONSTRAINT_NOT_SATISFIED", indicating that a mandatory constraint could not be satisfied.	Attribute	gUM
MediaError.`message` A human-readable description of the error that occurred.	Attribute	gUM
MediaError.`constraintName` If the error name was "CONSTRAINT_NOT_SATISFIED", this attribute has as its value the constraint that caused the error.	Attribute	gUM

Stream Processing APIs and Description	Type	Ref
`NavigatorUserMediaErrorCallback` Application-settable to a function/method that accepts a `NavigatorUserMediaError` as a parameter. Used by `NavigatorUserMedia.getUserMedia()`.	Callback	gUM

Table 8.9 WebRTC Stream Processing APIs
(PC=Peer Connection [1], gUM=getUserMedia [2]

Track Processing APIs and Description	Type	Ref
`MediaStreamTrack` Represents a single track of a media source. Note that a track can consist of multiple channels, as with a 6-channel surround sound source encoded into a single track. Also, a track may only contain one kind of media regardless of how many channels it has.	Interface	gUM
`MediaStreamTrack.kind` Has the value `audio` or `video`.	Attribute	gUM
`MediaStreamTrack.id` A globally-unique identifier generated by the browser.	Attribute	gUM
`MediaStreamTrack.label` A browser-generated label string for this `MediaStreamTrack`, e.g., "Built-in microphone". It is optional for the browser to provide anything other than the empty string as the label.	Attribute	gUM
`MediaStreamTrack.enabled` Application-settable Boolean to disable and re-enable the output of the track.	Attribute	gUM
`MediaStreamTrack.muted` A Boolean indicating whether or not the track is muted.	Attribute	gUM
`MediaStreamTrackState.live` A possible value for `MediaStreamTrack.readyState` that indicates the track is active, i.e., capable of producing output. Note that even if active, the `MediaStreamTrack` may be disabled (see `MediaStreamTrack.enabled`) or muted (see `MediaStreamTrack.muted`) and thus not producing output.	Enum	gUM
`MediaStreamTrackState.new` A possible value for `MediaStreamTrack.readyState` that indicates the track is not yet connected to a source.	Enum	gUM
`MediaStreamTrack.onmute` Application-settable to a function/method that will be called whenever the `MediaStreamTrack` is muted.	Attribute	gUM

Track Processing APIs and Description	Type	Ref
MediaStreamTrackState.**ended** A possible value for `MediaStreamTrack.readyState` that indicates the track has ended, i.e., that it is no longer capable of producing output and never will be.	Enm	gUM
MediaStreamTrack.**onunmute** Application-settable to a function/method that will be called whenever the `MediaStreamTrack` is unmuted.	Attribute	gUM
MediaStreamTrack.**onstarted** Application-settable to a function/method that will be called when the `MediaStreamTrack` becomes active.	Attribute	gUM
MediaStreamTrack.**onended** Application-settable to a function/method that will be called when the `MediaStreamTrack` finishes.	Attribute	gUM
MediaStreamTrack.**readonly** A Boolean indicating whether or not the track is unconstrainable. Examples are a file or some tracks received over a Peer Connection.	Attribute	gUM
MediaStreamTrack.**remote** A Boolean indicating whether or not the track was originated remotely over a Peer Connection.	Attribute	gUM
MediaStreamTrack.**readyState** Indicates the state of the track: `new`, `live`, or `ended`. Defined in the "Media Capture and Streams" document. The "WebRTC 1.0" document explains how remote-originated track attributes must be set.	Attribute	gUM and PC
MediaStreamTrack.**clone()** Creates a duplicate of the track with its own id.	Method	gUM
MediaStreamTrack.**stop()** Ends the track. If there are no other tracks referencing the media source, the relevant source is stopped and any device-in-use notifications are turned off.	Method	gUM

Track Processing APIs and Description	Type	Ref
`MediaStreamTrackEvent` Returns a `MediaStreamTrack` when a track is added or removed. Handled by `onaddtrack` or `onremovetrack`.	Event	gUM
`AudioMediaStreamTrack` Subclass of MediaStreamTrack that can only hold media of sourceType "audio".	Interface	gUM
`AudioMediaStreamTrack.getSourceIds()` Static method that returns all available audio source ids.	Method	gUM
`VideoMediaStreamTrack` Subclass of MediaStreamTrack that can only hold media of sourceType "video".	Interface	gUM
`VideoMediaStreamTrack.getSourceIds()` Static method that returns all available video source ids.	Method	gUM
`MediaStream.getTrackById()` Returns the `MediaStreamTrack` in this `MediaStream` with the given id, or null if there is no such track.	Method	gUM
`MediaStream.addTrack()` Adds the track given as the parameter to the `MediaStream` if it doesn't already exist.	Method	gUM
`MediaStream.removeTrack()` Removes the track given as the parameter from the `MediaStream`.	Method	gUM
`MediaStream.onaddtrack` Application-settable to a function/method that will be called whenever a track is added to this `MediaStream`.	Attribute	gUM
`MediaStream.onremovetrack` Application-settable to a function/method that will be called whenever a track is removed from this `MediaStream`.	Attribute	gUM

Table 8.10 WebRTC Track Processing APIs
(PC=Peer Connection [1], gUM=getUserMedia [2])

.

Constraint and Capability APIs and Description	Type	Ref
`NavigatorUserMedia.getMediaDevices()` Returns source-distinguishing information an application can use to create functional audio/video input chooser dialogs.	Method	gUM
`MediaDeviceInfoCallback` Application-settable to a function/method that accepts a `MediaDeviceInfo` as a parameter. Used by `NavigatorUserMedia.getMediaDevices()`.	Callback	gUM
`Constrainable` Adds methods and attributes for manipulating constraints, capabilities, and settings. Implemented by `MediaStreamTrack`.	Interface	gUM
`Constrainable.getConstraints()` Returns the current constraints, if any, applied to this object.	Method	gUM
`Constrainable.getSettings()` Returns the current values of all constrainable properties.	Method	gUM
`Constrainable.getCapabilities()` Returns the supported values for all constraints possible on this object.	Method	gUM
`Constrainable.applyConstraints()` Attempts to replace the object's current constraints with those given as argument.	Method	gUM
`Constrainable.onoverconstrained` Application-settable to a function/method that will be called whenever this object becomes *overconstrained*.	Attribute	gUM
`MediaStreamTrack.getConstraints()` See `Constrainable.getConstraints()`.	Method	gUM
`MediaStreamTrack.getSettingsow ()` See `Constrainable.getSettings()`.	Method	gUM

Constraint and Capability APIs and Description	Type	Ref
MediaStreamTrack.`getCapabilities()` See `Constrainable.getCapabilities()`.	Method	gUM
MediaStreamTrack.`applyConstraints()` See `Constrainable.applyConstraints()`.	Method	gUM
MediaStreamTrack.`onoverconstrained` See `Constrainable.onoverconstrained`.	Attribute	gUM
MediaErrorEvent Returns a `MediaError` object containing the error name and message, along with the unsatisfied mandatory constraint if the error name is "CONSTRAINT_NOT_SATISFIED".	Event	gUM
MediaDeviceInfo Contains simple info about a source or sink useful for disambiguation.	Dictionary	gUM
MediaDeviceInfo.`deviceId` A unique id for this source or sink. See `MediaStreamTrack.id`.	Attribute	gUM
MediaDeviceInfo.`kind` Either "audioinput", "audiooutput", or "videoinput".	Attribute	gUM
MediaDeviceInfo.`label` A browser-provided label for the source or sink. See `MediaStreamTrack.label`.	Attribute	gUM

Table 8.11 WebRTC Constraint and Capability APIs (PC=Peer Connection [1], gUM=getUserMedia [2])

8.2 WEBRTC Recommendations

None of the WEBRTC specifications have reached Recommendation status yet.

8.3 WEBRTC Drafts

All the WEBRTC documents are in the Working Draft stage. They are described in the following subsections. Note that the descriptions below are intended to be read in conjunction with the specification documents themselves – they do not repeat everything given in the specifications.

8.3.1 "WebRTC 1.0: Real-time Communication Between Browsers"

This document [1] is the primary document for the WebRTC work, informally known as the Peer Connection draft. It defines the RTCPeerConnection interface and extensions to the MediaStream interface defined in the "Media Capture and Streams" (getusermedia) specification. There are many bits of functionality defined in the RTCPeerConnection interface. To simplify life for the reader of the specification, related functionality has been grouped into separate sections, giving the naïve reader the impression that there are only a small number of methods and attributes in the RTCPeerConnection definition. In this section, we explain each of these grouped functionality sets. They include: the core RTCPeerConnection itself, the Data API, the DTMF API, the Statistics API, and the Identity API.

8.3.1.1 RTCPeerConnection Interface

The RTCPeerConnection interface is the primary API of the WebRTC effort. The function of this API is to set up a media connection path between two browsers. Although the API is strongly tied to the JavaScript Session Establishment Protocol (JSEP, described in Section 11.3.8) for media negotiation, most of the details for JSEP are handled by the browser.

The constructor for the RTCPeerConnection object takes an RTCConfiguration object with several useful properties. The first one, IceServers, can be set to an array of addresses of servers that assist in establishing sessions through NATs and firewalls (STUN and TURN servers, described in Section 10.2.5 and 10.2.6). The IceTransports property can be set to one of three values: all, indicating that any of the retrieved candidates may be used for ICE; relay, indicating that only relay candidates may be used for ICE; or none, indicating that none of the candidates may be used for ICE. The requestIdentity property is used by the identity functionality (see Section 8.3.1.5) to determine under what conditions the local browser needs to obtain an identity for the peer user and can have the value yes, no, or ifconfigured. This configuration object can be retrieved at a later point using the RTCPeerConnection's getConfiguration() method.

The RTCPeerConnection object can have associated media streams, of course. These are added and removed using the addStream() and removeStream() methods, respectively. Note that the media streams are not created by these methods; these methods add and remove existing local streams from the set of streams being sent to the remote peer. The getLocalStreams() and getRemoteStreams() methods can be used to fetch arrays tracking the complete set of local and remote streams, respectively. A not very obvious but significant aspect of the Peer Connection API is that it is the responsibility of the web application to manage SDP session negotiation. In other words, addStream() and removeStream() do not cause media to flow or stop flowing. They change the internal state of the local RTCPeerConnection object, but an explicit session negotiation is needed to coordinate the media change with the remote end. To trigger the application code to do the negotiation, the addStream() and removeStream() methods cause a negotiationneeded event to be thrown. When the application catches this event (or sets the onnegotiationneeded callback), the application must then negotiate media by:

1) Calling createOffer() - the user agent will examine the internal state of the Peer Connection and generate an appropriate RTCSessionDescription object (an offer).
2) Calling setLocalDescription() with the RTCSessionDescription object.
3) Sending the generated SDP session description to the remote peer. Note that the specification does not define or mandate the mechanism to send SDP session descriptions to and from the remote peer. The specification refers to this undefined channel as the "signaling channel", described in more detail in Chapter 4.

Of course, if the remote peer were the one to send the offer, the application would need to call createAnswer() instead and send the generated RTCSessionDescription object back. The call to setRemoteDescription() must be done by the application when the remote offer (or answer) is received on the signaling channel in order for the offer/answer negotiation to be completed. In either case, local or remote, the actual media state change occurs when a final answer is successfully applied in the browser.

An obvious question at this point is why the setup and parsing of the signaling channel, as well as all of the negotiation, were left to the application. The primary reason is flexibility. With respect to signaling, many browser-to-browser communication applications will have both browsers using exactly the same source code from the same web server, making it logical to have the signaling done through the server. Others may want to signal through gateways. With respect to the SDP session negotiation, the two biggest advantages of leaving it to the application are the ability to do "trickle" ICE, where ICE processing can begin even before all ICE candidates have been generated (see Section 11.5.1), and the ability to modify the SDP if necessary. Since SIP/SDP interoperability is still not at 100%, it is not uncommon to need to adjust the SDP, especially when a browser is communicating with a non-browser endpoint. It is likely that libraries will be developed to support the most common use cases for both signaling and negotiation.

A complexity in the Peer Connection mechanism is that it has two processes, an ICE process and an offer/answer media negotiation process, each of which has its own state machine. The offer/answer state machine is controlled by the JavaScript process, while the ICE state machine is controlled by the browser. The session description reflected in the SDP carries the media offered or answered, as well as the candidates for ICE "hole punching". However, the ICE process is not dependent upon the offer/answer process, which allows for the sometimes slow-moving ICE process to continue checking additional candidates after the media negotiation has completed, i.e., when no more SDP needs to be exchanged in order to agree upon the media. Although in reality there may be more than one underlying ICE state machine, depending on the way the media transport is specified, the WebRTC API exposes a combined state machine. In the specification, the progress of ICE processing is actually split into two pieces – candidate gathering, and checking and connection – because they can proceed somewhat in parallel. The iceGatheringState values are simply new, gathering and complete. The iceConnectionState values are new, checking, connected, completed, failed, disconnected, closed. Again, progression through these states occurs largely without the involvement of the JavaScript code. However, the ability to check these state variables can be useful when building robust applications. The signalingState variable tracks the offer/answer exchange status, with values of stable, have-local-offer, have-remote-offer, have-local-pranswer, have-remote-pranswer, and closed. The specification contains state transition diagrams for both signalingState and iceConnectionState. The JSEP signaling state machine diagram in Figure 11.9 is very similar to the transition diagram for signalingState.

Since an application may need to change the set of ICE servers it wants to use, or which transports are allowed, there is also now an `iceUpdate()` method that will accept the same `RTCConfiguration` object that the `RTCPeerConnection` constructor does.

8.3.1.2 DataChannel Interface

A key piece of functionality defined in the WebRTC specification is the `RTCDataChannel` interface, an API for a bi-directional data channel for use over a Peer Connection. To create the `RTCDataChannel`, the aptly-named `RTCPeerConnection.createDataChannel()` method is provided. In addition to an application-settable `label`, the method also takes an optional `dataChannelDict` configuration object. The different properties of this object allow for control of two primary characteristics: reliability of the channel and whether ordering matters. In an ideal world, there would be no cost to having reliable, ordered delivery. In practice, however, perfect reliability would require infinite retransmissions, and ordered delivery would require an infinite buffer to collect out-of-order messages. The two attributes `maxRetransmitTime` and `maxRetransmits` are used to limit the reliability. The first allows the application to specify the maximum amount of time, in milliseconds, that the browser will continue retransmitting. The second allows the application to specify the maximum total number of retransmission attempts. Only one may be specified (without causing an error). The Boolean `ordered` attribute allows the application to specify, as you might have guessed, whether or not the data channel is to deliver the messages in order. The configuration object also allows for the application to set an `id` (or have it chosen automatically by the browser) and to specify that negotiation of new data channels will be handled by the browser (the default for `negotiated`) rather than by the application.

The progress of the creation of a new `RTCDataChannel` is tracked by its `readyState` property, with values of `connecting` (the data channel is being established), `open` (the data channel is ready to be used), `closing` (the data channel is being shut down), and `closed` (the data channel has been shut down or was never established in the first place). Clearly there is a `close()` method on `RTCDataChannel`, as well as handlers that can be set for `onopen`, `onclose`, and `onerror`.

Once established, the data channel behaves similarly to a WebSocket, with a `send()` method for sending data and an ability to set an `onmessage` handler for incoming messages. Some of the details of data channels are still being finalized, but the general structure is fairly stable now.

8.3.1.3 DTMF API

Audio communication channels, when connected to today's phone networks, need to be able to convey DTMF (Dual Tone Multi-Frequency) tones. In particular, a JavaScript application sending audio into a SIP infrastructure will need a way to generate DTMF tones, since the audio may come from a generic microphone or other device without a DTMF keypad. However, it is during the negotiation of media for a Peer Connection that an ability to also send RFC 4733 DTMF packets is arranged. The specification thus provides an interface on RTCPeerConnection to associate DTMF capability with a designated MediaStreamTrack for that RTCPeerConnection. This section adds a method createDTMFSender() to the RTCPeerConnection interface that takes a MediaStreamTrack as argument. After that, DTMF tones can be sent on that MediaStreamTrack over the Peer Connection via the insertDTMF() method on the new RTCDTMFSender object. Note that DTMF is inserted only via an RTCDTMFSender and not directly via any method on the original MediaStreamTrack itself.

8.3.1.4 Statistics API

The WebRTC specification defines an API for collecting statistics from the tracks being transported over a Peer Connection. This can be important for determining how many packets are getting through, for example. The API works as follows: getStats() takes a MediaStreamTrack as input, along with a callback to be executed when the statistics are available. The callback is given an RTCStatsReport containing RTCStats objects. Statistics are grouped into these objects by type, but all types contain id, type, and timestamp properties. Currently the only defined types are inbound-rtp and outbound-rtp, both of which are instances of the RTCRTPStreamStats subclass that additionally provides remoteId and ssrc properties. The outbound-rtp object type is represented by subclass RTCOutboundRTPStreamStats, which provides packetsSent and bytesSent properties. The inbound-rtp object type is, unsurprisingly, represented by the subclass RTCInboundRTPStreamStats that provides analogous packetsReceived and packetsSent properties. Together, these properties can be used to track both how much data is being sent on the track and how much is being received. Note that the remoteId property can be used directly as a key into the RTCStatsReport to pull out the report for the remote end of the current track. Regardless of type, objects in the report can easily be processed using a for loop to access each one.

8.3.1.5 Identity API

The Identity API in the WebRTC specification is slightly different from the other APIs in that the underlying use of a web Identity Provider is not supposed to require any action on the part of the web application, assuming that the browser has already been configured with a claimed identity and an identity provider. In theory, all the application needs to do is to set the `onidentityresult` handler that will be called whenever an identity has been verified since on one end the browser can automatically generate a signature for the configured identity and on the other end the browser can automatically pull up the Identity Provider's verification page to verify the signature. In practice, however, the IETF draft (see Section 13.4) describing the underlying protocol requirements suggests that the signature itself needs to be transported using the signaling channel. Since the signaling channel is only used by the application JavaScript code directly, the application code would at least need to be involved in this step. In short, the specification is still vague in several respects. However the signing process is initiated, the signature conveyed, and the signature verified, the Identity API does provide a way for the application code to override the browser's configured identity and Identity Provider – the `setIdentityProvider()` method on the Peer Connection. The API also provides the `getIdentityAssertion()` method for applications that wish to start the identity checking process in advance of the offer/answer exchange (when it would occur automatically on its own). This may improve the user interface responsiveness if the time to verify an identity is long due to user login time needs. The Identity mechanism is very much in flux at the moment and not reliably implemented anywhere yet, so it is best not to rely on it at this time.

8.3.1.6 MediaStream Interface Extensions

The WebRTC specification also defines extensions to the `MediaStream` interface defined in the "Media Capture and Streams" specification (Section 8.3.2). First, each `MediaStream` has an `id` attribute to distinguish it from others sent through the `RTCPeerConnection` API. Second, the remote addition or removal of a `MediaStreamTrack` to an existing `MediaStream` will generate local `addtrack` and `removetrack` events. Similarly, remote track muting and unmuting is duplicated locally as well.

8.3.2 "Media Capture and Streams"

This document [2] is under the control of the Media Capture Task Force, which is composed of members of both the WEBRTC Working Group and the Device APIs and Policy (DAP) Working Group. Formerly known as the getusermedia draft, it defines the getUserMedia() method, the API for requesting and obtaining a local media stream from a device such as a camera or microphone.

8.3.2.1 getUserMedia() method

This API is intended to be the primary API used by all web application developers to obtain access to local device media. As such, it requires the browser to obtain user permission before accessing the device. However, the mechanism for obtaining this permission, the specificity of the permission, the duration of the permission, and all other details regarding permission are left up to the user agent. User agents are encouraged to indicate in a prominent manner when local devices are recording. There are two separate callbacks, successCallback and errorCallback, for the cases of a successful setup and a failure, respectively. The latter returns a MediaError, which is an object containing the name (error name), message (human-readable error string), and constraintName (the name of the unsatisfied mandatory constraint, if there is one) properties. There is some confusion still around precisely which errors will be available, but current thinking is that one error name will be ConstraintNotSatisfiedError.

A recent addition to the specification is the getMediaDevices() method, which replaces the prior getSourceInfos() method. The new method allows an application to get an initial list of the external sources and sinks available to the application. Note that an actual physical device could be presented by the browser as multiple different sources. getMediaDevices() takes a callback that, when called, has a list of MediaDeviceInfo objects. Each object contains the following properties: deviceId (this is the same as sourceId), kind (indicating audio/video and in/out), label, and groupId. Since the beginning of this work there have been significant concerns with and significant discussion around the privacy and user fingerprinting implications of an application being able to obtain a list of devices. The MediaDeviceInfo object is the current compromise. The label it gives is intended to be suitable for use in a selector that the application would show the user, but without sufficient detail to use for fingerprinting. The groupId is interesting and is directly connected with the change in name from getSourceInfos to getMediaDevices. Although the Media Capture specification defines how to select and control input media sources, there have been many requests for output device selection and control as well. Since other W3C working groups have also expressed interest in this, the most we decided to do at this time was to make it possible to obtain a list of both input sources and output sinks and to provide a groupId that would link together connected inputs and outputs. For example, a headset/microphone combination would likely be

180

presented as one input source and one output sink, each with a different deviceId, but with the same groupId.

8.3.2.2 Settings, Capabilities, and Constraints

The format and processing of the constraints argument to getUserMedia() warrants a separate explanation. This parameter consists of a JavaScript object with one property for each media type (currently only audio and video). The value for each type can be a Boolean value (explained in a moment) or an object. The object has two optional properties: mandatory and optional. The former contains a ConstraintSet, a set of constraint keys and values that must be satisfied – if not, an error will be returned. The second contains a priority-ordered list of ConstraintSet objects. Failure to satisfy one or more of these optional constraints does not result in an error, but there is a requirement that when conflicting constraints exist, the one occurring earlier in the sequence is to be satisfied. If, instead of an object value, a Boolean value of true is given for a media type, e.g., video:true, then either a video track must be obtained or an error returned. The list of possible constraints is extensible and could yet change before the specification is finalized, but here is the current list. For both audio and video, sourceId identifies the source with an identifier that will remain the same across sessions from the same origin yet distinguish the source from others available to the browser. The video constraints are width, height, frameRate, aspectRatio, and facingMode. The specification defines these fairly well, but it's worth explaining facingMode. There was quite a bit of discussion over what options should be available for the direction the camera faces. Although "front", "back", "left", and "right" were considered, only the last two were kept unmodified. Instead of "front" and "back" we now have "environment" (facing away from the user) and "user" (facing toward the user). The current audio constraints are volume, sampleRate, sampleSize, and the Boolean echoCancelation.

The ability to select and control track and other properties via constraints has two advantages over an earlier proposal for a simpler API that used optional hints: an ability for the application to indicate in advance whether certain tracks would be unacceptable, and an ability to indicate whether some constraints are more important than others. For these reasons, and to allow for extensibility going forward, getUserMedia() accepts the constraints parameter described in the preceding paragraph.

Each constraint has an associated capability and an associated settings, both described fairly extensively in the Media Capture and Streams specification. The capability is the valid range for the constraint. The setting is the current setting/value of the source for that constraint.

181

Although capabilities, settings, and constraints are all accessed via the methods and attributes of a `MediaStreamTrack`, the first two are rightly properties of the media source feeding the track. In other words, two tracks that share the same source will have the same state value. Let's look at video width as an example.

Used in a constraint specification:

```
{
  mandatory: {
    width: { max: 1280 }
  },
  optional: [
    { width: 1000 },
    { width: { min: 640 }}
  ]
}
```

In this example, the structure is requesting that the video track have a width of exactly 1000 pixels if possible (meaning min of 1000 and max of 1000). If that fails, it should at least have a width greater than or equal to 640. Most importantly, the width must not exceed 1280 pixels. If the source cannot provide a width of no more than 1280 pixels the constraint request must fail.

As a setting value:

`mytrack.getSettings().width` returns the track's video width

As a capability:

`mytrack.getCapabilities().width` might return a structure such as

`{ max: 1920, min: 640, supported: true }`

An important track method in the specification is `applyConstraints()`, which allows for constraints to be changed on the fly. Since tracks impose constraints on sources and these constraints can be changed dynamically, it is possible for a track to become *overconstrained*. This is even more likely in the case where multiple tracks are associated with the same source, since each track has the opportunity to impose constraints on the source that may conflict. The specification discusses this topic fairly extensively. The main thing to realize is that a track can become *overconstrained* at any time, in which case an `overconstrained` event will be generated for the track and the track will be muted. This event can of course be caught and handled.

The constraint, capability and setting functionalities have undergone quite a bit of change in how they are specified, although the core of how constraints work is almost identical to how they were first proposed. When reading the specification, it can be confusing to figure out what is defined where. The constraint mechanism has been pulled together into a separable

Constrainable interface defined at the end of the specification. The only hint that tracks support all of these methods now is that the MediaStreamTrack specification implements the Constrainable interface. This separation was done so other WebRTC-related specifications could also make use of the constraint mechanism.

8.3.2.3 MediaStream Interface

This document also defines the MediaStream interface, an API for creating objects representing streams of media data and the MediaStreamTrack interface. These are described in some detail in Sections 3.1.1 and 3.1.2.

8.3.2.4 MediaStreamTrack Interface

The foundational unit of the API is a MediaStreamTrack. This track represents the media of a single type that a single device or recording could return. A single stereo source or a 6-channel surround sound audio signal could be treated as a single track, even though both consist of multiple channels of audio. Note that the specification does not define a means to access or manipulate media at the channel level, although it does roughly define channels as having a "well known relationship to each other". From a practical standpoint, the contents of a track are defined in the WebRTC document as "intended to be encoded together for transmission as, for instance, an RTP payload type." In other words, the channels of a track are treated together as a single unit when being transported using a Peer Connection, and even locally with respect to being enabled/disabled or muted.

Until very recently there has been no way to create a MediaStreamTrack directly; there was no constructor for this object. Although no browser yet implements this, the specification does now define the AudioMediaStreamTrack and VideoMediaStreamTrack subclasses, both of which have constructors. At some point soon it is likely that the getUserMedia() method will accept as an input parameter one or more newly-created tracks and/or streams that will be attached to the media being acquired. The other (currently-implemented) means of creating tracks will be covered in the following section describing media streams. An interesting aspect of a MediaStreamTrack is that it is essentially just a handle to an underlying browser-managed media source. As such, it is possible for a MediaStreamTrack object to become disassociated from its underlying source. Additionally, different MediaStreamTrack objects can represent the same media source, which will be explained more fully in the following section describing MediaStream objects. There are two ways in which tracks can have their media suspended – via muting and via disabling.

The muting/unmuting of a track is something done by the user and/or browser, indicating that the track's underlying media source is temporarily unable to provide media. This can happen, for example, if the end user has suspended permission to use the media source by clicking a mute button in the browser chrome or toggling a switch on the side of their phone. In general, the application does not have control over when a track is muted. It can, however, check the value of the track's `muted` attribute. When muted, an audio track will have silence and a video track will show blackness. Separately, tracks can be disabled individually by setting the track object's `enabled` attribute to `false`. Both of these attributes are separate from the `readyState` attribute of a track that indicates its status — `new`, `live` or `ended`. A new track is one which has not yet been connected to media, while an ended track is one whose source is not providing and can never again provide more data. This could occur, for example, if a camera in use is then unplugged. A live track is one that could produce media. Since these attributes are independent, as an example one could perhaps have a track that is `live`, `unmuted`, and `disabled`.

8.3.3 "MediaStream Capture Scenarios"

This document [3] is the requirements and use cases document for media capture and media streams. It contains requirements in the following four categories: permissions, local media, remote media, and media capture. The requirements are still under review and will likely soon include requirements from the IETF RTCWEB use cases and requirements draft document (see Section 11.3.2) as well.

8.4 Related Work

There are areas in W3C that are under active discussion, either for inclusion into one of the WebRTC specifications or but have not yet been included in either an editor's draft or public draft of a specification. They are covered briefly in the following subsections. For more information on the W3C standards process, see Appendix A.

8.4.1 MediaStream Recording API Specification

The WebRTC APIs provide a handle to a device track but no access to the content (data) itself. It is of course possible for the contents of the track to be sent over a Peer Connection to an entity that can record the content, but there are valid use cases for having direct access to the data. One such use case is for Interactive Voice Response systems, the systems that answer the phone and play a voice menu. Many such IVR systems allow callers to use their voices to speak their menu choices. A recording API would allow the

JavaScript code access to the content for saving, additional manipulation, or posting to an automatic speech recognition system. Early Working Drafts of this document are now available [4].

8.4.2 Image Capture API

During the discussion of what constraints should be defined in the Media Capture and Streams specification, it became clear that there are many kinds of processing and control that application developers might want over video `MediaStreams`. A proposal for controlling cameras and capturing still images from them [5] is likely to become an official Working Draft at some point.

8.4.3 Futures

There have been requests recently to revise all of the API methods that use callbacks to be futures instead. Roughly speaking, in computer science a *future* is a variable that does not yet have a value but will at some unspecified point in the future. The futures being defined for the HTML DOM [6] have a non-blocking semantics in which handlers can be defined to take action when the future obtains a value. As an example, instead of calling

```
createOffer(gotSDP(), didntGetSDP())
```

you would call

```
createOffer().done(gotSDP(), didntGetSDP())
```

This minor syntactic difference, along with a few other features, could allow for combinations of asynchronous results to be checked for in a convenient manner. For example, if both `getUserMedia()` and `createSignalingChannel()` were defined as futures,

```
Future.every(getUserMedia({video:true, audio:true}),
             createSignalingChannel()
             ).done(executeMe())
```

would wait until both had completed before calling `executeMe()`. Although this programming paradigm has been in use in a variety of languages for many years, it is new to HTML standards. For this reason, and because a strong effort is being made to finalize the technical content of the WebRTC specifications at this time, this relatively new feature may not be incorporated into the first versions of the WebRTC standards. Note that no official W3C Working Drafts yet exist for DOM Futures, so syntax, content, and even the name can change. An alternate name being considered, for example, is Promises (rather than Futures). Since ECMAScript version 6 has just added Promises natively, we may see this sooner rather than later.

8.4.4 Media Privacy

One additional feature defined in the Media Capture and Streams Specification is the `peerIdentity` attribute permissible in a `getUserMedia()` constraints structure. When set, this attribute causes the resulting `MediaStream`, and its tracks, to be isolated from any application. In particular, this means that the tracks can be rendered/displayed in audio and video elements, but only if the browser provides the same restrictions on application access that it does for cross-origin content. (See Section 13.2.3). The `MediaStream` and its tracks can also be sent over a Peer Connection, but they will have to comply with additional requirements that are in the works for the WebRTC specification. Yes, this is a Work in Progress.

8.4.5 MediaStream Inactivity

The behavior of a `MediaStream` when attached to an HTML element such as `<video>` has now been defined. In particular, since it is possible to add a new track to a `MediaStream` even after its existing tracks have ended, the behavior in this case needed to be specified. When a `MediaStream` contains non-ended tracks it is called *active*, and when all of the tracks have ended it is called *inactive*. Adding new `live` tracks would make it *active* again.

The consequence for the `<video>` element is this: when the `MediaStream` attached to a `<video>` element becomes *inactive* the element ends, with its `ended` attribute set to `true`. At this point the element will not restart the playing of media, even if new live tracks are added to the `MediaStream`, unless the application specifically restarts the playing (e.g., by calling `play()`) or the `autoplay` attribute is set to `true`.

8.5 References

[1] Public Working Draft: http://www.w3.org/TR/webrtc, Editors' Draft: http://dev.w3.org/2011/webrtc/editor/webrtc.html

[2] Public Working Draft: http://www.w3.org/TR/mediacapture-streams, Editors' Draft: http://dev.w3.org/2011/webrtc/editor/getusermedia.html

[3] Public Working Draft: http://www.w3.org/TR/capture-scenarios, Editor's Draft: http://dvcs.w3.org/hg/dap/raw-file/tip/media-stream-capture/scenarios.html

[4] http://www.w3.org/TR/mediastream-recording

[5]   http://gmandyam.github.io/image-capture

[6]   http://dom.spec.whatwg.org/#futures

9 NAT AND FIREWALL TRAVERSAL

WebRTC uses unique peer-to-peer media flows, where voice, video, and data connections are established directly between browsers, as discussed in Chapter 5. Unfortunately, Network Address Translation (NAT) and firewalls make this difficult and require special protocols and procedures to work. Peer-to-peer media is also sometimes referred to as end-to-end media.

9.1 Introduction to Hole Punching

The nature of NAT makes establishing direct peer-to-peer sessions difficult. However, using a technique known as "hole punching" [BRYAN], it can be successfully done in many cases, perhaps as much as 85% of the time on average. However, this is an average of many users across many networks. Certain networks will have a higher success rate, and others will typically have a much lower success rate. For example, mobile data networks in the U.S. reportedly have a lower success rate of about 30%.

There are a number of pre-requisites for hole punching. They are:

1) The two browsers trying to establish a direct connection must both send "hole punching" packets at the same time. As a result, they must both be aware of the to-be-established session and know the addresses to which to send the packets. Note that there is nothing special about a hole punching packet – it is an ordinary IP packet that is sent to test to see if a particular destination address is reachable through the NATs.

2) The two browsers need to know as many possible IP addresses as possible that could be used to reach them. These

189

addresses are often described as "private" (or inside the NAT) addresses, "public" (or on the outside of the NAT) addresses, and relay addresses, depending on privacy settings (see Chapter 13.)

3) As a last resort, a media relay, which has a public IP address (is not behind a NAT) and hence is reachable by both browsers, is needed.

4) Symmetric flows must be used. That is, UDP traffic must appear to operate in a similar manner to a TCP connection.

Requirement 1) is met by using the Web Server to coordinate the hole punching. That is, the Web Server knows that a session is to be established between the browsers, so it ensures that both browsers begin hole punching at approximately the same time.

Requirement 2) is met by using a STUN (Session Traversal Utilities for NAT) Server, as described in Section 5.3. A Virtual Private Network (VPN) connection could provide an additional address. Other NAT traversal protocols such as Universal Plug and Play (UPnP) could be used, although these are uncommon.

Requirement 3) is met using a TURN (Traversal Using Relay around NAT) Server, described Section 5.4. The media relay address is a public IP address that will forward packets received to and from the browser that set up the relay address. This address is then added to the candidate list.

Requirement 4) is met by the browser sending media from the same UDP port that the browser is using to listen for incoming media. This makes the two one-way RTP sessions over UDP appear to the NAT to be one bi-directional RTP session. Symmetric RTP is described in Section 12.3.2.

9.1.1 Relayed Media Through TURN Server

In most cases, the hole punching will result in a direct peer-to-peer connection being established. However, in certain cases of a very restrictive NAT or firewall, the direct paths will fail and the only one that succeeds will be the address of the TURN server. This will result it the media being relayed through the TURN server, as shown in Figure 5.9. Although this figure shows the TURN server as a separate server, a TURN server is actually a STUN server with added relaying functionality, and in many cases are combined. While all TURN servers also have STUN functionality, not every STUN server has TURN functionality.

9.2 Interactive Connectivity Establishment

Interactive Connectivity Establishment, or ICE, is a standardized protocol for hole punching. It uses STUN and TURN to help endpoints establish connectivity. The basic steps in ICE are shown in Figure 9.1.

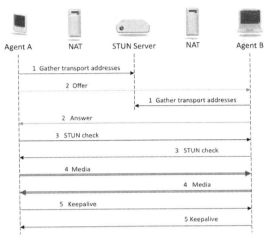

1) Gather Candidate Transport Addresses
2) Exchange Candidates over Signaling Channel
3) Perform Connectivity Checks
4) Choose Selected Pair and Begin Media
5) Send Keepalives
If either side detects a change in IP address in use, ICE is restarted (back to Step 1)

Figure 9.1 High Level ICE Call Flow

The following sections will cover these steps.

9.2.1 Gather Candidate Transport Addresses

The first step is to gather candidate transport addresses. A candidate address is an IP address and port where media might be able to be received for a Peer Connection. These addresses must be gathered at the time of the call – they cannot be gathered ahead of time in many cases. In the example of Figure 9.1, ICE Agent A begins gathering candidate addresses as soon as the user at A initiates a Peer Connection with B. ICE Agent B begins gathering candidate addresses as soon as the Peer Connection request from A is received in the signaling channel.

There are four types of address candidates, shown in Table 9.1. A host candidate address is an address obtained through the operating system that represents an actual address on a network interface card (NIC). If the ICE Agent is behind a NAT, this address will be a private IP address and not be routable outside the subnet. The next two types of candidate addresses are known as reflexive addresses since they represent addresses that are reflected back to the ICE Agent by a STUN check, as if the client is looking in a mirror through the STUN server to learn their actual IP addresses. A server reflexive candidate is an address learned from a response to a STUN check sent to a STUN server. If the ICE Agent is behind a NAT, this address will be the outside address of the outermost NAT. That is, there could be multiple layers of NAT between the ICE Agent and the STUN server, but this check only allows discovery of the last NAT before the STUN server.

Candidate Type	Use
Host	Local transport address obtained from the network interface card (NIC). If behind a NAT, this will be a private address
Server Reflexive	Transport address obtained by a STUN check sent to a STUN server. If behind a NAT, this will be the public IP address of the outermost NAT.
Peer Reflexive	Transport address obtained from a STUN connectivity check sent by the other ICE Agent (peer). This is a new candidate which is discovered during the connectivity checks, not sent over the signaling channel
Relayed	Transport address of a media relay server. Usually obtained using a TURN allocation request.

Table 9.1 ICE Candidate Address Types

A peer reflexive candidate is an address learned from a received STUN check sent by the other ICE Agent (a peer). This type of candidate address is not exchanged over the signaling channel but is discovered during the STUN connectivity checks of Step 3.

A relayed candidate is an address of a media relay. Usually this is obtained using the TURN protocol. The transport address obtained using a TURN allocate request is a relayed candidate.

Browsers are configured with the STUN and TURN servers used in this gathering candidates step. This is done using STUN URIs [RFC7064] and

TURN URIs [RFC7065] in the iceServers property of the RTCConfiguration object. Note that access to a TURN server means having STUN server functionality as well in most cases.

It is important to note that just learning public IP address candidates using STUN is not enough on its own to traverse the NATs. NATs are complicated and vary widely in operation between networks and service providers. As a result, the full functionality of ICE is needed to ensure NAT traversal.

9.2.2 Exchange of Candidates

The second step is the exchange of candidate addresses over the signaling channel. Candidates are exchanged between the browsers over the signaling channel, as described in Chapter 4. Once received, the candidates are first ordered or prioritized. In general, the highest priority are host candidates, followed by reflexive addresses, followed lastly by relayed candidates. If there is a preference between IPv4 and IPv6, this can be expressed by different priority settings. Candidates are associated with a particular media stream in SDP. The default behavior with WebRTC is to multiplex all media, including voice, video, and data, over the same transport address. As such, a single set of candidates is all that is needed.

9.2.3 STUN Connectivity Checks

The ICE Agents begin connectivity checks as soon as they have sent and received the candidates. In figure 9.1, for Agent A, this is when the SDP answer is received from Agent B. For Agent B, this is when the SDP answer is sent to Agent A. During this phase, the ICE Agents generate STUN responses to any STUN connectivity requests they receive from their peer that pass authentication.

The number of connectivity checks performed is minimized through a process of pairing and analyzing the candidates. This reduces the time needed by ICE to obtain a working candidate. For example, one step is to pair candidates based on IP address type (IPv4 or IPv6) since it does not make sense to test an IPv4 address against an IPv6 address, or vice versa.

Peer reflexive candidate addresses can be discovered during this step and are automatically paired as they are discovered. There are five possible connectivity states, as shown in Figure 9.2.

Queued candidate pairs start in the "frozen" state (a joke on the name of the protocol) – a holding state until the checks are ready to be performed. When the ICE connectivity check algorithm determines that a check should be performed, it is "unfrozen" and moves to the "waiting" state. A pair could stay in the waiting state due to pacing considerations for the checks, so that a flood of packets is not sent at once. When the pacing allows for the check to be made, the state moves to "in-progress" when the STUN connectivity check is sent to the other peer. If a response comes back, the state moves to "succeeded", while if the check times out without a response, it moves to "failed".

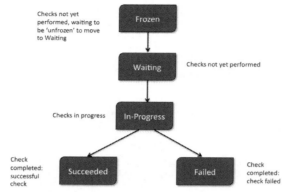

Figure 9.2 ICE Connectivity Check State Machine

There is an optimization of ICE known as Trickle ICE (see Section 11.5.1) where instead of all of the candidates being provided at the start of ICE processing, ICE is started with a minimal set, and additional candidates are added, or trickled in, as processing continues. These new candidates are paired and queued, and go through the same steps as Figure 9.2. Currently, only Chrome supports Trickle ICE.

9.2.4 Choose Selected Pair and Begin Media

The connectivity checks continue until either all possible checks have completed (all have moved from the "frozen" state to either "succeeded" or "failed") or one pair has been chosen. Choosing a pair is done by the controlling ICE Agent. The ICE protocol has an algorithm to choose which browser is the Controlling ICE Agent and which is the Controlled ICE Agent. The Controlled ICE Agent learns that the other ICE Agent has chosen a candidate pair when a STUN connectivity check is received with an attribute indicating that this pair is to be used. The Controlled ICE Agent then replies to the connectivity check echoing that the pair will be used. Media is now sent by both browsers using the chosen candidate pair.

9.2.5 Keep-Alives

To ensure that NAT mappings and filter rules do not time out during the media session, ICE continues to send STUN connectivity checks at 15 second intervals over the candidate pairs in use. This ensures that packets are sent, even when media is on hold or otherwise not being sent. If the media session is still active, the other ICE Agent generates a STUN response. The receipt of this STUN response by the other ICE Agent is taken as an indication that media can continue to be sent. If the STUN response is not received, the media flows are stopped. ICE would need to be restarted, per the next section. Note that this behavior is not defined in the original ICE protocol specification, but is defined in the ICE extension of Section 11.3.10.

9.2.6 ICE Restart

An ICE restart is triggered if either ICE Agent detects a change in the base transport address. Recall that the base address is the transport address which was used to generate the candidate pair which is in use. This will cause the ICE Agent to go back to Step 1, gather candidates and send those candidates in an SDP offer to the other ICE Agent. That will cause the other ICE Agent to also go back to Step 1 and the whole process will repeat.

Note that this will occur if a browser page involved in an active Peer Connection is reloaded by a user. This is sometimes described as "rehydration," and is an active area of discussion in the standards on how to best handle this situation.

9.3 WebRTC and Firewalls

Firewalls, named after the fire-proof walls used to stop the spread of fires or heat in buildings and cars, are also frequently found in the Internet. They are used at a network boundary to enforce security policies. They can implement any type of policy and do any type of IP packet filtering or blocking. Most commonly, firewalls implement simple packet filter rules similar to those used in NAT. Firewalls act as a "one way gate", allowing access from "inside" the network to the "outside" (the Internet), but blocking arbitrary traffic from the Internet from entering the network. Essentially, firewalls try to allow normal IP traffic originating from inside the network, but block malicious traffic from the Internet.

One type of policy is to allow only outgoing traffic, with the exception of packets from the outside that are determined to be valid responses to requests from the inside. For example, a firewall might allow TCP connections if they are opened from a host inside the network. Once the connection is open, packets can flow in either direction until the connection is closed. TCP connections from the outside will be blocked. Handling of UDP traffic is more difficult since the UDP packets are not part of a connection, and there is no signaling indicating the start and stop of a UDP flow. Outgoing UDP packets might also be allowed, and certain incoming

UDP packets if they are destined for a host that recently sent out a UDP packet. Note that this firewall behavior is very similar to the filter rules used by most NATs to restrict the usage of mappings between public and private IP addresses and ports. Some firewalls block all UDP traffic, with the exception of DNS lookups. In these circumstances, running media over TCP might be the only way to establish the media flow.

Firewalls are often combined with NAT and implemented in the same box, although they are separate functions. Most home routers and enterprise routers have firewall functionality built in. It is becoming increasingly common for PCs themselves to have firewall functionality, since IP access is handled by the operating system.

9.3.1 WebRTC Firewall Traversal

Hole punching techniques used to traverse NATs often also work for traversal of firewalls. However, some firewalls have stricter rules that cause hole punching to fail. Some firewalls even block all UDP traffic entirely. (For these cases, there have been some discussions of standardizing the transport of SRTP media over TCP or even HTTP.)

There are a number of different approaches used to help today's VoIP and video traffic traverse firewalls. One approach is to build awareness of the VoIP signaling and media protocols into the firewall, so that it can open "pin holes" for the media only for the duration of the media session. This approach is sometimes known as the Application Layer Gateway or ALG approach. This approach is not usable with WebRTC since there is no standardized signaling protocol used – the signaling is just part of the exchange over HTTP between the browser and the web server.

Another approach uses a special-purpose VoIP and video firewall which is trusted by the firewall. These elements are commonly known as Session Border Controllers or SBCs [RFC5853]. They terminate the VoIP and video signaling and media traffic and apply policy. The SBC is connected to the firewall using a trusted link known as a DMZ (for De-Militarized Zone). Again, this approach will not work unless WebRTC is gatewayed to a standard signaling protocol such as SIP.

One approach that could be used is to utilize a media relay which is trusted by the firewall. The media relay would also be connected via the DMZ and would be responsible for authenticating the flows. A TURN Server provides this functionality in a way that is compatible with the ICE hole punching used in WebRTC. Essentially, an enterprise that wanted to be able to control and monitor WebRTC media flows would implement firewall policies that would cause all the hole punching candidates with the exception of the enterprise TURN server to fail. As a result, all flows would be authenticated and relayed by the TURN server. The TURN server could be configured in a web browser in the same way (and for the same reason) as web proxies are configured today.

Alternatively, a firewall could implement an ICE ALG. This would allow the firewall to use the ICE hole punching as signaling for the UDP flows to come. The pinhole could be kept open as long as the ICE keep-alive packets continue.

Figure 9.3 shows media through a firewall using a TURN Server.

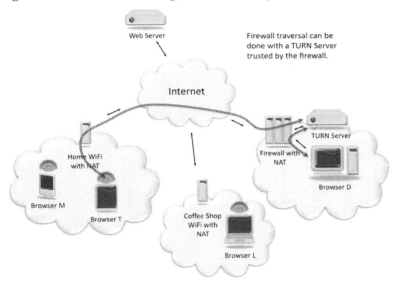

Figure 9.3 Media Relayed through Firewall Traversal TURN Server

For more information about media traversal through firewalls, see [IEEE-COMS] and [draft-hutton-rtcweb-nat-firewall-considerations].

9.4 References

[BRYAN]   http://www.brynosaurus.com/pub/net/p2pnat

[RFC7064]   http://tools.ietf.org/html/rfc7064

[RFC7065]   http://tools.ietf.org/html/rfc7065

[RFC5853]   http://tools.ietf.org/html/rfc5853

[IEEE-COMS] Alan Johnston, John Yoakum and Kundan Singh, Taking on WebRTC in an Enterprise, IEEE Communications Magazine, Vol. 51, No. 4, April 2013

[draft-hutton-rtcweb-nat-firewall-considerations]
   http://tools.ietf.org/html/draft-hutton-rtcweb-nat-firewall-considerations

10 PROTOCOLS

There are a number of protocols related to WebRTC. The most important ones are listed in Table 6.1 below. Their usage is discussed in this chapter. They are shown in the protocol stack of Figure 10.1.

Protocol	Use	Specification
HTTP	Hyper-Text Transport Protocol	RFC 2616
WebSocket	Socket between Web Browser and Server	RFC 6455
SRTP	Secure Real-time Transport Protocol	RFC 3711
SDP	Session Description Protocol	RFC 4566
STUN	Session Traversal Utilities for NAT	RFC 5389
TURN	Traversal Using Relays around NAT	RFC 5766
ICE	Interactive Connectivity Establishment	RFC 5245
TLS	Transport Layer Security	RFC 5246
TCP	Transmission Control Protocol	RFC 793
DTLS	Datagram Transport Layer Security	RFC 4347
UDP	User Datagram Protocol	RFC 768
SCTP	Stream Control Transport Protocol	RFC 4960
IP	Internet Protocol, version 4 and version 6	RFC 791, RFC 2460

Table 10.1 WebRTC Protocols

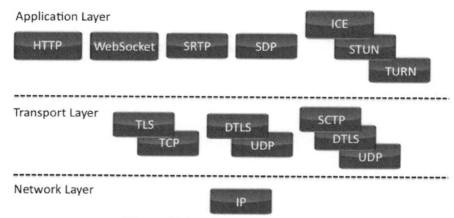

Figure 10.1 Protocols in WebRTC

10.1 Protocols

The preceding sections have discussed the WebRTC APIs as standardized by W3C. Web developers will interact directly with these APIs in their applications and web sites to add communication capabilities. The following sections will discuss the protocols utilized by WebRTC. These protocols are the "bits on the wire" that allow two browsers to communicate, or a browser and a server to communicate. A web developer in general will never directly interact with protocols, as the default settings and configurations of the protocols will usually meet their needs. However, in some cases, especially when a WebRTC client is communicating with a non-WebRTC client, some configuration and knowledge of the protocols used by WebRTC is necessary. Additionally, if there arises a need to adjust the `RTCSessionDescription` object in the WEBRTC API, such as may occur if there are SDP interoperability problems between user agents, the application author will need to have a deeper understanding of how the negotiation works. In any case, a basic understanding of the protocols used by WebRTC is useful for the developer – this is provided in this chapter. A telephony developer who wants to utilize WebRTC, on the other hand, will need to have a detailed understanding of the protocols used. For them, subsequent chapters of this book contain a detailed description of how they work together.

10.1.1 Wireshark Notes

Wireshark [WIRESHARK] is an open source tool for viewing protocols on the wire. It can be a very useful way to troubleshoot and learn about protocols of WebRTC. The easiest way to use Wireshark is to run it on the machine which is running a browser participating in the peer

200

connection. For the main protocols of WebRTC, notes on how to observe this protocol are provided in the following sections. These examples are based on version 1.10.5 of Wireshark and the screen captures are from the Mac version.

10.2 WebRTC Protocol Overview

10.2.1 HTTP (Hyper-Text Transport Protocol)

Of course, WebRTC uses HTTP, Hyper-Text Transport Protocol [RFC2616]. This is the protocol of the World Wide Web and is used between a web browser and a web server. WebRTC uses HTTP the same as any web application. As such, no specific knowledge of HTTP is needed. The current version of HTTP is 1.1. There is work in the IETF to define the next version of HTTP, known as 2.0. This protocol will likely increase the speed and efficiency of web downloads and applications. WebRTC will be able to use this and any other future version of HTTP. See Section 4.3.3 for examples of how to use HTTP for the WebRTC signaling channel.

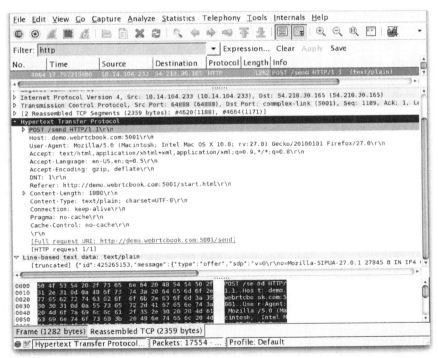

Figure 10.2 Wireshark HTTP Capture of Signaling (SDP) Data

HTTP can be monitored using Wireshark by setting the Display Filter to `http` or by filtering TCP on the port used for HTTP, either port 80, the default HTTP port, or, for the demo code in this book, port 5001, as shown in Figure 10.2. Note that the Chrome Tools/Developer Tools and Firefox Tools/Web Developer menus can be used to inspect HTTP within the browser.

10.2.2 WebSocket Protocol

The WebSocket protocol [RFC6455] allows a browser to open additional bi-directional TCP connections to a web server. The connection opening is signaled using HTTP has similar security properties to the HTTP web session, and can reuse existing HTTP infrastructure. This avoids HTTP polling and the opening of multiple HTTP connections between a browser and web server. The browser indicates the application using the WebSocket in the opening. This is known as the WebSocket sub-protocol. The SIP WebSocket sub-protocol or XMPP WebSocket sub-protocol are examples, described in Sections 4.3.6 and 4.3.7.

Wireshark can be used to detect WebSocket traffic by setting the Display Filter to `http` then looking for the `HTTP/1.1 101 Switching Protocols` response. Note that currently Wireshark does not have the ability to directly decode WebSocket traffic.

10.2.3 RTP (Real-time Transport Protocol) and SRTP (Secure RTP)

The most important protocol used by WebRTC is the Real-time Transport Protocol, or RTP [RFC3550]. WebRTC uses only the secure profile of RTP or Secure RTP, SRTP [RFC3711]. SRTP is the protocol used to transport and carry the audio and video media packets between WebRTC clients. The media packets contain the digitized audio samples or digitized video frames generated by a microphone or camera or application, and are rendered using a speaker or display. A successful setup of a Peer Connection, along with a complete offer/answer exchange, will result in an SRTP connection being established between the browsers or a browser and a server, and an exchange of media information.

SRTP provides information essential for successfully transporting and rendering media information: the codec (coder/decoder used to sample and compress the audio or video), the source of the media (the synchronization source or SSRC), a timestamp (for correctly timed play-out), sequence number (to detect lost packets), and other information needed for playback. For non-audio or video data, SRTP is not used. Instead, a call to the `RTCDataChannel` API will result in a data channel being opened between the browsers allowing any arbitrarily formatted data to be exchanged.

The RTP header is shown in Figure 10.3.

- **Version (V)** - (2 bits) Set to 2
- **Padding (P)** - (1 bit) Padding octets are present in payload
- **Extension (X)** - (1 bit) Header extension present
- **CSRC Count (CC)** - (4 bits) Number of CSRC identifiers present – 0 for non-mixed media
- **Marker (M)** – (1 bit) Profile defined marker
- **Payload Type (PT)** – (7 bits) Codec in payload
- **Sequence Number** - (16 bits) Count incremented for each packet sent
- **Timestamp** - (32 bits) Sampling instant for first octet in payload
- **Synchronization Source (SSRC)** - (32 bits) Identifies the sender of the packet, unique for each session
- **Contributing SSRC (CSRC)** - (32 bits) Optional contributing sources in payload due to mixing

Figure 10.3 RTP Header

The set of extensions to RTP used by WebRTC is shown in Table 10.2.

Extension	Description	Reference
SAVPF Profile	Extended Secure Audio and Video Profile with Feedback uses Secure RTP and early RTCP feedback	Section 12.1.4
Multiplexing RTP and RTCP	RTCP received on same UDP port as RTP	Section 12.1.5
Multiplexing Audio & Video	All media received on same UDP port, media type (audio or video) identified by SSRC and Payload Type	Section 11.5.4
Symmetric RTP	RTP media sent and received from same UDP port to help NAT traversal	Section 12.3.2
Congestion Avoidance & Control	Avoiding Congestion by stopping sending RTP or adjusting bandwidth usage	Section 11.5.5

Table 10.2 WebRTC RTP Extension Summary

RTP cannot be automatically analyzed by Wireshark. Simply setting the Display Filter to `rtp` will not, in general, result in any RTP packets displayed. Instead, first set the Display Filter to `udp` to find the UDP traffic. After the Peer Connection is established, there will be UDP traffic sent regularly between the browsers. RTP over UDP traffic will begin with 90 hexadecimal (or 80 hexadecimal if no RTP header extensions are present), the first octet of the RTP header. By selecting one of these UDP packets, and selecting Analyze/Decode As then selecting RTP, Wireshark will process the packets as RTP, as shown in Figure 10.4. By examining the SDP, you can determine the payload types (PT) for audio and video. Audio packets will be small (just over 100 octets) and sent every 20-60 ms. Video packets will be large (around 1000 octets) and sent four to five times as frequently. RTCP and data channel packets will also be interpreted as RTP packets. To see RTCP packets, select Analyze/Decode As RTCP. (If you have already performed a Decode As operation, such as to view as RTP, then you will first need to first clear that by selecting Analyze/Decode As then clicking the radio button "Do not decode.") Again, all packets will be interpreted as RTCP, including RTP and data channel traffic. To find the actual RTCP traffic, look for 'Sender Report' or 'Receiver Report' under the Info column, as shown in Figure 10.5. If RTP packets are only found in one direction for bi-directional media, TURN might be in use – see Section 10.2.6. Since WebRTC uses only SRTP, the RTP media payload will not be decipherable.

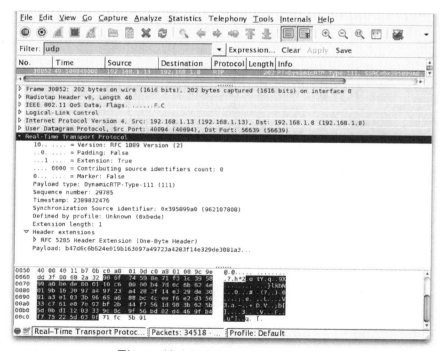

Figure 10.4 RTP Wireshark Capture

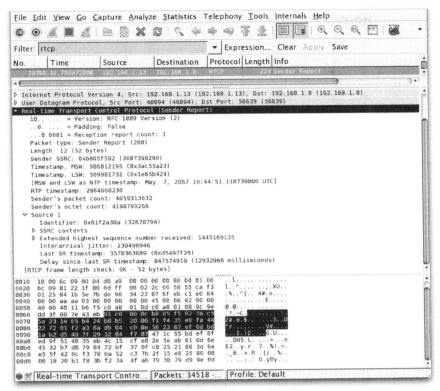

Figure 10.5 RTCP Wireshark Capture

10.2.4 SDP (Session Description Protocol)

WebRTC session descriptions are described using the Session Description Protocol, SDP [RFC4566]. An SDP session description (encoded as an RTCSessionDescription object) is used to describe the media characteristics of the Peer Connection. There is a long and complicated list of information that must be exchanged between the two ends of the SRTP session so that they can communicate. API calls to RTCPeerConnection will result in an SDP session description, a set of data formatted in a particular way, being generated by the browser and accessed using JavaScript by the web application. An application that wants to have tight control over the media may make changes to the session description before sharing it with the other browser. When changes are made to a Peer Connection, this will result in changes to the session description which the two peers will exchange. This is known as an offer/answer exchange (see Section 6.2. Any developer wishing to have fine-grained control over the media sessions needs to understand SDP.

Both SRTP and SDP are protocols standardized by the IETF and widely used by Internet Communications devices and services on the Internet, such as Voice over IP (VoIP) phones, clients, and gateways, and video conferencing and collaboration devices. As a result, communication between one of these devices or clients and a WebRTC client is possible. However, few VoIP or video devices or clients today support the full set of capabilities and protocols of WebRTC. These devices will need to be upgraded to support these new protocols, or a gateway function used between the WebRTC client and the VoIP or video client to do the conversion. Telephony and Internet Communication developers can use the descriptions of these protocols in this book to guide their development efforts with WebRTC compatible clients or gateways.

The SDP offer/answer exchange between the browsers will be sent over the signaling channel. If Wireshark captures the signaling channel unencrypted, then the SDP can be examined, for example see Figure 10.2. Alternatively, the demo application in this book displays the SDP offers and answers in the window below the video windows, as shown in Figure 6.3.

10.2.5 STUN (Session Traversal Utilities for NAT)

Session Traversal Utilities for NAT, STUN [RFC5389], is a protocol used to help with NAT traversal. In WebRTC, a STUN client will be built into the browser user agent, and web servers will run a STUN server. STUN test packets are sent prior to session establishment to allow a browser to learn if it is behind a NAT and to discover the mapped addresses and port. This information is then used to construct candidate addresses in ICE "hole punching". STUN can be transported over UDP, TCP, or TLS. The port number for STUN can be determined using a DNS SRV lookup; the default UDP port for STUN is 3478.

The format of the STUN header is shown in Figure 10.6. The first two bits are set to zero to help distinguish a STUN packet from an RTP packet (which will have the first two bits set to zero and one). The next 14 bits are the message type, which includes the class and method. The next 16 bits contain the message length, which has the entire size of the STUN packet including the header and any padding. The next 32 bits are a "magic cookie" which is a unique string to aid in the identification of STUN packets. The value of the magic cookie is 0x2112A442 in hexadecimal. The last field in the header is the Transaction ID, which is a cryptographic random number used to correlate a response to a request.

- **First two bits are 0's** – (2 bits) Differentiate from RTP
- **Message Type** - (14 bits) set to indicate end of event
  - Identifies the Class and Method of a message
- **Message Length** - (16 bits) Total length of the STUN packet including the 20 octet header.
- **Magic Cookie** – (32 bits) Unique string to aid in identification of STUN packets:
  - Value of 0x2112A442
- **Transaction ID** – (96 bits) Cryptographically random number used to correlate responses to requests

Figure 10.6 STUN Header Format

STUN is a client/server protocol. There are two types of STUN requests: request/response and indication. In a request/response request, the STUN client originating the request expects a response from the STUN server that received the request so requests are retransmitted if necessary to ensure delivery. When used over UDP, request/response request messages are retransmitted using an exponential back-off timer known as RTO (Retransmission Time Out). RTO is configurable, but must be greater than 500ms. The first retransmission is sent after RTO expires, the second after twice RTO, the third after three times RTO, etc. Retransmissions end after a total of seven requests have been sent. In an indication request, no response is expected.

In the core STUN protocol, there is only one method called Binding. Binding is used by a STUN client to create and discover NAT mappings. If a STUN client is behind a NAT, and the STUN server is outside the NAT, sending a STUN Binding request will cause the NAT to create a mapping and assign a public IP address and port. In addition, this creates a filter rule in the NAT about who is permitted to use this mapping to send packets to the private network. When the STUN server receives a STUN Binding request, it records the IP address and port number that it received the STUN Binding request from. This address and port number is then returned to the client in the STUN Binding response. The STUN client receiving the STUN Binding response compares the IP address and port received in the response to the IP address and port that it sent the request from. If they are the same, there is no NAT between the client and the server. If they are different, there is at least one NAT, and the client is able to learn the IP address and port assigned by the outer most NAT. Note that there could be multiple NATs between the STUN client and server, but only information about the outer most NAT is learned.

A STUN Binding request sent as an indication can be used to prevent NAT mappings from timing out if sent at regular intervals. The indication request will cause the NAT to reset its UDP timer. As long as the interval of sending out the STUN Binding indications is less than the shortest NAT UDP timer between the client and server, the NAT mapping will be maintained.

STUN has two authentication mechanisms: short term authentication and long term authentication. Short term authentication uses a username/password which is valid for a single session. This approach is used by ICE to make authentication unique for each set of connectivity checks. Long term authentication uses a challenge/response mechanism which allows a long term credential to be used. For example, a SIP authentication credential can be reused.

The format of STUN attributes is shown in Figure 10.7. Attributes are optional after the STUN header. Attributes are encoded as TLV (Type, Length, and Value). Type and Length are two octets long, but the Value is variable length. The Value is always padded out so that the length is a multiple of four octets.

- **Type** - (16 bits) Type of attribute
- **Length** - (16 bits) Total length of the Attribute
- **Value** – (variable length) All Value fields must be a multiple of 4 octets in length, and are padded

Figure 10.7 STUN Attribute Format

The list of STUN attributes in the core protocol is shown in Table 10.3. In Binding responses, the IP address and port number seen by the STUN server will be returned in a XOR-MAPPED-ADDRESS attribute. The XOR-MAPPED-ADDRESS attribute obfuscates the IP address and port number by performing an exclusive OR operation on it. This is because some NATs have functions known as general application layer gateways (ALGs) which look for IP addresses and ports associated with NAT mappings and rewrite them on the fly. (These ALGs can cause major problems with many protocols and should be disabled or removed whenever possible from a network). The presence of these ALGs can be determined if the server includes both attributes and the information as seen by the client is different in the two attributes. The MAPPED-ADDRESS attribute is only used if backwards compatibility with the original STUN protocol is needed.

Attribute	Use
XOR-MAPPED-ADDRESS	Exclusive ORed reflexive transport address of client
MAPPED-ADDRESS	Reflexive transport address of client seen by server
USERNAME	Username as used in message integrity
MESSAGE-INTEGRITY	Keyed message authentication code for STUN message
FINGERPRINT	Cyclic Redundancy Code (CRC) of STUN message
ERROR-CODE	Error code and reason phrase for error responses
REALM	Realm to be used for long-term authentication
NONCE	Nonce to be used for long-term authentication
UNKNOWN-ATTRIBUTES	Unknown attribute in 420 error response
SOFTWARE	Manufacturer and version of STUN for debugging
ALTERNATE-SERVER	Alternative STUN server in 300 error response

Table 10.3 STUN Attributes

Failure responses are carried in an ERROR-CODE attribute in a response. The set of STUN error codes is shown in Table 10.4. If a 420 Unknown Attribute code is used, the UNKNOWN-ATTRIBUTES attribute will list the attributes that were not understood. If a 300 Try Alternative code is used, the ALTERNATIVE-SERVER attribute will contain the IP address and port of the other STUN server to be used.

STUN servers do not implement any authentication mechanism. This is because the effort needed to authenticate requests is greater than the level of effort needed to simply respond to the requests.

New extensions are being developed for STUN in the newly formed IETF TRAM (TURN Revised and Modernized) Working Group. See Section 11.5.9 for the details.

Error Code	Reason Phrase	Usage
300	Try Alternative	STUN
400	Bad Request	STUN
401	Unauthorized	STUN
403	Forbidden	TURN
420	Unknown Attribute	STUN
437	Allocation Mismatch	TURN
438	Stale Nonce	STUN
441	Wrong Credentials	TURN
442	Unsupported Transport Protocol	TURN
486	Allocation Quota Reached	TURN
487	Role Conflict	ICE
500	Server Error	STUN
508	Insufficient Capacity	TURN

Table 10.4 STUN Error Codes

   Wireshark can find STUN by setting Display Filter to stun, as shown in Figure 10.8. However, this will find STUN, ICE, and TURN packets. By examining the message type and attributes present, you can distinguish STUN packets from ICE and TURN packets. Also, to find just STUN binding requests and responses, you can filter on port 3478. ICE STUN packets will be present on the same ports as the RTP media. The WebRTC book demo application uses STUN by default to generate server reflexive candidates. To turn STUN off, add the attribute 'stunuri=0' to the URL.

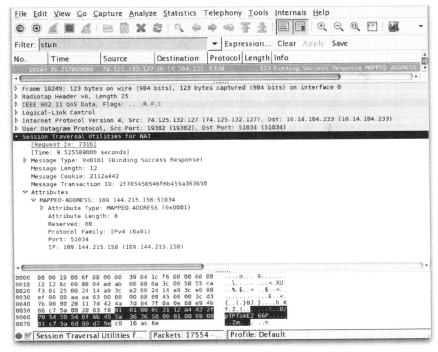

Figure 10.8 STUN Wireshark Capture

10.2.6 TURN (Traversal Using Relays around NAT)

Traversal Using Relays around NAT, TURN [RFC5766], is an extension to the STUN protocol that provides a media relay for situations where ICE "hole punching" fails. In WebRTC, the browser user agent will include a TURN client, and a web server, service provider, or enterprise will provide a TURN server. The browser requests a public IP address and port number as a transport relay address from the TURN server. This address is then included as a candidate address in the ICE "hole punching". TURN can also be used for firewall traversal, as described in Section 9.3. The port number for TURN can be determined using a DNS SRV lookup; the default UDP port for TURN is 3478.

TURN can be used to establish relayed transport addresses that use UDP, TCP, or TLS transport. However, the communication between the TURN server and the TURN client (through the NAT) is always UDP.

The set of STUN attributes defined for TURN are shown in Table 10.5. The TURN error codes for STUN are listed in Table 10.4.

Attribute	Use
CHANNEL-NUMBER	Channel number for Channel binding or refreshing
LIFETIME	Allocation, Channel, or Permission must be refreshed within this time or it will expire in server
XOR-PEER-ADDRESS	Peer's Server Reflexive Address which has permission to use the Relayed Address
DATA	Contains relayed application data in Send and Data
XOR-RELAYED-ADDRESS	Allocated relay address in Allocate response
EVEN-PORT	Request even port for RTP and next higher for RTCP
REQUESTED-TRANSPORT	Requested transport between relay and peer, usually UDP
DONT-FRAGMENT	Set don't fragment bit for application data sent to peer
RESERVATION-TOKEN	Uniquely identifies a relayed transport address

Table 10.5 TURN STUN Attributes

TURN defines a whole new set of STUN methods, in addition to the Binding, shown in Table 10.6. The `Allocate` method is used to request a relayed transport address from the STUN server. The `Refresh` method is used to refresh and keep alive an existing transport allocation. The `CreatePermission` method is used to set filtering rules on the relayed address, similar to those used by NATs. TURN has two ways in which data can be relayed through the TURN server. One is to use the `Send` and `Data` methods, where the relayed data is carried in the STUN message. Another method is to establish a channel between the TURN client and the TURN server, and the data is sent using a `ChannelData` message which does not use the STUN header and the 36 octets of overhead. For audio or video media, a channel is usually used. The `ChannelBind` method is used to establish the channel.

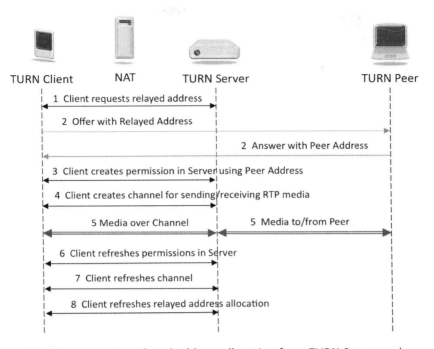

1) Client requests relayed address allocation from TURN Server and receives in response
2) In Offer, Client sends Relayed Address to Peer. In Answer, Peer sends Peer Address to Client
3) Client creates permission in Server using Peer Address to Server
4) Client creates channel for sending and receiving RTP media
5) Client sends and receives media over channel. Peer sends and receives media with TURN Server
6) Client refreshes permissions in Server
7) Client refreshes channel with Server
8) Client refreshes relayed address allocation with Server

Figure 10.9 High Level TURN Call Flow

- **Channel Number** - (16 bits) CHANNEL-NUMBER attribute from CreateChannel request
- **Length** - (16 bits) Total length in octets of the Application Data field
- **Application Data** – (variable length) The application data sent to or received from the Peer

Figure 10.10 TURN ChannelData Format

STUN Method	Use	Spec
Binding	Create and maintain NAT mapping	STUN
Allocate	Client receives allocated relayed transport address	TURN
Refresh	Regular keep alives for allocation from client	TURN
Send	Application data from client to server (not used for RTP)	TURN
Data	Application data from server (peer) to client (not used for RTP)	TURN
CreatePermission	Sets permissions in the server to allow a particular IP address to use a relayed address	TURN
ChannelBind	Create or refresh a channel for exchange of RTP data	TURN

Table 10.6 STUN Methods

TURN servers commonly use the STUN long-term authentication. A TURN request can be challenged with a 401 Unauthorized response containing a REALM and NONCE attribute. These are used by the TURN client to resend the request with the USERNAME attribute containing the username of the user, and the MESSAGE-INTEGRITY attribute, which is keyed using an MD5 hash of the concatenation of the username, realm, and password. This is similar to (but not identical to) the challenge/response authentication of SIP Digest and HTTP Digest.

See Section 11.5.9 for some of the new extensions being developed for TURN in the TRAM Working Group.

TURN packets can be found in Wireshark by setting Display Filter to stun and looking for methods such as Allocate, Refresh, etc shown in Table 10.6. A TURN Allocate request is shown in Figure 10.11 and an

`Allocate` response is shown in Figure 10.12. In addition, media may be running over TURN. Look for STUN packets sent regularly labeled as `ChannelData` messages, as in Figure 10.10, as shown in Figure 10.12. Note that the TURN `ChannelData` payload in Figure 10.13 is a complete RTP packet (begins with 90 hexadecimal). TURN is not used by default in the WebRTC book demo, but can be turned on using 'turnuri=1' URL attribute. Note that TURN is currently only supported in Chrome, but turning it on for Firefox seems to cause failures. For example, the URL `"http://demo.webrtcbook.com:5001/start.html?turnuri=1"` would add a TURN relayed candidate. To force the use of a TURN server for the media, if both browsers are on different networks and behind NATs (so that host candidates will not work), the following URL could be used: `"http://demo.webrtcbook.com:5001/start.html?turnuri=1&stunur i=0"` which will result in only host and relayed candidates being used.

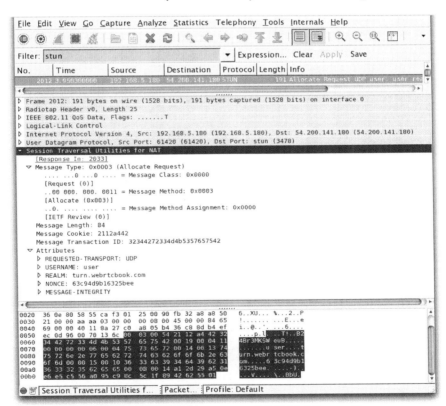

Figure 10.11 Wireshark Capture of TURN Allocate Request

215

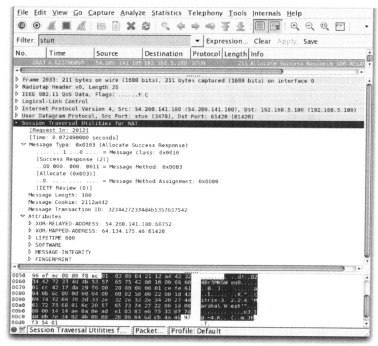

Figure 10.12 Wireshark Capture of TURN Allocate Response

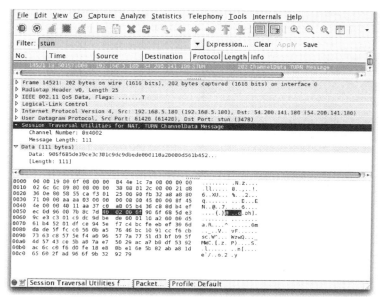

Figure 10.13 Wireshark Capture of TURN ChannelData Message

10.2.7 ICE (Interactive Connectivity Establishment)

Another key protocol used in WebRTC is Interactive Connectivity Establishment, or ICE [RFC5245]. ICE has two important functions:

1) ICE allows WebRTC clients to exchange media across devices that perform Network Address Translation or NAT.
2) ICE provides a verification of communication consent. This means that media packets will only be sent to a browser that is expecting the traffic. A malicious web application might try to trick a browser into sending media to an Internet host that is not a party to communication. This type of attack is known as a Denial of Service or DOS flooding attack. ICE will prevent this from succeeding since media will never be sent unless the ICE exchange completes successfully.

ICE uses a technique known as "hole punching" (see Section 9.2), which was pioneered by online gamers who needed to exchange packets directly between PCs playing multiplayer games despite the presence of NATs in-between. ICE is run at the start of a session prior to establishing the SRTP session between the browsers. It is also used for the non-media data channel establishment as well.

The operation of ICE is described in Chapter 9 in detail. This section will discuss the way ICE utilizes the STUN and TURN protocols. Note that the demultiplexing of STUN, SRTP, and DTLS when a single port is used is described in Section 5.1.2 of [RFC5764].

ICE utilizes the short term authentication mechanism of STUN. A username and password are randomly generated for each session and exchanged in the offer/answer exchange. Each side contributes half of the session username (carried in the a=ice-ufrag SDP attribute) and a password (carried in the a=ice-pwd SDP attribute). The session username is the concatenation of each of the username fragments, and the key used is the password sent by the other ICE Agent. The MESSAGE-INTEGRITY attribute contains a keyed message authentication code (keyed HMAC or keyed hash function) over the entire STUN message.

Gathered candidate addresses are categorized in two ways. All non-host candidates have a base. The base is the IP address and port that was used to generate the candidate. For a reflexive candidate, it is the host address from which the STUN check was sent. For a relayed candidate, the base is the IP address and port where the relayed traffic will be forwarded. Each candidate also has a foundation associated with it. A foundation is a unique string used to group candidates that are the same connection address (IPv4 or IPv6), base IP address, and transport protocol (usually UDP), and that were derived using the same STUN or TURN server. For example, candidates that include both IPv4 addresses, use UDP transport and utilize the same STUN and TURN server, would have the same foundation.

ICE provides a keep-alive functionality by sending packets at periodic intervals. There is an extension (see Section 11.3.10) to turn this into a continuing consent functionality by requiring a response and restarting ICE if the response does not come.

ICE peer-to-peer connectivity checks are sent over the same ports as the RTP media session. To help de-multiplex the protocols, ICE requires the use of the STUN FINGERPRINT attribute. The FINGERPRINT attribute contains a Cyclic Redundancy Code across the entire STUN message. ICE also requires the use of the PRIORITY STUN attribute. The PRIORITY attribute carries the chosen priority of the candidate, and is used by the other ICE Agent to determine the priority of any peer reflexive candidates generated from this connectivity check.

Table 10.7 shows the new STUN attributes defined for ICE. The USE-CANDIDATE attribute is used by the Controlling ICE Agent to select a candidate pair for use in a connectivity check. The Controlled ICE Agent includes the attribute in a response to confirm the chosen candidate pair. The ICE-CONTROLLED attribute is included in all connectivity checks by the Controlled ICE Agent. The ICE-CONTROLLING attribute is included in all connectivity checks by the Controlling ICE Agent. ICE includes mechanisms for choosing which ICE Agent is Controlling and which is Controlled. Should both Agents choose the same role, they will discover this using these attributes, send a 487 Role Conflict response, and choose again.

Attribute	Use
USE-CANDIDATE	Controlling ICE Agent indicates candidate is to be used
ICE-CONTROLLED	Attribute included by Controlled ICE Agent
ICE-CONTROLLING	Attribute included by Controlling ICE Agent

Table 10.7 STUN Attributes defined for ICE

To select a particular candidate pair to be used for media, the Controlling ICE Agent sends a connectivity check containing the USE-CANDIDATE attribute. The Controlled ICE Agent responds to the connectivity check echoing the USE-CANDIDATE attribute. If the Controlling ICE Agent wants to choose the best candidate pair to use, the Controlling ICE Agent would complete all connectivity checks, then select the highest priority successful pair. If the Controlling ICE Agent wants to use the first successful candidate pair, the Controlling ICE Agent would include the USE-CANDIDATE attribute in every connectivity check sent. The first successful connectivity check received by the Controlled ICE Agent will contain the USE-CANDIDATE attribute and the first successful response received by the Controlling ICE Agent will also contain the attribute.

ICE used in WebRTC will support the Trickle ICE extension discussed in 8.5.1.

ICE packets can be found in Wireshark by setting the Display Filter to stun and looking for the ICE attributes of Table 10.7, as shown in Figure 10.14. ICE packets will be multiplexed over the same ports as the media packets.

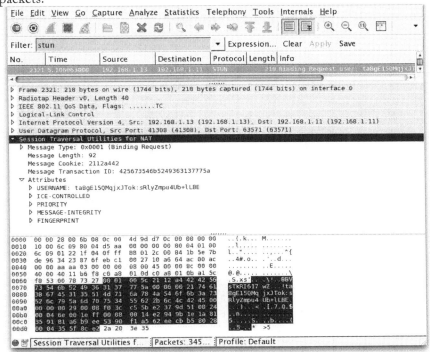

Figure 10.14 Wireshark Capture of ICE Message

10.2.8 TLS (Transport Layer Security)

Transport Layer Security, TLS [RFC5246], whose older versions were known as Secure Sockets Layer or SSL, is a shim layer between TCP and the application that provides confidentiality and authentication services. Confidentiality is provided by encrypting the "over the wire" packets. Authentication is provided using digital certificates. Secure web browsing today (HTTPS) utilizes only TLS transport. WebRTC can take advantage of TLS for signaling and user interface security. There is also a version of TLS that runs over UDP, called Datagram TLS (DTLS, see Section 10.2.10), and a version that can be used to generate keys for SRTP known as DTLS-SRTP [RFC5764].

Wireshark can show the TLS handshake by setting the Display Filter to tcp and looking for Protocol of TLSv1 or TLSv1.2, but cannot decode the actual TLS packets since they are encrypted with a key not known to Wireshark.

10.2.9 TCP (Transmission Control Protocol)

Transmission Control Protocol, TCP [RFC793], is a transport layer protocol in the Internet Protocol stack that providers reliable transport with congestion control and flow control. TCP is used to transport web (HTTP) traffic but is not suitable for carrying real-time communications traffic such as RTP, as retransmissions used to implement reliability introduce unacceptably long delays. Like UDP, TCP uses a concept of ports, a 16-bit integer number, to separate flows and protocols. TCP is provided by the operating system under the browser.

Wireshark can find TCP packets by setting the Display Filter to tcp, which will include HTTP, WebSocket, and often signaling traffic. Media, in general, will use UDP transport.

10.2.10 DTLS (Datagram TLS)

Datagram TLS [RFC6347] is a version of TLS that runs over UDP. The same confidentiality and authentication properties are provided. UDP is easier to get through NAT and can be better suited to peer-to-peer applications.

Wireshark can show the DTLS handshake by setting the Display Filter to udp and looking for a Protocol of DTLSv1.0. Actual DTLS packets, such as data channel messages just appear to Wireshark as encrypted UDP packets.

10.2.11 UDP (User Datagram Protocol)

User Datagram Protocol, UDP [RFC768], is a transport layer protocol in the Internet Protocol stack that provides an unreliable datagram service for upper layers. UDP is commonly used to transport small, short packet exchanges (for example DNS, Domain Name Service packets) or to transport real-time media such as RTP. UDP provides for very fast and efficient exchange of information; however, users of UDP must deal with possible packet loss. In addition, UDP has no congestion control, so users must be sensitive to packet loss and congestion to avoid overloading Internet connections. Like TCP, UDP uses a concept of ports, a 16-bit integer number, to separate flows and protocols.

Most Internet applications use a reliable transport, such as TCP, Transmission Control Protocol, in which lost packets are automatically retransmitted. Web browsing, email, and streaming audio and video use reliable transport. Received packets are acknowledged, and the lack of an acknowledgement after a certain amount of time triggers a retransmission of the packets until an acknowledgement is received. Real-time communication cannot take advantage of this type of reliable transport due to the time delay involved in detecting packet loss and receiving retransmitted packets. Lost packets in a web page load could result in a page taking an extra second or two to fully load. A real-time communication session cannot pause for a second or two in the middle of a voice conversation, or freeze playing back video for a second while awaiting the retransmission of the missing information. Instead, real-time communications systems just have to do the best they can when information is lost. Techniques to cover up loss or minimize the effects are known as packet loss concealment or PLC.

The average packet loss in general over the Internet is extremely low, on the order of fractions of a percent. Although occurring infrequently, packet loss occurs in a burst, resulting in high packet loss over short intervals. The ability to handle these short-duration loss events has a major impact on the perceived quality of a communication system. Advanced codecs, especially the Opus audio codec (see Section 11.3.9), are designed to provide a good user experience, even during high packet loss. In addition, real-time feedback from the receiver of media also provides the ability to reduce bandwidth or resolution during packet congestion, providing a better user experience and sharing bandwidth fairly with other Internet users.

UDP is provided by the operating system under the browser.

Wireshark can find UDP packets by setting the Display Filter to udp which will find media packets (RTP), control packets (RTCP), data channel packets (encrypted DTLS), and other assorted traffic including DNS queries.

10.2.12 SCTP (Stream Control Transport Protocol)

The data channel is built using the Stream Control Transport Protocol (SCTP) [RFC4960]. SCTP was originally designed for transporting PSTN telephony protocol Signaling System #7 (SS7) messages over IP networks. It provides useful features not available in TCP including:

- Reliable or semi-reliable delivery
- Non-ordered delivery of packets
- Multiple streams within an SCTP association
- Ability to send messages

The reliable or semi-reliable delivery option is one that is extremely useful for web developers. For some applications, reliability is the most important property, such as when performing a file transfer. For others, semi-reliability is good enough, such as cases where the information conveyed is only useful for a limited duration of time. In semi-reliable mode, SCTP will attempt to retransmit but give up after a set number of retransmissions or a set amount of time. For example, both real-time position information, such as a tracking application, and speaker identification such as in a conference would be a good candidates for semi-reliable transport.

Non-ordered delivery avoids a well known TCP problem known as "head of line blocking." In TCP, the stream data is always delivered to the user application in sequence, i.e. in byte stream order. If a segment is lost, data handoff by the TCP stack to the user halts until the missing segment has been received, even if other segments are being received in the meantime. SCTP in a similar situation will continue to handoff data to the user while retransmissions are occurring. Not every application can make use of this non-ordered delivery, but some can, and SCTP provides this feature.

SCTP has the concept of streams within a single SCTP association. These streams are treated independently and can even have different reliability properties. There is no head of line blocking between streams. Streams are identified by a stream number and provide a level of multiplexing without having to open multiple SCTP connections.

SCTP is message oriented, as compared to TCP which is stream oriented. This means that applications using SCTP do not have to manage their own framing when individual messages are sent and received.

SCTP also has some properties that are not utilized in WebRTC, such as multi-homing, where an SCTP association can be established between more than two IP addresses, allowing for fallback and redundancy. Since a data channel is part of a WebRTC Peer Connection, it is always a point-to-point connection between two browsers or a browser and another device.

SCTP has built-in congestion control, just as TCP does. Congestion control is important in protocols so that different users of the Internet share limited bandwidth fairly and react to congestion in ways that reduce congestion and not add to it. Standards work is underway in the IETF in the RMCAT Working Group to add congestion avoidance and control to RTP which will be designed in such a way as to work well with TCP and SCTP congestion control.

10.2.12.1 Transporting SCTP over DTLS

SCTP is a transport protocol, just like TCP or UDP, and theoretically can run directly on top of IP. For a number of reasons, this is not how SCTP is used in WebRTC. The wide use of Network Address Translators or NATs (explained in detail in Chapter 9) makes use of transport protocols other than TCP or UDP difficult, as every NAT in the path must understand that transport protocol. The limited deployment of SCTP and other new transport protocols, such as Datagram Congestion Control Protocol (DCCP) means that almost no NATs support them today. Also, transport protocols that run on top of IP are generally run and managed by a computer's operating system (OS). An OS implementation of SCTP would not provide the flexibility of configuration and usage of SCTP that WebRTC needs. As a result, SCTP is implemented in the browser, in so-called "user-land."

In WebRTC, SCTP is run on top of the Datagram Transport Layer Protocol (DTLS). DTLS provides privacy, integrity protection, and authentication for SCTP. The transport of SCTP over DTLS is described in [draft-ietf-tsvwg-sctp-dtls-encaps]. A DTLS connection is first established and authenticated, then the SCTP association is established. The details of how the Maximum Transmission Unit discovery by DTLS and SCTP is performed is described in [draft-ietf-tsvwg-sctp-dtls-encaps].

Wireshark cannot decode the SCTP used in data channel packets since they are transported over the encrypted DTLS session. To find data channel SCTP packets, find the RTP packets (see Section 10.2.3), then look for packets with invalid RTP version 0.

10.2.13 IP (Internet Protocol)

Internet Protocol, IP, is the network layer protocol that underlies the Internet. IP version 4, IPv4 [RFC791], the current version, is running out of unique address identifiers, known as IP addresses. IP version 6, IPv6 [RFC2460], was defined to greatly extend the address space to allow the Internet to continue its phenomenal growth into the 21st century. Unfortunately, support and deployment of IPv6 continues to proceed slowly, although many Internet backbones and services and web sites currently support it. Not all Internet Service Providers (ISPs) support it today, unfortunately. Negotiating media and data transport over the different versions of IP can be done using ICE. It is perfectly possible for a dual-stack WebRTC browser to run HTTP over IPv4 and the media over IPv6, or vice versa.

Wireshark can decode IPv4 or IPv6 packets by setting the Display Filter to ip.

10.3 References

[WIRESHARK]   http://wireshark.org

[RFC2616]   http://tools.ietf.org/html/rfc2616

[RFC6455]   http://tools.ietf.org/html/rfc6455

[RFC3550]   http://tools.ietf.org/html/rfc3550

[RFC3711]   http://tools.ietf.org/html/rfc3711

[RFC4566]   http://tools.ietf.org/html/rfc4566

[RFC5389]   http://tools.ietf.org/html/rfc5389

[RFC5766]   http://tools.ietf.org/html/rfc5766

[RFC5245]   http://tools.ietf.org/html/rfc5245

[RFC5246]   http://tools.ietf.org/html/rfc5246

[RFC5764]   http://tools.ietf.org/html/rfc5764

[RFC793]   http://tools.ietf.org/html/rfc793

[RFC6347]   http://tools.ietf.org/html/rfc6347

[RFC768]   http://tools.ietf.org/html/rfc768

[RFC4960]   http://tools.ietf.org/html/rfc4960

[RMCAT-WG]   http://tools.ietf.org/wg/rmcat

[draft-ietf-tsvwg-sctp-dtls-encaps] http://tools.ietf.org/html/draft-ietf-tsvwg-sctp-dtls-encaps

[RFC791]   http://tools.ietf.org/html/rfc791

[RFC5764]   http://tools.ietf.org/html/rfc5764

[RFC2460]   http://tools.ietf.org/html/rfc2460

11 IETF DOCUMENTS

There are a number of standards documents that define the protocols used in WebRTC. Some are Internet-Drafts – working documents in the IETF that will continue to be refined and developed before final publication. Others have already been published as RFCs (Request for Comments), the standards documents of the IETF. The draft documents are grouped according to the working group currently discussing and editing each document. Other RFCs that are related to WebRTC such as RTP and SDP are covered in the next chapter.

11.1 Request For Comments

IETF Request For Comments or RFCs are referenced by their RFC number, and do not change with time. There are numerous sources for RFCs including the RFC Editor's Page [RFC-EDITOR]. The RFC links provided in this book are to a conveniently hyperlinked version stored at the IETF website.

Currently, no IETF WebRTC documents have been published as RFCs.

11.2 Internet-Drafts

IETF Internet-Drafts are the work-in-progress documents in the IETF. They change frequently before being finalized as RFCs. Internet-Drafts can be working group documents or individual submissions. Individual documents are likely to undergo the largest changes and will very likely change document names before being published as an RFC. For more information on the IETF standards process, see Appendix B.

11.3 RTCWEB Working Group Internet-Drafts

The main documents of the IETF RTCWEB Working Group are listed in Table 11.1. The documents are discussed in the following sections.

Document	Title	Section
Overview	"Overview: Real Time Protocols for Browser-based Applications"	11.3.1
Use Cases and Requirements	"Web Real-Time Communication Use-cases and Requirements"	11.3.2
RTP Usage	"Web Real-Time Communication (WebRTC): Media Transport and Use of RTP"	11.3.3
Security Architecture	"RTCWEB Security Architecture"	11.3.4
Threat Model	"Security Considerations for RTC-Web"	11.3.5
Data Channel	"RTCWeb Data Channels"	11.3.6
Data Protocol	"WebRTC Data Channel Establishment Protocol"	11.3.7
JSEP	"JavaScript Session Establishment Protocol"	11.3.8
Audio	"WebRTC Audio Codec and Processing Requirements"	11.3.9
Consent Freshness	"STUN Usage for Consent Freshness"	11.3.10
Transports	"Transports for RTCWEB"	11.3.11

Table 11.1 IETF RTCWEB Working Group Documents

11.3.1 "Overview: Real Time Protocols for Brower-based Applications" [draft-ietf-rtcweb-overview]

The Overview working group Internet-Draft [draft-ietf-rtcweb-overview] provides an overview of the protocols and architecture used by WebRTC.

The high level goal is to build into a standard HTML5 browser the capabilities for real-time communication with audio, video, and data communications. Codecs for encoding and decoding media streams will be built-in, as will media processing such as echo cancellation (allowing for hands-free or speakerphone operation without a headset or push-to-talk button) and packet loss concealment. A key goal is the establishment of a multimedia session between two browsers with the media packets being sent directly between the browsers ("peer-to-peer"). This reduces load, processing, and bandwidth requirements on servers, and minimizes latency (delay) and packet loss on the media path. APIs (Application Programming Interfaces) will be used to expose the browser RTC functions to JavaScript web applications downloaded as part of a web page. This document provides an overall view of the architecture and approach to the WebRTC problem.

11.3.2 "Web Real-Time Communication Use-cases and Requirements" [draft-ietf-rtcweb-use-cases-and-requirements]

This working group Internet-Draft [draft-ietf-rtcweb-use-cases-and-requirements] details the requirements and use cases for WebRTC. The requirements include the ability to traverse NAT (Network Address Translation), work with IPv4 and IPv6 and dual stack browsers, utilize wideband and narrowband Internet connections and deal with congestion and packet loss. Use cases include audio and video with multiple sources and streams. Multiparty communication is also described. Applications include conventional telephony calling, meet-me video chat, gaming with peer-to-peer exchange of information, and distributed music making. Interworking with the PSTN (Public Switched Telephone Network) and existing VoIP (Voice over IP) and multimedia systems using SIP and other signaling protocols is also discussed.

This document will be published as an Informational RFC, which will document the thinking and logic behind the design of the actual protocol documents.

11.3.3 "Web Real-Time Communication (WebRTC): Media Transport and Use of RTP" [draft-ietf-rtcweb-rtp-usage]

This working group Internet-Draft [draft-ietf-rtcweb-rtp-usage] describes the usage of the Real-time Transport Protocol (RTP) in WebRTC. Browsers will have a full RTP stack built-in as part of the RTC function, as shown in Figure 1.2. The use of the RTP Control Protocol (RTCP) is also specified for the exchange of session information and sender and receiver reports on quality and congestion. Besides the core RTP specification described in Section 10.2.3, WebRTC implements a number of extensions and additions to RTP. Some of these extensions are common, while others are uncommon. This document does not define any new RTP extensions, but references other RFCs and Internet-Drafts that do. The most important difference between regular RTP and RTP as used by WebRTC relates to multiplexing. Normally, each RTP media stream uses a unique UDP port number, and the RTCP session associated with a given RTP stream uses another unique port number. So a multimedia session involving audio and video and associated RTCP sessions would normally require four separate UDP ports. In WebRTC, only one UDP port will be used: all media, voice and video, and the corresponding RTCP sessions will be multiplexed over the same port. This greatly reduces the effort needed to traverse Network Address Translation (NAT) boxes. The multiplexing of RTP and RTCP packets on a single port is described in Section 12.1.5.

For backwards compatibility with non-WebRTC endpoints (such as SIP or Jingle clients), browsers will be required to fall back to using multiple UDP ports, as part of normal media negotiation.

A number of conferencing and header extensions are also referenced in this document.

This document will be published as a standards track RFC as it documents the required usage of RTP and RTCP for WebRTC.

11.3.4 "RTCWEB Security Architecture" [draft-ietf-rtcweb-security-arch]

This working group Internet-Draft [draft-ietf-rtcweb-security-arch] describes the security architecture for WebRTC. The basic security model of web browsing is applied to real-time communications. In its simplest form, the human user must trust their web browser. The user relies on their web browser to protect them against potentially malicious sites they might visit. Before a site is given access to a microphone or camera, the browser must get permission from the user. Figure 11.1 shows an example of an actual WebRTC browser (Google Chrome Canary on Mac OS) requesting user consent when a WebRTC application (Meetecho collaboration [MEETECHO]) requests permission from the user to use the microphone and camera. The permission request is located under the URL bar.

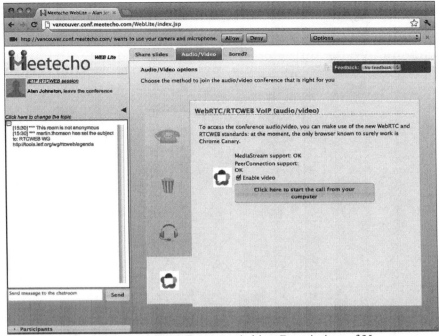

Figure 11.1 WebRTC Browser Asking Permission of User

In addition, the fact that a microphone or camera is being used by a web site must also be indicated to the user. This is shown in Figure 11.2 for the Meetecho WebRTC application.

The document also discusses the ways in which protocols such as TLS (Section 10.2.8), SRTP (Section 10.2.3), and DTLS-SRTP [RFC5764] can be used to provide security in WebRTC. For example, the use of security provided by HTTPS is discussed, as shown in Figure 11.3.

WebRTC security, and the use of an Identity Provider is discussed in detail in Chapter 13.

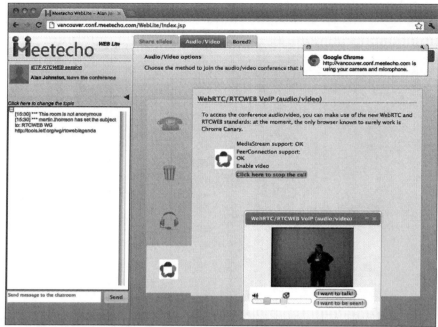

Figure 11.2 WebRTC Browser Providing Indication to User that Microphone and Camera are in Use

HTML/CSS/JavaScript

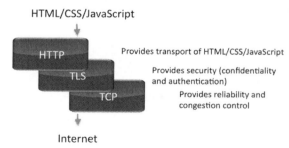

Provides transport of HTML/CSS/JavaScript

Provides security (confidentiality and authentication)

Provides reliability and congestion control

Internet

Figure 11.3 HTTPS Security Layers in WebRTC

11.3.5 "Security Considerations for RTC-Web" [draft-ietf-rtcweb-security]

This working group Internet-Draft [draft-ietf-rtcweb-security] describes the threat model for WebRTC in support of the RTCWEB Security Architecture document. This threat model will be used to evaluate the security mechanisms in the protocol specifications. WebRTC security is discussed in detail in Chapter 13.

11.3.6 "RTCWeb Data Channels" [draft-ietf-rtcweb-data-channel]

This working group Internet-Draft [draft-ietf-rtcweb-data-channel] discusses the requirements and protocols used for non-RTP, non-media data exchanged between browsers. The proposal is to use Stream Control Transport Protocol (SCTP) (see Section 10.2.12) over Datagram Transport Layer Security Protocol (DTLS) (see Section 10.2.10), over User Datagram Protocol (UDP) as shown in Figure 11.4. This somewhat complicated protocol stack is designed to provide NAT traversal, authentication, confidentiality, and reliable transport of multiple streams. While SCTP is a transport layer protocol, it cannot be used directly on top of IP (Internet Protocol) due to the presence of NAT. Instead, the whole stack is tunneled over UDP so that NAT will not drop packets. ICE is used while establishing the data channel to provide communication consent and hole punching to enable NAT and firewall traversal. Note that SCTP will be implemented in the browser itself (so called "user-land") as opposed to relying on an operating system (kernel) implementation.

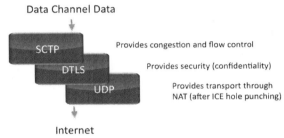

Figure 11.4 Protocol Layers of the WebRTC Data Channel

11.3.7 "WebRTC Data Channel Establishment Protocol" [draft-ietf-rtcweb-data-protocol]

The Data Channel Establishment Protocol (DCEP) is defined in [draft-ietf-rtcweb-data-protocol].

Each SCTP message contains a Protocol Payload Identifier (PPID) which allows multiple protocols to share an SCTP association. Two WebRTC PPIDs are defined, one for the sending of JavaScript strings and one for the sending of binary data. For a JavaScript string encoded in UTF-8 the PPID "WebRTC String" is used. For JavaScript binary data (ArrayBuffer or Blob) the PPID "WebRTC Binary" is used. An additional PPID is defined for signaling in the Data Channel Establishment Protocol (DCEP) used to open and close SCTP streams.

An SCTP connection is known as an association, and can be established as part of a WebRTC Peer Connection. The SDP signaling used to establish a data channel is described in [draft-ietf-mmusic-sctp-sdp] which uses the m=application media type. Streams within an SCTP association are unidirectional and are identified by a 16 bit number, the SCTP stream identifier. DCEP defines how to combine two *uni*directional SCTP streams into a single *bi*directional WebRTC data channel. DCEP messages use the SCTP PPID or "WebRTC Control" or "WebRTC DCEP."

DCEP defines two message types DATA_CHANNEL_OPEN and DATA_CHANNEL_ACK. To open a data channel, an SCTP stream ID is chosen. If the side opening the data channel was the DTLS server (i.e., performed a passive open) for the DTLS connection over which this SCTP association was established, then an odd numbered session ID is chosen. If this side was the DTLS client (i.e., performed an active open), then an even numbered session ID is chosen from among the unused stream IDs. This avoids any race condition conflicts (known as "glare") where both sides try to open a channel at the same time using the same session ID number.

A DATA_CHANNEL_OPEN message containing the fields shown in Figure 11.5. The Channel Type field indicates the desired reliability, which must be one of the options shown in Table 11.2 below. A Priority field indicates the relative priority of this channel with respect to other channels established over this SCTP association. A label field is used to set a label for this channel.

- **Message Type** – (8 bits) Type of attribute
- **Channel Type** – (8 bits) Type of reliability for the channel
- **Priority** – (16 bits) Relative priority of this channel
- **Reliability Parameter** – (32 bits) If the channel is partially reliable, controls the reliability
- **Label Length** - (16 bits) Length of the label field
- **Protocol Length** - (16 bits) Length of the protocol field
- **Label** – (variable) Name of the channel
- **Protocol**- (variable) Protocol of the channel

Figure 11.5 DATA_CHANNEL_OPEN Message

Channel Type	Use
DATA_CHANNEL_RELIABLE	Reliable
DATA_CHANNEL_RELIABLE_UNORDERED	Reliable Unordered
DATA_CHANNEL_PARTIAL_RELIABLE_REXMIT	Partial Reliable with Fixed Number of Retransmissions
DATA_CHANNEL_PARTIAL_RELIABLE_REXMIT_UNORDERED	Partial Reliable Unordered with Fixed Number of Retransmissions
DATA_CHANNEL_PARTIAL_RELIABLE_TIMED	Partial Reliable with Timed Retransmissions
DATA_CHANNEL_PARTIAL_RELIABLE_TIMED_UNORDERED	Partial Reliable Unordered with Timed Retransmissions

Table 11.2 Data Channel Reliability Options

The other side responds with a DATA_CHANNEL_ACK message, completing the channel open sequence, although the opener does not have to wait for the acknowledgement message before sending data using the channel. This message is shown in Figure 11.6.

Message Type	• **Message Type** – (8 bits) Type of attribute

Figure 11.6 DATA_CHANNEL_ACK Message

The complete sequence of steps to set up a data channel is shown in Figure 11.7 below. Note that if media sessions are being opened at the same time, the DTLS connection is used for DTLS-SRTP to generate the keys for the SRTP media session that is being established in parallel.

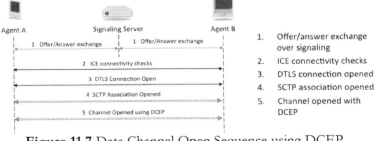

Figure 11.7 Data Channel Open Sequence using DCEP

11.3.8 "JavaScript Session Establishment Protocol" [draft-ietf-rtcweb-jsep]

The JavaScript Session Establishment Protocol (JSEP) [draft-ietf-rtcweb-jsep] is a new 'signaling protocol' developed for WebRTC. It is not really a signaling protocol in the way that SIP and Jingle are signaling protocols. Instead, JSEP describes how a JavaScript application running on a browser interacts with the built-in RTC function. It defines how the JavaScript can get information about the capabilities of the browser, including supported media types and codecs – the SDP `RTCSessionDescription` object. It also describes how JavaScript can manage the offer/answer negotiation of media between the browsers, and the ICE hole punching process running in the browser. It is very important to note that JSEP does not define any on-the-wire protocol – how the SDP objects are sent to and from the web server is not described. Any of the approaches described in Chapter 4 can be used.

Those experienced with signaling protocols may wonder where the 'state machine' is located. The state machine in WebRTC is kept in the browser, but it operates under complete control of the JavaScript code.

APIs are used to get candidate and capability information from the browser. The ICE state machine runs natively in the browser, and is decoupled from the JSEP state machine. The division of state between the browser and the server is shown in Figure 11.8.

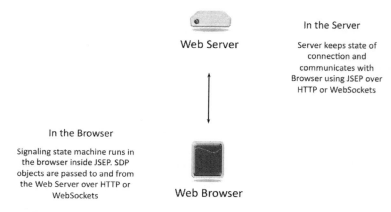

In the Server

Web Server

Server keeps state of connection and communicates with Browser using JSEP over HTTP or WebSockets

In the Browser

Signaling state machine runs in the browser inside JSEP. SDP objects are passed to and from the Web Server over HTTP or WebSockets

Web Browser

Figure 11.8 Division of State Between Browser and Server

JSEP currently uses SDP session descriptions, Section 10.2.4, as the syntax for offers and answers, although a JavaScript Object Notation (JSON) format could be defined in the future. Within the application JavaScript code, some form of an offer/answer state machine is needed. Some initial work was to use the existing SIP offer/answer model, defined in [RFC3264], but with a different encoding. (This was known as ROAP, RTCWEB Offer Answer Protocol, and was described in a number of individual Internet-Drafts.) However, this was viewed as too restrictive, and this current proposal tries to relax the offer/answer requirements as much as possible. In addition, this proposal tries to deal with the "refresh" or "rehydration" problem where a user manually reloads a web page during an RTC session, although this is still under discussion in the working group. This book does not cover the details of SDP offer/answer. To understand SDP offer/answer, see [SDP-OA].

The JSEP state machine is shown in Figure 11.9.

Consider the case where a browser is initiating a new Peer Connection. Starting from the Idle state, the browser generates and sends the offer to the other browser. This is the Local-Offer state. If an answer is received,

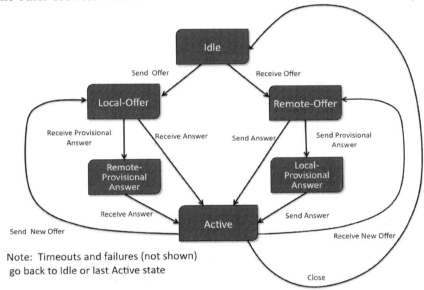

Figure 11.9 JSEP State Machine

the Peer Connection is established and the resulting state is Active. Alternatively, a provisional answer could be received. A provisional answer is identical to an answer except that resources associated with the offer should not be freed up. More than one provisional offer could be received, but the receipt of an answer establishes the Peer Connection, moving into the Active state. In the case where a browser receives an offer, the state machine is similar, except a browser should not normally send a provisional answer, but instead a full answer. Provisional answers are normally sent by gateways to other protocols such as SIP in order to handle special cases such as forking. Once in the Active state, a Peer Connection can be changed by either browser initiating a new offer, repeating the process.

11.3.9 "WebRTC Audio Codec and Media Processing Requirements" [draft-ietf-rtcweb-audio]

This Internet-Draft [draft-ietf-rtcweb-audio] discusses requirements for audio codecs and media processing. For example, the Opus codec [RFC6716] is the default audio codec between browsers, with PCM μ-law/A-law (G.711) [RFC3551] and telephone events [RFC4733] (for DTMF – dual tone multi frequency) for interoperation with the PSTN and SIP and Jingle clients. The recommended audio level is also discussed. Requirements for both near-end and far-end echo cancellation are also discussed.

The default video codec is currently under discussion with H.264 [draft-burman-rtcweb-h264-proposal], VP8 [draft-alvestrand-rtcweb-vp8], and others being considered by the working group.

Codec information is summarized in Table 11.3.

Codec	Use	Specification
Opus	Narrowband to wideband Internet audio codec for speech and music	RFC 6716
G.711	PCM audio encoding for PSTN interworking and backwards compatibility with VoIP systems	RFC 3551
Telephone Events	Transport of Dual Tone Multi Frequency (DTMF) tones	RFC 4733
H.264	Proposed video codec requiring licensing	RFC 6184
VP8	Proposed open source video codec	RFC 6386

Table 11.3 WebRTC Codec Summary

11.3.10 "STUN Usage for Consent Freshness" [draft-ietf-rtcweb-stun-consent-freshness]

This draft [draft-ietf-rtcweb-stun-consent-freshness] discusses some important potential changes to the way in which a browser determines whether a multimedia session is still alive, and whether the other party wishes to continue to receive the negotiated media. The document extensions to ICE to require that ICE keep-alive Binding responses be processed, and a failure to receive the response will result in an ICE restart.

236

11.3.11 "Transports for RTCWEB" [draft-ietf-rtcweb-transports]

This draft [draft-ietf-rtcweb-transports] discusses the transports used in WebRTC. Besides the usual UDP for RTP media and TCP for HTTP and WebSockets, it also discusses TCP for media and ICE TCP. If SRTP is sent over TCP, then [RFC4571] framing must be used. ICE TCP works reliably when other end is in the cloud or has a public IP address.

11.4 Individual Internet-Drafts

These documents have not yet been adopted as working group items but have had discussion and seem to have some level of support and interest in the IETF.

11.4.1 "IANA Registry for RTCWeb Media Constraints" [draft-burnett-rtcweb-constraints-registry]

This individual Internet-Draft [draft-burnett-rtcweb-constraints-registry] defines an Internet Assigned Numbers Authority (IANA) registry to track all media constraints and capabilities used in both the RTCPeerConnection and getUserMedia interfaces.

11.4.2 "RTCWEB Considerations for NATs, Firewalls and HTTP proxies" [draft-hutton-rtcweb-nat-firewall-considerations]

This individual Internet-Draft [draft-hutton-rtcweb-nat-firewall-considerations] discussed NAT and firewall considerations for WebRTC.

11.4.3 "DSCP and other packet markings for RTCWeb QoS" [draft-dhesikan-tsvwg-rtcweb-qos]

This individual Internet-Draft [draft-dhesikan-tsvwg-rtcweb-qos] discusses DiffServe Code Point (DSCP) settings for Quality of Service (QoS) for WebRTC. It replaces the earlier draft in the RTCWEB Working Group called draft-ietf-rtcweb-qos which is no longer progressing.

11.4.4 "A Google Congestion Control for Real-Time Communication on the World Wide Web" [draft-alvestrand-rmcat-congestion]

This individual Internet-Draft [draft-alvestrand-rmcat-congestion] describes Google's current implementation of congestion control used in their WebRTC open source project as submitted to the RTP Media Congestion Avoidance Techniques Working Group.

Congestion control is about the behavior of protocols and applications when packet loss occurs on the Internet. TCP has very advanced congestion control algorithms that have been developed over many decades of Internet experience. In very simple terms, TCP slowly ramps up its throughput. When packet loss occurs, TCP reduces its throughput and backs off, and slowly ramps up again. This allows a number of different TCP flows to share available bandwidth. UDP does not have any built-in congestion control, and WebRTC media flows utilize UDP transport.

This has not really been much of a problem so far in Internet-based communication for two reasons. First, these deployments have mainly been VoIP, where the audio bandwidth is quite small. Second most VoIP systems have used fixed-rate telephony codecs which cannot adapt even if they are aware of congestion.

WebRTC is likely to see a significant deployment of high definition video communications, which uses significant bandwidth and is also bursty (due to being a mixture of infrequent but large I-frames or key frames, with more frequent smaller P-frames and B-frames). In addition, WebRTC uses Internet codecs such as Opus that can operate over a wide range of bandwidths and can adapt without signaling. RTCP provides a feedback mechanism from the remote peer giving information about packet loss, delay, and delay variation in the connection.

There is significant work in the IETF to develop new congestion control algorithms suitable for RTP over UDP flows. These algorithms will use network statistics derived from the RTCP feedback to estimate conditions and detect congestion before packet loss occurs. This information will then be used to rate-limit the bandwidth used by the SRTP media flows and the data channel flows.

The approach described in this Internet-Draft uses RTCP feedback based on Temporary Maximum Media Stream Bit Rate Request (TMMBR, pronounced "timber", described in Section 9.1.11) . The approach uses signal processing to detect congestion before packet loss occurs. The approach uses the TCP Friendly Rate Control (TFRC) described in Section 12.1.10. Another draft [draft-alvestrand-rmcat-remb] describes RTCP messages for transporting the Receiver Estimated Max Bitrate (REMB).

The IETF will attempt to standardize a congestion control algorithm for RTP in the future suitable for use in WebRTC browsers. In July 2012, the Internet Architecture Board (IAB) held a workshop on "Congestion Control for Interactive Real-Time Communication". Information about the workshop including a link to the papers discussed is available on the IAB website [IAB-CCIRTC]. The RMCAT Working Group has been formed to work on congestion control for RTP media.

11.5 RTCWEB Documents in Other Working Groups

Some of the protocols being developed for use in WebRTC are being worked on in working groups other than RTCWEB, as discussed in Section

B.3. The Internet-Drafts are listed in this section.

11.5.1 "Trickle ICE: Incremental Provisioning of Candidates for the Interactive Connectivity Establishment (ICE) Protocol" [draft-ietf-mmusic-trickle-ice]

Trickle ICE [draft-ietf-mmusic-trickle-ice] is an optimization for ICE designed to shorten the time taken for ICE to complete. Trickle ICE is shown in Figure 11.10.

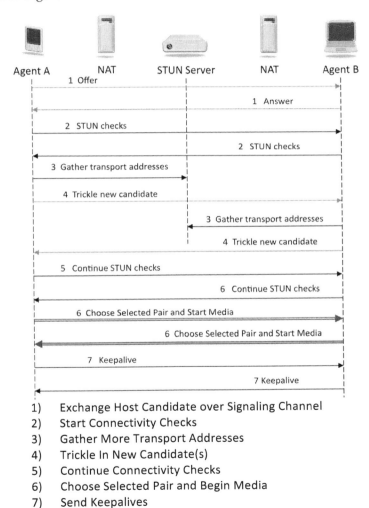

1) Exchange Host Candidate over Signaling Channel
2) Start Connectivity Checks
3) Gather More Transport Addresses
4) Trickle In New Candidate(s)
5) Continue Connectivity Checks
6) Choose Selected Pair and Begin Media
7) Send Keepalives

Figure 11.10 Trickle ICE

Instead of waiting until all candidates are gathered before beginning ICE, as shown in Figure 9.1, Trickle ICE begins ICE processing as soon as at least one candidate is available. A host candidate can be gathered the fastest, since it doesn't involve sending any STUN or TURN messages. The host candidates can be exchanged in the offer/answer exchange and ICE processing begun right away. In parallel, other candidates, such as server reflexive addresses from a STUN server, can be added later, or "trickled" in. If it appears that neither the host nor reflexive candidate pairs will work, a relay candidate can be obtained and also trickled in. This has an additional advantage of not reserving relay candidates, except when it is likely that they will be needed.

11.5.2 "Multiplexing Negotiation Using Session Description Protocol (SDP) Port Numbers" [draft-ietf-mmusic-sdp-bundle-negotiation]

This MMUSIC Working Group Internet-Draft [draft-ietf-mmusic-sdp-bundle-negotiation], discussed in the MMUSIC Working Group, defines a new SDP grouping framework extension called BUNDLE (a=group:BUNDLE). SDP grouping is defined in [RFC5888]. This grouping allows the grouped m= media lines to share the same port number. WebRTC will use this to signal the multiplexing of multiple media types on the same ports. This draft is still under development.

To use BUNDLE, an SDP offer or answer will contain a media grouping ID (a=mid) for each media line. There will also be a session level grouping attribute (a=group:BUNDLE) which lists the media grouping ID for each of the media lines which are bundled. Bundled media lines will use the same transport address for all RTP and RTCP and data defined by those media lines. BUNDLE can be included in any SDP offer and in an SDP answer where BUNDLE was included in the offer.

11.5.3 "Cross Stream Identification in the Session Description Protocol" [draft-ietf-mmusic-msid]

This MMUSIC Working Group Internet-Draft document [draft-ietf-mmusic-msid] defines the a=msid attribute extension which is used to convey the JavaScript MediaStream identifier string in SDP offers and answers. The draft also defines the a=msid-semantic attribute extension. A semantic token for WebRTC WMS for WebRTC Media Stream is defined. This extension is used to associate a MediaStream to an SSRC. As discussed in the WebRTC (Peer Connection) draft, a MediaStream is made up of multiple MediaStreamTracks. An example of this is shown in the example SDP of Section 12.2.1. More work is needed to finalize this extension. Note that the -00 version of this draft recommended msid information be carried inside an a=ssrc attribute. The Chrome browser version 32 appears to implement this version.

11.5.4 "Multiple Media Types in an RTP Session" [draft-ietf-avtcore-multi-media-rtp-session]

This Internet-Draft [draft-ietf-avtcore-multi-media-rtp-session] explains how RTP can be multiplexed, the issues discussed in RFC 3550 against multiplexing, and how the multiplexing can be accomplished. It is being discussed in the AVTCORE Working Group.

11.5.5 "Multimedia Congestion Control: Circuit Breakers for Unicast RTP Sessions" [draft-ietf-avtcore-rtp-circuit-breakers]

This Internet-Draft [draft-ietf-avtcore-rtp-circuit-breakers] discusses the congestion conditions under which RTP senders should stop sending to avoid making congestion worse. This protection is analogous to the use of circuit breakers to interrupt the flow of excessive current in an electrical circuit. WebRTC will also eventually have congestion control algorithms to reduce traffic before this condition is reached.

11.5.6 "Support for Multiple Clock Rates in an RTP Session" [draft-ietf-avtext-multiple-clock-rates]

This AVTEXT Working Group Internet-Draft [draft-ietf-avtext-multiple-clock-rates] provides guidance in the event that the clock rate changes for an SSRC in a media session. This could happen in WebRTC when switching between Opus and PCM codecs, for example, which use different clock rates.

11.5.7 "Stream Control Transmission Protocol (SCTP)-Based Media Transport in the Session Description Protocol (SDP)" [draft-ietf-mmusic-sctp-sdp]

Data channels can be established using an SDP offer/answer exchange, as defined in [draft-ietf-mmusic-sctp-sdp]. A data channel is established using an `m=application` SDP media line, along with a mandatory `a=sctpmap` attribute. For example:

```
m=application 54111 DTLS/SCTP 50002
a=sctpmap:50002 webrtc-datachannel 1
a=setup:actpass
a=connection:new
```

The application media line contains a UDP port number (`54111`) and the transport. Note that for SCTP running on top of DTLS on top of UDP, which we normally write as SCTP/DTLS, the protocol token in this case is

241

actually DTLS/SCTP which seems backwards. Next is a format (<fmt> in SDP syntax) which contains the SCTP port number, in this case, 50002. Next is the a=sctpmap attribute which identifies the protocol using DTLS/SCTP transport for this SCTP port number, in this case webrtc-datachannel. An optional maximum number of streams is present next, with a value of 1. If not present, the maximum number of streams is 16. Since DTLS is a connection-oriented protocol, the active/passive roles need to be negotiated, along with the new/existing status of the connection. The a=setup:actpass attribute indicates that this side is willing to either be active (DTLS client) or passive (DTLS server), leaving the choice up to the other side. The a=connection:new attribute indicates that a new DTLS connection is to be established.

This draft also defines SDP for DTLS/SCTP (again, the definition is seemingly backwards using the token SCTP/DTLS) and just SCTP, although these aren't used in WebRTC data channels.

Note that a single SCTP/DTLS association can be used for multiple protocols. For example, if both a WebRTC data channel and a Binary Floor Control Protocol (BFCP) session are to be used, the SDP changes to:

```
m=application 54111 DTLS/SCTP 50002 50006
a=sctpmap:50002 webrtc-datachannel 1
a=sctpmap:50006 bfcp 2
```

11.5.8 "Mechanisms for Media Source Selection in the Session Description Protocol (SDP)" [draft-lennox-mmusic-sdp-source-selection]

This individual Internet-Draft [draft-lennox-mmusic-sdp-source-selection] extends the Source Specific Media Attributes to allow selection of a media stream by source. The a=remote-ssrc SDP attribute is used to select a particular stream and set a particular attribute. This specification also defines a number of media attributes that can be set using this mechanism, including recv, framerate, imageattr, and priority. The recv attribute is used to enable (recv:on) or disable (recv:off) a source. If the recv attribute is not present, then recv:on is assumed. The framerate attribute is used to request a particular frame rate for a video stream. The imageattr attribute is used to set image resolution of a media source. The priority attribute is used to set the relative priory among the media sources. If bandwidth or other limitations prevent receiving all the requested sources, the priority is used to decide which sources should be omitted or scaled back.

This specification also defines two new parameters to be used for Source Specific Media attributes: information and sending. The information attribute is used to provide human readable text about a media source, in a similar way to the i= field in SDP. The sending attribute indicates the sending state of a particular source, either on or off. A source may be off due to it being disabled by the receiver, or the sender may just no longer wish to send the source.

In offer/answer SDP exchanges, all parties should list all available sources. Note that sources can be discovered via other mechanisms such as receipt of SSRC in RTP or through other conferencing notifications.

11.5.9 STUN and TURN Extensions in the TRAM Working Group

Extensions are being developed for STUN and TURN in the newly formed TRAM (TURN Revised and Modernized) Working Group [TRAM-WG] in the IETF. Despite the use of TURN in the name of this group, many of the extensions being developed are actually STUN extensions. A few individual Internet-Drafts under active discussion are listed in this section.

The TRAM Working Group plans to update both the STUN and TURN specifications. One important area is adding support to STUN and TURN for stronger cryptographic algorithms than the SHA1 hash currently supported. There are currently no Internet-Drafts defining this new crypto algorithms yet.

One extension is to define a DTLS transport for STUN and TURN in [draft-petithuguenin-tram-stun-dtls]. DTLS transport provides the benefits of TLS privacy and authentication but avoids the problems of having to transport the media over TCP. The use of TLS or DTLS also allows a browser to authenticate the TURN server by checking the certificate presented by the TURN server.

Another STUN extension proposed is to add an ORIGIN attribute to STUN and TURN requests in [draft-johnston-tram-stun-origin]. For browser implementations, the Origin would be the same as the HTTP Origin of the page that created the Peer Connection (HTTP or HTTPS, the domain name, and the port number). Origin information provides additional information for STUN and TURN servers in processing and authenticating requests, and also for logging/debugging purposes. For example, an enterprise STUN server could be configured to only respond to STUN binding requests sent from Origins associated with the enterprise. For a TURN server that supports multiple domains (e.g. a multi-tenanted server), the Origin provides a hint to the TURN server as to which REALM to include in an authentication challenge. This and other issues identified with TURN authentication are documented in [draft-reddy-behave-turn-auth]. Without this or some other approach, a TURN server would need to provide unique URIs for each domain (either a different IP address or port) to allow the proper REALM to be chosen.

Another TURN extension proposed is to add support for OAuth [RFC6749] authentication to TURN in [draft-reddy-tram-turn-third-party-

243

authz]. Two new attributes, THIRD-PARTY-AUTHORIZATION and ACCESS-TOKEN are proposed.

Two new ways to discover TURN servers are proposed in [draft-patil-tram-turn-serv-disc]. One approach uses Dynamic Host Configuration Protocol (DHCP) and Naming Authority Pointer Records (NAPTR) type Domain Name Service (DNS) records. The other approach proposes a standard anycast [RFC4786] address for TURN. Anycast routes a packet to a single host out of a group which is topologically nearest the sender.

Another draft proposes new extensions to STUN to enable communication about Quality of Service (QoS) between an application and the network in [draft-martinsen-tram-discuss]. The approach is called Differentiated prIorities and Status Code-points Using Stun Signalling (DISCUSS) and proposes a number of new attributes such as STREAM-TYPE, BANDWIDTH-USAGE, STREAM-PRIORITY, and NETWORK-STATUS.

Another draft proposes a BANDWIDTH attribute for TURN in [draft-thomson-tram-turn-bandwidth]. This allows a TURN client to indicate to a TURN server the maximum bandwidth it expects to send and receive through an allocated relayed address, and allows a TURN server to indicate to a client the maximum bandwidth allowed before rate limiting might be applied. This allows the fair sharing of TURN bandwidth between users, and also the TURN server to share policies with clients.

Note that currently all these Internet-Drafts are individual submissions. In the future, some will likely be adopted as TRAM Working Group documents, in which case the draft name will change. To find the latest versions of TRAM documents use this link [TRAM-WG].

11.6 References

[RFC-EDITOR]   http://www.rfc-editor.org

[draft-ietf-rtcweb-overview]   http://tools.ietf.org/html/draft-ietf-rtcweb-overview

[draft-ietf-rtcweb-use-cases-and-requirements]
    http://tools.ietf.org/html/draft-ietf-rtcweb-use-cases-and-requirements

[draft-ietf-rtcweb-rtp-usage]   http://tools.ietf.org/html/draft-ietf-rtcweb-rtp-usage

[draft-ietf-rtcweb-security-arch]   http://tools.ietf.org/html/draft-ietf-rtcweb-security-arch

[MEETECHO]   http://www.meetecho.com

[RFC5764]   http://tools.ietf.org/html/rfc5764

[draft-ietf-rtcweb-security]   http://tools.ietf.org/html/draft-ietf-rtcweb-security

[draft-ietf-rtcweb-data-channel]   http://tools.ietf.org/html/draft-ietf-rtcweb-data-channel

[draft-ietf-rtcweb-data-protocol]   http://tools.ietf.org/html/draft-ietf-rtcweb-data-protocol

[draft-ietf-mmusic-sctp-sdp]   http://tools.ietf.org/html/draft-ietf-mmusic-sctp-sdp

[draft-ietf-rtcweb-jsep]   http://tools.ietf.org/html/draft-ietf-rtcweb-jsep

[RFC3264]   http://tools.ietf.org/html/rfc3264

[SDP-OA]   Chapter 13 of SIP: Understanding the Session Initiation Protocol, 3rd Edition.

[draft-ietf-rtcweb-audio] http://tools.ietf.org/html/draft-ietf-rtcweb-audio

[RFC6716]   http://tools.ietf.org/html/rfc6716

[RFC3551]   http://tools.ietf.org/html/rfc3551

[RFC4733]   http://tools.ietf.org/html/rfc4733

[draft-burman-rtcweb-h264-proposal]   http://tools.ietf.org/html/draft-burman-rtcweb-h264-proposal

[draft-alvestrand-rtcweb-vp8] http://tools.ietf.org/html/draft-alvestrand-rtcweb-vp8

[draft-ietf-rtcweb-stun-consent-freshness]
     http://tools.ietf.org/html/draft-ietf-rtcweb-stun-consent-freshness

[draft-ietf-rtcweb-transports] http://tools.ietf.org/html/draft-ietf-rtcweb-transports

[RFC4571]   http://tools.ietf.org/html/rfc4571

[draft-burnett-rtcweb-constraints-registry]
     http://tools.ietf.org/html/draft-burnett-rtcweb-constraints-registry

[draft-hutton-rtcweb-nat-firewall-considerations]
     http://tools.ietf.org/html/draft-hutton-rtcweb-nat-firewall-considerations

[draft-dhesikan-tsvwg-rtcweb-qos]   http://tools.ietf.org/html/draft-dhesikan-tsvwg-rtcweb-qos

[draft-alvestrand-rmcat-congestion]   http://tools.ietf.org/html/draft-alvestrand-rmcat-congestion

[draft-alvestrand-rmcat-remb] http://tools.ietf.org/html/draft-alvestrand-rmcat-remb

[IAB-CCIRTC]   http://www.iab.org/activities/workshops/cc-workshop/

[draft-ietf-mmusic-trickle-ice] http://tools.ietf.org/html/draft-ietf-mmusic-trickle-ice

[draft-ietf-mmusic-sdp-bundle-negotiation]
     http://tools.ietf.org/html/draft-ietf-mmusic-sdp-bundle-negotiation

[RFC5888]   http://tools.ietf.org/html/rfc5888

[draft-ietf-mmusic-msid] http://tools.ietf.org/html/draft-ietf-mmusic-msid

[draft-ietf-avtcore-multi-media-rtp-session]
     http://tools.ietf.org/html/draft-ietf-avtcore-multi-media-rtp-session

[draft-ietf-avtcore-rtp-circuit-breakers]   http://tools.ietf.org/html/draft-ietf-avtcore-rtp-circuit-breakers

[draft-ietf-avtext-multiple-clock-rates]   http://tools.ietf.org/html/draft-ietf-avtext-multiple-clock-rates

[draft-ietf-mmusic-sctp-sdp]   http://tools.ietf.org/html/draft-ietf-mmusic-sctp-sdp

[draft-lennox-mmusic-sdp-source-selection]
http://tools.ietf.org/html/draft-lennox-mmusic-sdp-source-selection

[TRAM-WG] http://tools.ietf.org/wg/tram/

[draft-petithuguenin-tram-stun-dtls]   http://tools.ietf.org/html/draft-petithuguenin-tram-stun-dtls

[draft-johnston-tram-stun-origin]   http://tools.ietf.org/html/draft-johnston-tram-stun-origin

[draft-reddy-behave-turn-auth]   http://tools.ietf.org/html/draft-reddy-behave-turn-auth

[RFC6749]   http://tools.ietf.org/html/rfc6749

[draft-reddy-tram-turn-third-party-authz]
http://tools.ietf.org/html/draft-reddy-tram-turn-third-party-authz

[draft-patil-tram-turn-serv-disc]   http://tools.ietf.org/html/draft-patil-tram-turn-serv-disc

[RFC4786]   http://tools.ietf.org/html/rfc4786

[draft-martinsen-tram-discuss]   http://tools.ietf.org/html/draft-martinsen-tram-discuss

[draft-thomson-tram-turn-bandwidth]   http://tools.ietf.org/html/draft-thomson-tram-turn-bandwidth

12 IETF RELATED RFC DOCUMENTS

WebRTC uses a number of IETF standards and protocols documented in Request For Comments (RFCs). These RFCs were not specifically developed for or used by WebRTC. They are listed based on the protocol that they relate to.

12.1 Real-time Transport Protocol

12.1.1 "RTP: A Transport Protocol for Real-Time Applications" [RFC3550]

RFC 3550 [RFC3550] defines version 2 of the Real-time Transport Protocol, RTP, and the RTP Control Protocol, RTCP. RTP includes a bit-oriented header field which carries information such as the payload type (codec), timestamp, sequence number, and the synchronization source (SSRC). RTCP messages include Sender Reports (SR), Receiver Reports (RRs), and Source Description (SDES). (Note that the term SDES is an informal name for SDP Security Descriptions, defined in [RFC4568] – the two concepts are unrelated.) The SDES messages carry the Canonical Name (CNAME) which identifies the user in an RTP session. An RTP mixer can provide information about the senders whose media is included in the packet using the contributing source field (CSRC).

12.1.2 "RTP Profile for Audio and Video Conferences" [RFC3551]

RFC 3551 [RFC3551] defines the basic RTP Audio and Video Profile, known as AVP. Formats for a number of common audio and video codecs are defined, along with static payload types (values 0-95). Note that static payload types are no longer allocated – instead dynamic payload types (values 96-127) must be used. This document includes the definition of the

PCM G.711 audio codec, with both A-law and μ-law companding (a portmanteau of compressing and expanding, which results in level compression). This document will need to be updated for use by WebRTC as it recommends DVI4 as an audio codec in addition to G.711.

12.1.3 "The Secure Real-time Transport Protocol (SRTP)" [RFC3711]

RFC 3711 [RFC3711] defines the Secure Audio Video Profile for RTP, known as SAVP. This includes the use of Secure RTP (SRTP) and Secure RTCP (SRTCP). SRTP provides confidentiality and authentication to RTP, using symmetric keys to encrypt and decrypt the media and control messages. SRTP uses the Advanced Encryption Standard in Counter Mode, AES-CM. SRTP uses 128 bit keys, although it has been extended to allow 192 and 256 bit keys in [RFC6188]. SRTP requires a key management protocol to ensure the sender and receiver have the same symmetric key. WebRTC uses only DTLS-SRTP [RFC5764] for key management. SRTP generates an encrypted keystream, which is then Exclusive ORed with the media or control packets to encrypt them. This allows the keystream to be generated in parallel with the media or control packets, resulting in minimum added latency. The encryption is applied to the RTP body, leaving the RTP header in the clear, including RTP header extensions. Authentication is provided by an added authentication tag, which can be 0 to 10 octets in length. Each media stream needs to have a unique session key. If a browser sends two video and two audio streams in a session, there will be four unique session keys used to encrypt them.

12.1.4 "Extended Secure RTP Profile for RTCP-Based Feedback (RTP/SAVPF)" [RFC5124]

WebRTC uses the Extended Secure RTP Profile for RTCP-Based Feedback [RFC5124], known as SAVPF. In comparison, most Internet-based communication VoIP and video systems today either use the normal Audio Video Profile, AVP, or the Secure Audio Video Profile, SAVP. The SAVPF profile combines the security of SRTP from SAVP [RFC3711], and the timely feedback of the AVPF profile [RFC4585]. The basic AVP profile defined in [RFC3551] includes RTCP feedback messages and has a mechanism to ensure that excessive bandwidth is not used for these control messages, even for large conferences. One drawback of this is that feedback messages cannot always be sent by the receiver when they would be most useful to the sender. To improve the timeliness of this feedback, AVPF introduces the concept of early RTCP packets and an additional RTCP message known as a feedback message (FB) which can be useful for codecs. The a=rtcp-fb SDP attribute is used to signal which FB messages are to be used. Examples include ack (positive acknowledgements) and nack (negative acknowledgements). The AVPF profile can interoperate with AVP profiles. However, SAVP cannot interoperate with AVP profiles, due to the lack of support for best effort encryption.

12.1.5 "Multiplexing RTP Data and Control Packets on a Single Port" [RFC5761]

This document [RFC5761] describes how to multiplex RTP and RTCP on the same port. This is done for NAT traversal reasons, minimizing the number of times "hole punching" needs to be done. A method to negotiate this in SDP using the attribute a=rtcp-mux is described.

12.1.6 "A Real-time Transport Protocol (RTP) Header Extension for Mixer-to-Client Audio Level Indication" [RFC6465]

RFC 6465 [RFC6465] can be used by a mixer in WebRTC to indicate to a WebRTC user agent the audio levels in a mixed audio conference. An audio media mixer receives RTP streams and combines them into a single stream. The mixer usually implements a mixing policy such as the three loudest active speakers. The RTP packet can contain the CSRC (Contributing Source identifiers) for the participants that ultimately contributed to the mixed packet. This RTP header extension adds to this information by providing the audio level of each participant included in the mix. The level is encoded in 7 bits as dBov, which is the level, in decibels, relative to the overload point of the system (the maximum loudness). The presence of this RTP header extension is negotiated using the approach described in [RFC5285]. This information can be rendered against the conference participant roster, for example, for active speaker identification.

Support for this RTP header extension is indicated in the SDP by the presence of urn:ietf:params:rtp-hdrext:csrc-audio-level in the a=extmap attribute.

12.1.7 "A Real-time Transport Protocol (RTP) Header Extension for Client-to-Mixer Audio Level Indication" [RFC6464]

This specification [RFC6464] can be used to simplify the operation of a mixer in a WebRTC conference. This RTP extension provides a way for a participant in a conference to indicate the audio level of the packet sent to the mixer. This information is useful for a mixer to quickly select which streams to include in the mix, or a media selector to quickly choose which streams will be selected without having to decode the media packet. The level is encoded in 7 bits as dBov, which is the level, in decibels, relative to the overload point of the system (the maximum loudness). The presence of the RTP header extension is negotiated using the approach described in [RFC5285]. This information could be copied into a mixed packet using the approach of [RFC6465].

Support for this RTP header extension is indicated in the SDP by the presence of `urn:ietf:params:rtp-hdrext:ssrc-audio-level` in the `a=extmap` attribute.

12.1.8 "Rapid Synchronization of RTP Flows" [RFC6051]

At the start of an RTP session, there is a period of synchronization between the RTP senders and RTP receivers. For a simple two-party session, this occurs rapidly. However, for multiparty sessions, this can take longer. This document [RFC6051] discusses the issues in synchronization and redefines RTCP timing and new FB (FeedBack) messages to speed up this process. This could be useful in WebRTC sessions in which a centralized media selector is forwarding media packets from a large number of participants over a single Peer Connection.

12.1.9 "RTP Retransmission Payload Format" [RFC4588]

In cases where the latency requirements of a media stream are not strict, this technique for requesting retransmission of lost RTP packets can be used. The SAVPF profile is necessary, which allows for rapid RTCP FB (FeedBack) packets to be sent. Since WebRTC is about real-time communications, where low latency is necessary, it is far from obvious how this approach could be useful.

12.1.10 "Codec Control Messages in the RTP Audio-Visual Profile with Feedback RTP/AVPF" [RFC5104]

This document [RFC5104] describes how to send Codec Control Messages (CCM) using the AVPF profile. These codec control messages can be used for H.271 Video Back Channel, Full Intra Request (FIR), Temporary Maximum Media Stream Bit Rate (TMMBR), and Temporal-Spatial Trade-off. TMMBR can used for congestion control, as discussed in Section 11.4.4. The FIR is used by a video receiver to request that a video sender send an I-frame when video switching has taken place. The ccm parameter is defined for use in the `a=rtcp-fb` attribute. For example `a=rtcp-fb:98 ccm fir` would be used to indicate support of FIR CCM for payload 98.

12.1.11 "TCP Friendly Rate Control (TFRC): Protocol Specification" [RFC5348]

This document [RFC5348] describes a congestion control mechanism for real-time UDP traffic that shares bandwidth fairly with TCP flows. This mechanism relies on feedback from the receiver to the sender about the packet loss rate and round trip time (RTT). The sender then computes the

TCP throughput using the TCP Throughput Equation and adjusts its transmit rate to match this. WebRTC approaches incorporating congestion control will likely make use of this specification.

12.1.12 "A General Mechanism for RTP Header Extensions" [RFC5285]

The RTP specification [RFC3550] allows RTP header extensions, but does not specify how to signal or negotiate them or allow more than one extension per RTP packet. This document [RFC5285] partitions the RTP header extension, allowing for more than one, and describes how they can be signaled using the SDP a=extmap attribute. If RTP header extensions such as [RFC6464] and [RFC6465] are used, then this header extension mechanism will be required in WebRTC.

12.1.13 "Guidelines for the Use of Variable Bit Rate Audio with Secure RTP" [RFC6562]

This document [RFC6562] discusses issues with variable bit rate (VBR) encoding and encrypted media. Variations in the rate and size of variable bit rate audio packet streams can leak information about the information content, even when encrypted. The use of RTP padding to protect against this is discussed. PCM (G.711) is a constant bit rate (CBR) codec, while Opus can operate in VBR or CBR mode.

12.1.14 "Support for Reduced-Size Real-Time Transport Control Protocol (RTCP): Opportunities and Consequences" [RFC5506]

This document [RFC5506] discusses the conditions under which reduced-size RTCP packets (i.e. non-compound packets) can be sent. The use of the a=rtcp-rsize SDP attribute is used to indicate support for reduced-sized RTCP packets. This allows more RTCP packets to be exchanged using the same bandwidth percentage as full-sized RTCP packets. WebRTC uses RTCP feedback for a number of purposes.

12.1.15 "Encryption of Header Extensions in the Secure Real-Time Transport Protocol (SRTP)" [RFC6904]

Normal SRTP, described in Section 10.2.3, does not encrypt RTP header extensions, although header extensions are authenticated. This document [RFC6904] defines how to encrypt RTP header extensions. If RTP header extensions, such as those in Section 12.1.6 and Section 12.1.7, are used in WebRTC and need privacy, then this extension may be used by WebRTC. Encryption of the RTP header is specified using the a=extmap SDP extension.

12.1.16 "Guidelines for Choosing RTP Control Protocol (RTCP) Canonical Names (CNAMEs)" [RFC7022]

This specification [RFC7022] defines a new algorithm for generating random CNAMEs, canonical names which are sent over RTCP and used to identify RTP endpoints in a RTP session. This is important for media privacy in WebRTC where CNAMEs could be used to identify senders across sessions and across applications.

12.2 Session Description Protocol

12.2.1 "SDP: Session Description Protocol" [RFC4566]

This specification [RFC4566] defines version 0 of the Session Description Protocol, SDP. SDP session descriptions are used in WebRTC to represent a media stream offer or answer and are transported and manipulated using JSEP (Section 11.3.8). SDP provides a way to describe media sessions in terms of connection IP address and port, media types, codecs, and configuration information. However, a number of SDP extensions (not defined in this RFC) are needed in WebRTC. The SIP usage of SDP to negotiate sessions is known as the offer/answer protocol. The syntax of SDP and SDP extensions is defined using ABNF.

A minimal SDP session description is shown below, which includes an IPv6 address:

```
v=0
o=alice 2890844526 2890844526 IN IP4 client.digitalcodexllc.com
s=-
c=IN IP6 FF1E:AD32::72EF:8D21:B866
t=0 0
m=audio 49178 RTP/AVP 98
a=rtpmap:98 OPUS/48000
```

12.2.2 WebRTC SDP Examples From Browsers

Actual SDP offers and answers generated from Chrome and Firefox browsers will be examined in this section. The version numbers for the browsers are shown next to the SDP. For later versions of each browser, the SDP will likely be slightly different. See the WebRTC book website for updates.

Each section lists the SDP and then an explanation of the SDP.
These offers and answers were captured using the demo application in this book (http://demo.webrtcbook.com). The resulting SDP offer/answer exchange and candidate exchange over the signaling channel is listed below the video windows. The SDP is encoded in a JSON object starting with `{"type":"offer","sdp":"` and ending with `","type":"offer"}` or `","type":"answer"}` depending on whether it is an offer or answer. If

the SDP offer or answer contains no candidates, this means the browser is using Trickle ICE, (See Section 11.5.1) and the candidates will be sent over the signaling channel separately.

12.2.2.1 Session Between Chrome Windows and Firefox Mac

This session was established from Chrome 32 running on Windows to Firefox running on Macintosh. Chrome supports Trickle ICE but Firefox does not, so the Chrome offer does not show any candidates.

SDP offer generated by Chrome 32 Windows

```
v=0
o=- 3844610931104753979 2 IN IP4 127.0.0.1
s=-
t=0 0
a=msid-semantic: WMS bnybSNzYSljqzLw7pXPQaHCOoete5eYJXPkc
m=audio 1 RTP/SAVPF 109 0 8 101
c=IN IP4 0.0.0.0
a=rtcp:1 IN IP4 0.0.0.0
a=ice-ufrag:8NNHURsRlhAjOw/h
a=ice-pwd:6nZhTKpRwfJIXYbnLFz7qq3K
a=fingerprint:sha-256
DF:8C:B7:71:80:C7:66:09:48:D3:52:9E:96:19:8D:38:9A:9F:9C:DE
:E0:62:C0:85:22:98:AA:07:3A:76:BA:BD
a=setup:active
a=mid:audio
a=sendrecv
a=rtcp-mux
a=rtpmap:109 opus/48000/2
a=fmtp:109 minptime=10
a=rtpmap:0 PCMU/8000
a=rtpmap:8 PCMA/8000
a=rtpmap:101 telephone-event/8000
a=maxptime:60
a=ssrc:2842059344 cname:CtQf9S3X07RCWXSp
a=ssrc:2842059344 msid:bnybSNzYSljqzLw7pXPQaHCOoete5eYJXPkc
7b2095ed-0fb3-42ff-ac92-cd306e1ce6f0
a=ssrc:2842059344
mslabel:bnybSNzYSljqzLw7pXPQaHCOoete5eYJXPkc
a=ssrc:2842059344 label:7b2095ed-0fb3-42ff-ac92-
cd306e1ce6f0
m=video 1 RTP/SAVPF 120
c=IN IP4 0.0.0.0
a=rtcp:1 IN IP4 0.0.0.0
a=ice-ufrag:Adu8/KM8PcTGF0gm
a=ice-pwd:+TgOyZBGaTptyf3n2QI0R1H9
a=fingerprint:sha-256
DF:8C:B7:71:80:C7:66:09:48:D3:52:9E:96:19:8D:38:9A:9F:9C:DE
:E0:62:C0:85:22:98:AA:07:3A:76:BA:BD
```

```
a=setup:active
a=mid:video
a=sendrecv
a=rtcp-mux
a=rtpmap:120 VP8/90000
a=rtcp-fb:120 ccm fir
a=rtcp-fb:120 nack
a=ssrc:3018698479 cname:CtQf9S3X07RCWXSp
a=ssrc:3018698479 msid:bnybSNzYSljqzLw7pXPQaHCOoete5eYJXPkc
55832df1-abb9-4165-b1da-ff5ebabcbede
a=ssrc:3018698479
mslabel:bnybSNzYSljqzLw7pXPQaHCOoete5eYJXPkc
a=ssrc:3018698479 label:55832df1-abb9-4165-b1da-
ff5ebabcbede
m=application 1 DTLS/SCTP 5000
c=IN IP4 0.0.0.0
a=ice-ufrag:w+hx91AyIpbIxE0+
a=ice-pwd:VdyR8sgUk4+k0YC+nsD6NBPh
a=fingerprint:sha-256
DF:8C:B7:71:80:C7:66:09:48:D3:52:9E:96:19:8D:38:9A:9F:9C:DE
:E0:62:C0:85:22:98:AA:07:3A:76:BA:BD
a=setup:active
a=mid:data
a=sctpmap:5000 webrtc-datachannel 1024
```

The SDP begins with four required fields: version (v=), origin (o=), subject (s=), and time (t=). The version is set to 0, the only version of SDP in use. The origin contains a series of fields including user, a session id, version id, network type (IN for Internet) , address type (IP4 for IP version 4) and address, which strangely is the loopback address (127.0.0.1).

Next is an SDP attribute (a=) defining the media stream ID semantic used in this SDP object; in this case the semantic is WMS (Section 11.5.3), which stands for WebRTC Media Stream. Next, this SDP offer contains three media lines (m=) starting with the audio (m=audio), then video (m=video), and application (m=application) to establish a data channel. Next is a media level connection data field (c=), which is set to an invalid IP address (so-called "black hole" address of 0.0.0.0). This is because this and all other c= addresses in this session description are not really used, as only the IP addresses and ports in ICE candidates are used to set up the session.

The first media line for audio lists a port number (1, again not used, since the actual ports are in the a=candidate fields), the Extended Secure Audio/Video Profile (RTP/SAVPF) (Section 12.1.4), then a list of four possible codecs (payload types 109, 0, 8, and 101). These codecs, which are listed in order of preference, are: Opus, PCM mu-law, PCM A-law, and telephone-events (used for sending DTMF, see Section 8.3.1.3). The PCM codecs use a static payload (in the range 0-95) while Opus and telephone-events use a dynamic payload (in the range 96-127). Chrome includes an

RTP map attribute (a=rtpmap) for all four codecs, although this attribute is optional for static payloads. Opus uses a 48kHz sampling frequency, and is a stereo codec, as shown by the /2 in the a=rtpmap attribute. For Opus packets received, a minimum packetization time of 10ms is set (minptime=10) in a format payload attribute (a=fmtp). PCM uses standard 8kHz sampling frequency. For telephone-events, a maximum packetization time of 60ms is set (a=maxtime:60). An RTCP port and IP address attribute is included in an a=rtcp attribute, however it is set to an invalid IP address and port, so it is not clear what purpose this serves.

The ICE username fragment (a=ice-ufrag) and ICE password (a=ice-pwd) are included. Note that different usernames and passwords are included for each m= line. However, with bundling, only the first one is used. Next is the fingerprint (a=fingerprint), a SHA-256 hash of the self-signed certificate which will be used for the DTLS connection to be established. This field is encoded as hex digits separated by colons. Since DTLS is a client/server connection-oriented protocol, the determination of which side opens the connection must be negotiated. In this case, Chrome indicates that it is taking the active role (a=setup:active) and will open the connection. Next is the media ID attribute which labels this media line as "audio" (a=mid:audio). The send/receive attribute indicates that the audio session is bi-directional (a=sendrecv). The RTP multiplexing attribute indicates that RTCP will be multiplexed over the same port as the RTP (a=rtcp-mux). The final set of attributes for this audio line indicates that for this SSRC (a=ssrc), a particular RTCP CNAME will be used. The media stream ID, media stream label and label are set using more a=ssrc attributes. Note that Chrome appears to be following draft-ietf-mmusic-msid-00 which recommends putting this information in an a=ssrc attribute. The current version of the draft (see Section 11.5.3) recommends using an a=msid attribute instead.

For the media line for the video (m=video), only one codec is offered, VP8, using the dynamic payload 120. The same SAVPF profile is used. Also there is a media ID of "video" and indication of bi-directional media and RTCP multiplexing. For this video line, three RTCP feedback messages are declared (a=rtcp-fb, see Section 12.1.4):

1. ccm: Codec Control Messages (CCM), see Section 12.1.10
2. fir: Full Intra Request (FIR), see Section 12.1.10
3. nack (Negative ACKnowledgement), see Section 12.1.4

In the same way as for the audio media line, the SSRC, CNAME, media stream ID, media stream label, and label are declared for the video media line.

The last media line is for the data channel (m=application) which lists a dummy port (1), DTLS/SCTP transport and a format type (5000). As before, there are connection data, ICE username fragment and password, active setup, and a media ID (with value "data") selected. The last attribute sets the SCTP properties (a=sctpmap, see Section 11.5.7) for the format type of 5000 of the protocol (webrtc-datachannel) and the maximum number of channels (1024).

Next is the SDP answer generated by Firefox.

SDP answer generated by Firefox Mac

```
v=0
o=Mozilla-SIPUA-29.0a1 1653 0 IN IP4 0.0.0.0
s=SIP Call
t=0 0
a=ice-ufrag:c378ff48
a=ice-pwd:285af6088010426ea44b07a07a3458e1
a=fingerprint:sha-256
CA:6B:19:C3:50:48:FD:EE:98:9A:51:C1:DD:5D:35:E8:3C:15:CE:AE
:80:A0:08:C6:74:C7:B1:83:53:D6:59:43
m=audio 57463 RTP/SAVPF 109 0 8 101
c=IN IP4 109.144.215.158
a=rtpmap:109 opus/48000/2
a=ptime:20
a=rtpmap:0 PCMU/8000
a=rtpmap:8 PCMA/8000
a=rtpmap:101 telephone-event/8000
a=fmtp:101 0-15
a=sendrecv
a=setup:actpass
a=candidate:0 1 UDP 2130379007 192.168.1.8 57463 typ host
a=candidate:1 1 UDP 1694236671 109.144.215.158 57463 typ
srflx raddr 192.168.1.8 rport 57463
a=candidate:0 2 UDP 2130379006 192.168.1.8 49692 typ host
a=candidate:1 2 UDP 1694236670 109.144.215.158 49692 typ
srflx raddr 192.168.1.8 rport 49692
a=rtcp-mux
m=video 49912 RTP/SAVPF 120
c=IN IP4 109.144.215.158
a=rtpmap:120 VP8/90000
a=sendrecv
a=rtcp-fb:120 nack
a=rtcp-fb:120 nack pli
a=rtcp-fb:120 ccm fir
a=setup:actpass
a=candidate:0 1 UDP 2130379007 192.168.1.8 49912 typ host
a=candidate:1 1 UDP 1694236671 109.144.215.158 49912 typ
srflx raddr 192.168.1.8 rport 49912
a=candidate:0 2 UDP 2130379006 192.168.1.8 56941 typ host
a=candidate:1 2 UDP 1694236670 109.144.215.158 56941 typ
srflx raddr 192.168.1.8 rport 56941
```

```
a=rtcp-mux
m=application 59328 DTLS/SCTP 5000
c=IN IP4 109.144.215.158
a=sctpmap:5000 webrtc-datachannel 16
a=setup:actpass
a=candidate:0 1 UDP 2130379007 192.168.1.8 59328 typ host
a=candidate:1 1 UDP 1694236671 109.144.215.158 59328 typ
srflx raddr 192.168.1.8 rport 59328
```

The first four fields (version, origin, subject, and time) are required in SDP. The origin field uses a "black hole" IP address of 0.0.0.0. The subject is set to "SIP Call", probably because the original Mozilla RTC stack also included a SIP signaling stack. The next three attributes are session level attributes as they occur before the first media line; they set the ICE username fragment and password and the SHA-256 hash of the self-signed public key used for DTLS. These values are common to all the media lines in this session description.

There are three media lines, as the answer must contain the same number of m= lines as the offer. The first media line is audio, and contains a non-zero port number (57463) indicating that this media type has been accepted. The same SAVPF profile is used, and the same set of payload types is included. The payload types which can be used for the media session are given in the set included in the answer, which is a subset of the offered set. In this case, all four payloads can be used at any time during the session. Additional payload types not present in the offer can be included in the answer, but since they were not included in the offer, they cannot be used in this session without another offer/answer exchange. Also note that the dynamic payload types listed in the answer match the numbers in the answer (i.e., 109 for Opus and 101 for telephone events). The answer could use different dynamic payload types as long as they mapped to the same payloads (e.g., 108 for Opus and 103 for telephone events could be used) and be perfectly valid. The packetization time requested for receiving by this browser is 20ms (a=ptime:20). The connection data address (c=) field contains the server reflexive address, although this address isn't used; instead, the a=candidate candidates are used by ICE as described in Section 9.2. The audio session is bi-directional (a=sendrecv) and the directionality of the DTLS is set to either active or passive (a=setup:actpass). Since the offer was for active, this means this browser will be passive for this session. The next four attributes are the ICE candidates, the host and server reflexive candidates for RTP, and the host and server reflexive candidates for the RTCP. The preference is for RTCP to be multiplexed over the same ports as RTP due to the (a=rtcp-mux). Since both browsers support bundling and RTP/RTCP multiplexing, only the first set of candidates will be used.

The video media line has a non-zero port (49912) indicating that this media type has been accepted and the codec will be VP8 with payload 120. Again the connection data is set to the server reflexive address, and the video is send/receive. Four RTCP feedback messages are supported: `nack`, `pli` (picture loss indication), `ccm`, and `fir`. Again, the connection setting is active or passive, and four more ICE candidates are provided for RTP and RTCP. Again, these candidates will not be used since both browsers support bundling.

The final media line accepts the data channel with a non-zero port (59328). The SCTP map indicates that up to 16 channels of data channel are supported. Two additional unused ICE candidates are also included.

Note that although Firefox supports bundling, there is no indication in the SDP of this.

12.2.2.2 Session Between Chrome OS and Chrome Windows

This session was established from Chrome OS 32 running on a Chromebook to Chrome 32 running on Windows. Both browsers support Trickle ICE so there are no candidates in the SDP.

SDP offer generated by Chrome OS 32

This SDP offer generated by Chrome OS 32 is similar to one generated by Chrome Windows but there are a few differences. The session level attribute `a=group:BUNDLE` indicates that this browser supports the BUNDLE grouping framework. The BUNDLE group includes all three media lines, which are labeled audio, video, and data in `a=mid` attributes.

Note that all three media lines use the same (invalid) port of 1 and invalid (black hole) IP address of 0.0.0.0.

The client-to-mixer audio level indication RTP extension (see Section 12.1.7) is supported, as indicated by the presence of `urn:ietf:params:rtp-hdrext:ssrc-audio-level` in the `a=extmap` attribute.

The `a=ice-options:google-ice` attribute indicates that Chrome supports an earlier version of ICE. The absence of the attribute in an SDP offer indicates that standard (RFC 5245) ICE is used.

```
v=0
o=- 5476117230252359250 2 IN IP4 127.0.0.1
s=-
t=0 0
a=group:BUNDLE audio video data
a=msid-semantic: WMS yKbRQTdzN2DG8YAUsKNIJHOb0xC3ELyRIYoH
m=audio 1 RTP/SAVPF 111 103 104 0 8 106 105 13 126
c=IN IP4 0.0.0.0
```

```
a=rtcp:1 IN IP4 0.0.0.0
a=ice-ufrag:6faThXCg8GyVLdoE
a=ice-pwd:zyOJiitDHxS/jBmwi8zfoXWo
a=ice-options:google-ice
a=fingerprint:sha-256
DF:8C:B7:71:80:C7:66:09:48:D3:52:9E:96:19:8D:38:9A:9F:9C:DE
:E0:62:C0:85:22:98:AA:07:3A:76:BA:BD
a=setup:actpass
a=mid:audio
a=extmap:1 urn:ietf:params:rtp-hdrext:ssrc-audio-level
a=sendrecv
a=rtcp-mux
a=crypto:1 AES_CM_128_HMAC_SHA1_80
inline:xfx/v+memobaUvfbGkYAL9N6JEB6/Et2tpdNwc4P
a=rtpmap:111 opus/48000/2
a=fmtp:111 minptime=10
a=rtpmap:103 ISAC/16000
a=rtpmap:104 ISAC/32000
a=rtpmap:0 PCMU/8000
a=rtpmap:8 PCMA/8000
a=rtpmap:106 CN/32000
a=rtpmap:105 CN/16000
a=rtpmap:13 CN/8000
a=rtpmap:126 telephone-event/8000
a=maxptime:60
a=ssrc:2142953128 cname:NPMnExJy19ESBB9g
a=ssrc:2142953128 msid:yKbRQTdzN2DG8YAUsKNIJHOb0xC3ELyRIYoH
18e84811-abfb-47b2-b3d4-66c3295f5991
a=ssrc:2142953128
mslabel:yKbRQTdzN2DG8YAUsKNIJHOb0xC3ELyRIYoH
a=ssrc:2142953128 label:18e84811-abfb-47b2-b3d4-
66c3295f5991
m=video 1 RTP/SAVPF 100 116 117
c=IN IP4 0.0.0.0
a=rtcp:1 IN IP4 0.0.0.0
a=ice-ufrag:6faThXCg8GyVLdoE
a=ice-pwd:zyOJiitDHxS/jBmwi8zfoXWo
a=ice-options:google-ice
a=fingerprint:sha-256
DF:8C:B7:71:80:C7:66:09:48:D3:52:9E:96:19:8D:38:9A:9F:9C:DE
:E0:62:C0:85:22:98:AA:07:3A:76:BA:BD
a=setup:actpass
a=mid:video
a=extmap:2 urn:ietf:params:rtp-hdrext:toffset
a=extmap:3 http://www.webrtc.org/experiments/rtp-
hdrext/abs-send-time
a=sendrecv
a=rtcp-mux
a=crypto:1 AES_CM_128_HMAC_SHA1_80
inline:xfx/v+memobaUvfbGkYAL9N6JEB6/Et2tpdNwc4P
a=rtpmap:100 VP8/90000
a=rtcp-fb:100 ccm fir
```

```
a=rtcp-fb:100 nack
a=rtcp-fb:100 goog-remb
a=rtpmap:116 red/90000
a=rtpmap:117 ulpfec/90000
a=ssrc:3251765476 cname:NPMnExJy19ESBB9g
a=ssrc:3251765476 msid:yKbRQTdzN2DG8YAUsKNIJHOb0xC3ELyRIYoH
c81ec094-ff9f-4c0b-862f-408851892f1d
a=ssrc:3251765476
mslabel:yKbRQTdzN2DG8YAUsKNIJHOb0xC3ELyRIYoH
a=ssrc:3251765476 label:c81ec094-ff9f-4c0b-862f-
408851892f1d
m=application 1 DTLS/SCTP 5000
c=IN IP4 0.0.0.0
a=ice-ufrag:6faThXCg8GyVLdoE
a=ice-pwd:zyOJiitDHxS/jBmwi8zfoXWo
a=ice-options:google-ice
a=fingerprint:sha-256
DF:8C:B7:71:80:C7:66:09:48:D3:52:9E:96:19:8D:38:9A:9F:9C:DE
:E0:62:C0:85:22:98:AA:07:3A:76:BA:BD
a=setup:actpass
a=mid:data
a=sctpmap:5000 webrtc-datachannel 1024
","type":"offer"}
```

This offer has no ICE candidates in it. Instead, using Trickle ICE, a number of candidates were generated and exchanged over the signaling channel to the other browser.

Payload type 116 is red (RFC 2198 for audio) or redundant video while payload type 117 is ulpfec, Uneven Level Protection Forward Error Correction (RFC 5109).

SDP answer generated by Chrome 32 Windows

Here is the SDP answer from the Windows Chrome browser. Again, the SDP contains no ICE candidates. The ICE candidates are trickled in after the SDP is generated.

```
v=0
o=- 6377299728859741416 2 IN IP4 127.0.0.1
s=-
t=0 0
a=group:BUNDLE audio video data
a=msid-semantic: WMS B45cm6lwyRNVoE1zMlkijpbWUfL3rzNqscSq
m=audio 1 RTP/SAVPF 111 103 104 0 8 106 105 13 126
c=IN IP4 0.0.0.0
a=rtcp:1 IN IP4 0.0.0.0
a=ice-ufrag:wC9kk4acDp3y80J2
a=ice-pwd:IaFjOBjaCJB9+JG4Amr33Z15
a=fingerprint:sha-256
D4:31:EA:41:3E:B5:73:CB:DE:49:B5:E7:52:7F:0E:66:DE:D7:1D:41
```

```
:2B:DF:D8:94:39:42:76:E7:CE:BF:D8:45
a=setup:active
a=mid:audio
a=extmap:1 urn:ietf:params:rtp-hdrext:ssrc-audio-level
a=sendrecv
a=rtcp-mux
a=rtpmap:111 opus/48000/2
a=fmtp:111 minptime=10
a=rtpmap:103 ISAC/16000
a=rtpmap:104 ISAC/32000
a=rtpmap:0 PCMU/8000
a=rtpmap:8 PCMA/8000
a=rtpmap:106 CN/32000
a=rtpmap:105 CN/16000
a=rtpmap:13 CN/8000
a=rtpmap:126 telephone-event/8000
a=maxptime:60
a=ssrc:3453958609 cname:l45rMDOjvq7YHlyj
a=ssrc:3453958609 msid:B45cm6lwyRNVoE1zMlkijpbWUfL3rzNqscSq
905731da-ee01-4314-9577-05a4f1d31101
a=ssrc:3453958609
mslabel:B45cm6lwyRNVoE1zMlkijpbWUfL3rzNqscSq
a=ssrc:3453958609 label:905731da-ee01-4314-9577-
05a4f1d31101
m=video 1 RTP/SAVPF 100 116 117
c=IN IP4 0.0.0.0
a=rtcp:1 IN IP4 0.0.0.0
a=ice-ufrag:wC9kk4acDp3y80J2
a=ice-pwd:IaFjOBjaCJB9+JG4Amr33Z15
a=fingerprint:sha-256
D4:31:EA:41:3E:B5:73:CB:DE:49:B5:E7:52:7F:0E:66:DE:D7:1D:41
:2B:DF:D8:94:39:42:76:E7:CE:BF:D8:45
a=setup:active
a=mid:video
a=extmap:2 urn:ietf:params:rtp-hdrext:toffset
a=extmap:3 http://www.webrtc.org/experiments/rtp-
hdrext/abs-send-time
a=sendrecv
a=rtcp-mux
a=rtpmap:100 VP8/90000
a=rtcp-fb:100 ccm fir
a=rtcp-fb:100 nack
a=rtcp-fb:100 goog-remb
a=rtpmap:116 red/90000
a=rtpmap:117 ulpfec/90000
a=ssrc:379840342 cname:l45rMDOjvq7YHlyj
a=ssrc:379840342 msid:B45cm6lwyRNVoE1zMlkijpbWUfL3rzNqscSq
b69d0186-c4bc-4980-bdae-b4729e38eebe
a=ssrc:379840342
mslabel:B45cm6lwyRNVoE1zMlkijpbWUfL3rzNqscSq
a=ssrc:379840342 label:b69d0186-c4bc-4980-bdae-b4729e38eebe
m=application 1 DTLS/SCTP 5000
```

```
c=IN IP4 0.0.0.0
a=ice-ufrag:wC9kk4acDp3y80J2
a=ice-pwd:IaFjOBjaCJB9+JG4Amr33Z15
a=fingerprint:sha-256
D4:31:EA:41:3E:B5:73:CB:DE:49:B5:E7:52:7F:0E:66:DE:D7:1D:41
:2B:DF:D8:94:39:42:76:E7:CE:BF:D8:45
a=setup:active
a=mid:data
a=sctpmap:5000 webrtc-datachannel 1024
```

The audio media line contains many more payload types than just Opus, G.711 mu-law and A-law. Also included are ISAC at 16k and 32k sampling rates and Comfort noise (CN) at 16k and 32k sampling rates.

The video media line contains an ICE options attribute of `google-ice`. Also, two RTP header extensions are indicated: `toffset` (transmission time offset, defined in RFC 5450) and an experimental `abs-send-time` (absolute sender time, defined in [draft-alvestrand-rmcat-remb]). This video media line also contains a now deprecated `a=crypto` attribute which is used if SDP Security Descriptions is used to key SRTP instead of DTLS-SRTP as is now mandatory for WebRTC. RTCP Feedback messages supported include `ccm`, `fir`, `nack`, and `goog-remb`. RED and ULPFEC are supported as well.

12.2.3 "Session Description Protocol (SDP) Bandwidth Modifiers for RTP Control Protocol (RTCP) Bandwidth" [RFC3556]

This specification [RFC3556] defines new SDP bandwidth modifiers useful for specifying the bandwidth for RTCP. Normally, RTCP bandwidth is capped at 5% of total bandwidth. The `b=RS` and `b=RR` fields defined in this specification allow for direct specification of RTCP sender bandwidth and RTCP receiver bandwidth, respectively. Note that `b=CT` and `b=AS` are defined in [RFC4566] and represent the conference total and application specific bandwidth.

12.2.4 "Source-Specific Media Attributes in the Session Description Protocol (SDP)" [RFC5576]

This specification [RFC5576] allows for the properties of individual media sources in a stream to be specified in SDP. Note that the term "media stream" is slightly confusing. In some contexts, it means a media object defined in SDP by an m= line. In other contexts, it means a source of RTP packets. In WebRTC, a number of media sources may be associated with a single m= line – this could be multiple streams from the same user, or multiple users contributing streams. This specification defines a media source as an SSRC in RTP. This specification defines the `a=ssrc` attribute which allows the properties of an SSRC to be declared. Properties such as

CNAME (cname), previous SSRC (previous-ssrc), and format-specific parameters (fmtp) are defined.

12.2.5 "Negotiation of Generic Image Attributes in SDP" [RFC6236]

This specification [RFC6236] defines the a=imageattr SDP attribute used to negotiate image attributes. For example, consider:

```
a=imageattr:97 send [x=800,y=640,sar=1.1,q=0.6]
[x=480,y=320] recv [x=330,y=250]
```

This attribute sets for payload 97 the send and receive image sizes, in pixels. For sending, two possible image sizes are offered. The first has a storage aspect ration (sar) of 1.1 and a preference value of 0.6. The second one has the default sar (1.0 for square pixels) and a default preference of 0.5. In addition, the range of acceptable picture aspect ratio (par) values can also be set.

12.3 NAT Traversal RFCs

12.3.1 "Interactive Connectivity Establishment (ICE): A Protocol for Network Address Translator (NAT) Traversal for Offer/Answer Protocols" [RFC5245]

As described in Chapter 9, WebRTC uses Interactive Connectivity Establishment (ICE) [RFC5245] for NAT traversal and media authorization. ICE is a standardized protocol for "hole punching" – a technique developed in the gaming world to establish a peer-to-peer connection between two hosts behind NAT. Each host gathers potential address candidates: local addresses (read from its NIC, network interface card, interfaces), reflexive addresses (determined from a STUN server), and relay addresses (obtained from a TURN server or other media relay), as shown in Figure 9.1. These candidates are prioritized, encoded as a=candidate lines in SDP, then exchanged using a server located in the public Internet known as a rendezvous server. Both hosts then begin sending test packets, sometimes referred to as "hole punching packets", at roughly the same time. As they attempt to send test packets to the other host's candidate addresses, the packets create NAT mappings and filter rules. In many cases, after a few test packets, an end-to-end path through the NATs is obtained, and this connection is then used for the duration of the session. In some cases, due to strict NAT or firewalls, there is no peer-to-peer connection possible. In this case, the TURN media relay address will be used instead. Non-published statistics from service providers who have used ICE or other similar hole punching approaches report that a direct connection can be obtained up to 85% of the time. A TURN server address could be configured in a web browser in a similar way (and for a similar reason) as a web proxy can be configured in browsers today to enable firewall traversal, as described in Section 9.2.

Since a candidate address in ICE will only be used if an authenticated reply hole punching packet is received from the other host, this provides the media authorization needed. Only if the candidate address is expecting and actively trying to establish a session will the candidate succeed and be used for the session. This prevents the "voice hammer" attack where a candidate address of another host is provided in an attempt to have that host flooded with unwanted traffic.

Connection address candidates are carried in an SDP attribute a=candidate along with the type of address. For example:

```
a=candidate:2 1 UDP 1694498815 192.0.2.3 45664 typ srflx
raddr 10.0.1.1 rport 8998
```

This specification defines the values host, srflx, prflx, and relay for host, server reflexive, peer reflexive, and relayed candidates, respectively.

12.3.2 "Symmetric RTP / RTP Control Protocol (RTCP)" [RFC4961]

This document [RFC4916] defines symmetric RTP and RTCP, and provides guidance on when it should be used. RTP is symmetric if packets are sent from and received on the same UDP port in a bi-directional RTP session. This is important for traversal of NAT and traversal through TURN and other media relays, such as those provided by SBCs. All media in WebRTC is symmetric.

12.4 Codecs

12.4.1 "Definition of the Opus Audio Codec" [RFC6716]

Opus [RFC6716] is the Internet low latency codec for audio and music. Opus incorporates elements and technology from Skype's SILK [SILK] codec and the open source CELT (Constrained Energy Lapped Transform) [CELT] codec. Opus is extremely flexible, supporting bit rates from 6 – 510 kb/s, constant or variable bit rate, sampling rates from 8 – 48 kHz, support for speech and music, mono and stereo, frame sizes from 2.5ms to 60ms, and floating point or fixed-point implementation. Opus also has very good packet loss concealment (PLC) and good quality even during packet loss. The RTP payload for Opus is defined in [draft-ietf-payload-rtp-opus].

12.4.2 "VP8 Data Format and Decoding Guide" [RFC6386]

VP8 [RFC6386] is an open source video codec used in WebRTC. The RTP Payload for VP8 is defined in [draft-ietf-payload-vp8].

12.5 Signaling

12.5.1 "The WebSocket Protocol as a Transport for the Session Initiation Protocol (SIP)" [RFC7118]

This document [RFC7118] defines a WebSocket transport for SIP. WebSockets, described in Section 10.2.2, allows a Web browser to open a new connection to the web server. While this specification is not required for WebRTC, it is related in that it allows Session Initiation Protocol (SIP) to be used as the signaling protocol. The SIP User Agent (UA) stack would be written, for example, in JavaScript and downloaded by the web server. The SIP UA would then open a new WebSocket connection to the SIP Proxy Server. The media from the SIP signaling would use the normal WebRTC methods, e.g. a Peer Connection to establish media sessions. This specification defines a new Via transport token WS (WebSocket) and new SIP URI transport parameters ws (WebSocket) and wss (Secure WebSocket); the latter uses TLS transport.

Note that SIP signaling between Web Servers, as shown in the WebRTC Trapezoid of Figure 1.4, would most likely not use WebSocket transport, and instead would use normal SIP transport such as TCP or UDP.

12.6 References

[RFC3550]   http://tools.ietf.org/html/rfc3550

[RFC4568]   http://tools.ietf.org/html/rfc4568

[RFC3551]   http://tools.ietf.org/html/rfc3551

[RFC3711]   http://tools.ietf.org/html/rfc3711

[RFC6188]   http://tools.ietf.org/html/rfc6188

[RFC5764]   http://tools.ietf.org/html/rfc5764

[RFC5124]   http://tools.ietf.org/html/rfc5124

[RFC4585]   http://tools.ietf.org/html/rfc4585

[RFC5761]   http://tools.ietf.org/html/rfc5761

[RFC6465]   http://tools.ietf.org/html/rfc6465

[RFC5285]   http://tools.ietf.org/html/rfc5285

[RFC6464]   http://tools.ietf.org/html/rfc6464

[RFC6051]   http://tools.ietf.org/html/rfc6051

[RFC4588]   http://tools.ietf.org/html/rfc4588

[RFC5104]   http://tools.ietf.org/html/rfc5104

[RFC5348]   http://tools.ietf.org/html/rfc5348

[RFC5285]   http://tools.ietf.org/html/rfc5285

[RFC6562]   http://tools.ietf.org/html/rfc6562

[RFC5506]   http://tools.ietf.org/html/rfc5506

[RFC6904]   http://tools.ietf.org/html/rfc6904

[RFC7022]   http://tools.ietf.org/html/rfc7022

[RFC4566]   http://tools.ietf.org/html/rfc4566

[draft-alvestrand-rmcat-remb] http://tools.ietf.org/html/draft-alvestrand-rmcat-remb

[RFC3556]   http://tools.ietf.org/html/rfc3556

[RFC5576]   http://tools.ietf.org/html/rfc5576

[RFC6236]   http://tools.ietf.org/html/rfc6236

[RFC5245]   http://tools.ietf.org/html/rfc5245

[RFC4961]   http://tools.ietf.org/html/rfc4961

[RFC6716]   http://tools.ietf.org/html/rfc6716

[RFC6386]   http://tools.ietf.org/html/rfc6386

[SILK]   http://developer.skype.com/silk

[CELT]   http://www.celt-codec.org

[draft-ietf-payload-vp8]   http://tools.ietf.org/html/draft-ietf-payload-vp8

[RFC7118]   http://tools.ietf.org/html/rfc7118

13 SECURITY AND PRIVACY

WebRTC security has a number of aspects that will be introduced and discussed in this chapter. They include:

1) New attacks and compromises that can be launched against a browser by a malicious website.
2) Whether sessions established by WebRTC are secure, and what types of attacks can be launched against them.
3) Whether WebRTC compromises a user's privacy when browsing.
4) Whether allowing WebRTC sessions to cross an enterprise border is secure.

For a complete discussion of the security threats and concepts relating to WebRTC, see [draft-ietf-rtcweb-security] and [draft-ietf-rtcweb-security-arch].

This chapter assumes basic familiarity with security concepts such as privacy and authentication, and security approaches such as encryption, digital signatures, and certificates. Refer to [APPLIED-CRYPTO] for an in depth introduction to these topics.

13.1 Browser Security Model

Any discussion of WebRTC security must begin with the basic web browser security model. In this model, the user must trust their web browser. A malicious browser could redirect a user to web pages they do not wish to visit, log browsing history and data and share that with unauthorized third parties, or gain access to the computer microphone and webcam without telling the user. In short, no security measures provided by protocols or APIs are of any value if they are ignored or implemented incorrectly. Note that this applies to any software installed by users.

271

Web sites, however, are not necessarily trusted. A user must be able to browse malicious sites and not suffer any harm. While users avoid visiting sites they believe may potentially be malicious, it cannot always be prevented. For example, a user might follow a shortened URL link that results in that user accessing a malicious web site. Or, a link or a website can connect or redirect a user to a malicious site. While a user is visiting a website, that site has control over the screen and can display arbitrary images or text, and can also initiate video or audio streaming. Of course, the user can simply close the browser tab or window to end everything. If a website attempts to download a file, the browser will not allow it unless a user authorizes it by clicking a dialog box. Some operating systems will also warn a user before executing software that has been downloaded using the browser. All of these features are designed to help protect the user against malicious sites.

13.1.1 WebRTC Permissions

WebRTC provides some similar protections. In particular, a browser is required to verify user consent before providing access to the user's microphone or camera. For many browsers, this means that a WebRTC application wishing to access a user's microphone or camera will not be given access until the user has been prompted and authorization is given. This authorization dialog is handled by the browser itself, and is not under the control of the JavaScript. An example browser confirmation is shown in Figures 13.1 and 11.1. This permission is asked for each session – an application is not given the ability to access the microphone or camera at any time, but just when the user wants to participate in a real-time session. Also, this permission is granted on a per-domain basis. This is important since it is common for a given web window view to have content rendered from many different sites, including additional frames, ads, and tracking software. If multiple domains on a given page wish to have access to the media, then individual permission will need to be obtained for each. This prevents domains piggy-backing on another domain's permission grant.

Figure 13.1 Browser Prompting User for Permission

Interestingly, WebRTC JavaScript calls to establish only a data channel do not require user permission. The logic behind this is that by visiting a web site, a user has given the site permission to send arbitrary data to the browser, which is what the data channel allows. A permissions check is needed only to acquire user media, not to transmit it once it has been acquired.

Enforcing permission grants is only useful if a browser can securely determine which web site is requesting permission. This is discussed in the next section.

13.1.2 Web Site Identity

Early in the history of the World Wide Web, a need was recognized to be able to determine the identity of a web site, and to have encrypted, authenticated sessions with a web site. This led to the development of Secure Sockets Layer or SSL, which has evolved into the TLS protocol, Section 10.2.8. The use of secure web browsing, when Secure HTTP or HTTPS is used between the browser and a web site, is increasingly common today. In the past it was mainly used just during login and for sensitive financial transactions. Today, however, it is becoming the default, and browser plug-ins such as the Electronic Frontier Foundation's HTTPS Everywhere [HTTPS-EVERY] make it easy to ensure the highest level of privacy in web browsing.

The identity of a website providing a WebRTC service or application can be determined if secure browsing (Secure HTTP which utilizes TLS transport) is used rather than regular browsing (plain HTTP which just uses TCP transport). Through the TLS handshake performed when the connection is opened, the browser can learn the identity of the site. In this approach, the web site provides a digital certificate which has been issued by a Certificate Authority (CA), a trust anchor in the browser. Browsers come pre-configured with a set of trust anchor certificate authorities. These certificate authorities issue digital certificates to the holder of a specific domain name, upon proof of ownership and control of that domain name. For example, the owner of the example.com domain can purchase a digital certificate (X.509 certificate) from a certificate authority. A web server in the example.com domain is then able to use the certificate as part of the TLS handshake to prove that it is in the example.com domain. The browser can validate the certificate with the certificate authority to make sure it is authentic.

If the identity validates, the browser displays the padlock or other user interface hint to indicate that this is a secure and authenticated web session. If not, the browser displays a warning and recommends the user disconnect. These types of warnings are most often encountered during login WiFi redirects.

One major problem with this web site authentication model is that a browser will trust any certificate for that website that passes validation. There is no way to know that this is, in fact, the right certificate for the web site. DANE, DNS-Based Authentication of Named Entities [DANE], is a new security mechanism that uses DNSSEC, DNS Security [DNSSEC], to verify that a digital certificate received in a TLS connection is the correct certificate used by that site.

WebRTC benefits from these web security mechanisms when the JavaScript is provided over an HTTPS connection and the signaling channel is provided over HTTPS or Secure WebSockets (a WSS URI). For example, a long term permission for use of the camera or microphone can be stored if the WebRTC site uses HTTPS. For a non-HTTPS WebRTC site, only a short term, per use, permission grant is possible, possibly requiring the browser to prompt the user for each session in order to verify consent.

13.1.3 Browser User Identity

Unfortunately, the same techniques for web site authentication described in the previous section cannot be used for browser user identity. While it is possible for a browser to present a digital certificate during the TLS handshake, browsers in general do not have installed digital certificates. This is due to cost, ease of use, and the fact that a user has multiple identities, each of which would require a separate certificate. For example, an inexpensive certificate from a trusted certificate authority can cost between $60 and $100 per year – this would be a major expense for most service and application providers.

Instead, other approaches are typically used on the web such as prompting a user for a username/password combination, or the use of a "cookie" from a previously authenticated session. Sometimes a third party identification service is also used. WebRTC can reuse these authentication techniques, as will be discussed later in this chapter.

13.2 New WebRTC Browser Attacks

WebRTC does introduce many new potential attacks on browsers, due to the new APIs, protocols, and the signaling channel. The attacks on each will be described.

13.2.1 API Attacks

WebRTC introduces a number of new JavaScript APIs. Each of these is a potential new attack vector into a browser.

We have already discussed the user consent requirements in order for

JavaScript code to request access to the user's camera and microphone. The media capture APIs do not actually give access to the data flowing in a `MediaStreamTrack`, only a handle to the track that can be passed to other page elements. However, it is relatively simple to access the data flowing on the track. By creating a `<canvas>` containing the user's video, it is then possible to sample the canvas at regular intervals. This allows for some interesting JavaScript-coded effects to be applied to a user's video stream, but it does mean that user consent to access the camera implicitly provides access to the data from the camera as well.

It is also possible to take any stream, whether from camera, microphone, local file, or other source, and stream it over a Peer Connection to another endpoint which can do anything with it that it wants. The Recording API provides even more direct access, allowing for easy saving of streams.

One new capability, not yet widely implemented, is the `noaccess` flag that can be set on a track. When set, the browser is expected to ensure that no access is given to the data in the track, whether used in a video element in a canvas, or whether sent over a Peer Connection. It is expected that the new Identity APIs will allow for identity-restricted track access at some point in the future.

The Media Capture and Streams APIs around capabilities determination are still in flux, but it is likely that an application will be able to get device names in advance of user consent and details about any device for which the user gives consent.

Users must be cautious about the permissions they give. It is likely that, over time, browsers will have settings enabling users to give longer-term permissions for certain sites to access their cameras and microphones. Keep in mind that any permission lasting beyond the time a user is actively operating the device could result in an application using the device at an inopportune time for the user, such as at night or while in a private conversation near the device.

Aside from the general concerns described above, the APIs should not provide new major threats beyond those of any use of JavaScript in a web application. However, these APIs are new, and there is always the possibility of implementation bugs that could turn these APIs into potential attacks on browsers and WebRTC sessions.

13.2.2 Protocol Attacks

Figure 6.1 shows the new protocols present in WebRTC. Each of these protocols provides a new opportunity for attackers. For example, since WebRTC uses SDP, a malformed SDP object could be used to try to crash a browser. WebRTC uses RTP for media transport, and so any attack based on RTP could be utilized. In addition, during an established session, the browser will utilize a codec to decode received audio or video samples.

Malformed media samples could be used to try to compromise a browser.

The new architecture of WebRTC also makes some of these attacks even more severe. Before WebRTC, the browser only communicated with the web server. With WebRTC, browsers can establish peer-to-peer connections directly with other browsers, or other devices. This means that the browser needs to not only protect against malicious web sites but malicious browsers. A perfectly safe WebRTC application could enable an attack by another browser through the Peer Connection.

Another aspect is the potential for a malicious web site to use WebRTC to launch denial of service attacks on other hosts. On possible attack is shown in Figure 13.2.

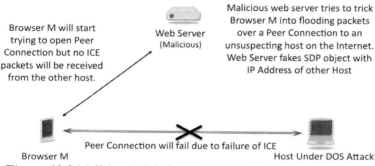

Browser M will start trying to open Peer Connection but no ICE packets will be received from the other host.

Web Server (Malicious)

Malicious web server tries to trick Browser M into flooding packets over a Peer Connection to an unsuspecting host on the Internet. Web Server fakes SDP object with IP Address of other Host

Peer Connection will fail due to failure of ICE

Browser M

Host Under DOS Attack

Figure 13.2 Malicious Web Server DOS Attack using WebRTC

A malicious web server could attempt to trick a browser into sending a high bandwidth stream (such as high definition video) to another host. Fortunately, WebRTC requires ICE to indicate consent by the remote site before starting any media stream. A web server cannot spoof those ICE packets, preventing this kind of DOS attack. It is still possible for WebRTC to generate considerable Internet traffic, though, producing a type of DOS attack on the browser. A user might, for example, authorize a WebRTC session, not realizing how much bandwidth would be consumed. For example, a site could cause a browser to initiate ten HD video streams to a server which would just drop the traffic, leaving the user wondering why their Internet connection is so slow. This could interfere with other Internet activity on that host or other hosts that share a common infrastructure.

ICE is yet another protocol implemented in the browser, so attacks using ICE are also possible, such as malformed ICE packets. Also, the nature of ICE hole punching is such that during this phase of peer connection establishment, the browser will accept and process incoming packets from any destination. Fortunately, once the ICE handshake is complete, the session is locked down to a particular IP address. However, malicious STUN or TURN servers used with ICE could still attempt to disrupt sessions.

13.2.3 Signaling Channel Attacks

WebRTC relies on the signaling channel to establish media and data channels. If the signaling channel or signaling server is compromised, an attacker can do a number of things. For example, the attacker could prevent a media or data channel session from being established. Or, the attacker could downgrade the security on the connection. Or, the attacker could redirect the connection to another user, or through a man-in-the-middle device which could record, inject or modify media or data, or otherwise interfere with the session. As such, securing the WebRTC signaling channel is very important.

The way in which the signaling channel for WebRTC is implemented affects what attacks are possible. For example, if WebSockets are used, then potential attacks on WebSockets are possible. If SIP or Jingle is used, then known and new vulnerabilities in these protocol implementations are possible. For a full security analysis of SIP, refer to [VOIP-SEC].

The same origin security model is used in web servers to protect against handling unwanted web traffic. However, having signaling forced through the Web Server is not ideal for bandwidth and performance reasons. As a result, the same origin policy can be relaxed for WebRTC signaling using Cross-Origin Resource Sharing (CORS) [CORS]. WebSockets (Section 10.2.2) allow for a relaxation of the same origin policy. This allows a SIP Proxy or XMPP Server or WebSocket Proxy to be run independently from the Web Server.

For HTTP requests generated by XHR [XHR-API], CORS can also be used to allow HTTP signaling messages to be routed to a different server than the Web Server. If HTTPS is used, then this server can be authenticated by the browser prior to sending signaling information.

13.3 Communication Security

Communication security represents the security of the real-time communications session established using WebRTC. Privacy and authentication are two important security properties that are enabled with WebRTC.

13.3.1 Communication Privacy

Privacy prevents a third party from eavesdropping on a voice or video communication session. Privacy can be provided by end-to-end encryption.

For audio and video sessions, this is provided by default in WebRTC using Secure RTP [RFC3711]. SRTP uses symmetric secret keys to encrypt and decrypt media packets, and commonly uses the AES encryption cipher in Counter Mode. For the data channel, DTLS provides the encryption. Data channel data can also be encrypted and decrypted in the JavaScript, providing an additional layer of security.

The encrypted and authenticated parts of the SRTP header are shown in Figure 13.3. Note that the RTP header is authenticated, but not encrypted. This means that SRTP packets can be identified as RTP but the media cannot be played or recorded without the key. Allowing SRTP traffic to be detected allows networks to apply policy, and provide Quality of Service (QoS) and monitoring services.

- Encryption covers only payload
  - Uses AES in Counter Mode with 128 bit symmetric keys
  - Also covers header extensions, but only encrypted if RFC 6094 extension is supported
- Authentication covers header, optional header extensions, and payload
  - Authentication hash is HMAC-SHA1 carried in 32 or 80 bit tag at end of packet

Figure 13.3 Encrypted and Authenticated parts of SRTP Packet

The security of SRTP depends strongly upon the keying method. There are two approaches to keying SRTP: sending the key over the signaling channel, or generating the key in the media path. SDP Security Descriptions is an example of the former, while DTLS-SRTP is an example of the latter.

13.3.2 Key Transport over the Signaling Channel

Sending the key over the signaling channel places security requirements on the signaling channel. If the signaling channel is not encrypted, then the entire SRTP media session will not have privacy. This encryption could be provided by Secure HTTP (HTTPS) or Secure WebSockets (WSS) transport for the signaling channel. In addition, since signaling usually goes through a signaling server, that signaling server must be trusted and must be protected against compromise. In particular, if logging is performed on a signaling server used to transport SRTP keys, those logs must be secured and encrypted or else SRTP keys could be revealed.

SDP Security Descriptions [RFC4568], informally known as SDES, is the most commonly used signaling protocol for VoIP and video systems that use SRTP. SDP Security Descriptions carries the SRTP master key and salt in the a=crypto SDP attribute. For example:

```
a=crypto:1 AES_CM_128_HMAC_SHA1_32 inline:a0RgdmcmVCspeWpVLFJhfHAQ
```

This configures SRTP to use AES Counter Mode with 128 bit keys and a 32 bit HMAC SHA-1 authentication tag. Inline contains the key and salt encoded in base 64. Note that SDP Security Descriptions is not allowed in WebRTC.

13.3.3 Key Agreement in the Media Path

Key agreement in the media path does not rely on the security of the signaling channel or trust of the signaling server. Instead, keys are generated using a public key operation in the media path (over the same transport IP address and port number as the resulting media session). One example of this public key operation is a Diffie-Hellman (DH) key agreement. DTLS-SRTP is a media path key agreement that performs this operation during the DTLS handshake. The DTLS handshake occurs after ICE connectivity checks have completed and the candidate pair chosen for the media session. The operation of DTLS-SRTP is shown in Figure 13.4.

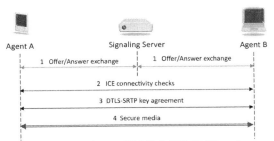

Figure 13.4 Operation of DTLS-SRTP Key Agreement

13.3.4 Authentication

Authentication for the communication session is the ability to determine that a media packet comes from the other party in the session. The HMAC carried inside the authentication tag is part of SRTP's media authentication, as shown in Figure 13.3.

13.3.5 Identity

There are a few ways that the identity of a participant in a WebRTC session can be determined. Both approaches rely on the DTLS-SRTP keying approach. If the browser has a client certificate which is part of a PKI, then this certificate can be passed in the DTLS handshake and validated. Having a PKI browser certificate is not common.

If a PKI certificate is not used, a browser uses a so-called self-signed certificate. This is a digital certificate which is not issued by a certificate authority, and is not part of a chain of trust. Essentially, it is just a container for a public key which is associated with the private key which will be used for public key operations during the SRTP key negotiation. A finger print, the output of a hash function, of that certificate is included in the SDP offer or answer message. If the signaling channel has end-to-end integrity protection, this can provide authentication, but this is not very common.

13.4 Identity in WebRTC

There are two types of identity that apply in WebRTC. The first is the identity of the website that is providing the WebRTC application. This is applicable for any type of web site, and WebRTC can simply make use of existing browser-based approaches described in Section 13.1.2. The other is the identity of the end user at the other end of the Peer Connection. With the addition of WebRTC, this is new to browsers, as most websites only involve interaction directly with a web server, not another browser as WebRTC allows.

WebRTC defines a new identity scheme that is an extension of existing cross-web site ID and single sign on approaches. Some common web-based approaches are listed in Table 13.1. The Identity Provider (IdP) defined in [draft-ietf-rtcweb-security-arch] is a framework for a generalized web identity scheme to be used to provide identity in WebRTC. In theory, each of these approaches could be used with an Identity Provider.

Approach	Used By	URL
OpenID	OpenID Foundation	http://openid.net/foundation
BrowserID	Mozilla, part of Persona	https://login.persona.org/
Facebook Login	Facebook	http://developers.facebook.com/docs/facebook-login

Table 13.1 Common Web Identity Schemes

An Identity Provider fulfills a similar role as a trust anchor in server identity. Figure 13.5 shows a simple case of an Identity Provider in the WebRTC triangle. Both browsers are connected to the same Web Server and also use the same Identity Provider. Note that there does not need to be any interaction or cooperation between the web site and the identity service – they can be completely independent. This allows a WebRTC provider to completely stay out of providing any identity.

A more general case of Identity Provider in the WebRTC trapezoid is shown in Figure 13.6. In this case, there are two separate Web Servers, with a signaling connection between them to allow the establishment of a Peer Connection between browsers in each of their web pages. There are also two separate Identity Providers, each unassociated with the web domain.

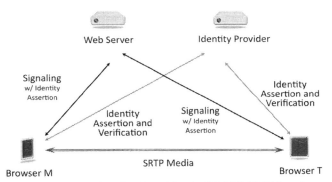

Figure 13.5 Identity Provider in WebRTC Triangle

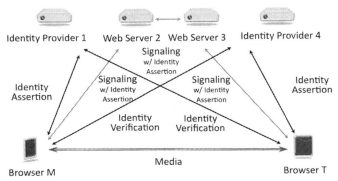

Figure 13.6 WebRTC Identity Provider in WebRTC Trapezoid

Figure 13.7 shows another possible architecture with the WebRTC triangle but separate Identity Providers. This architecture will be used to explain how the Identity Provider mechanism works. This figure shows a single web domain with two Identity Providers.

In this example, the user at browser M has an account with Identity Provider 1, and has configured his browser to use Identity Provider 1 as his identity provider. The user signs in to Identity Provider 1. When the user at browser M initiates a WebRTC session, the browser contacts Identity Provider 1 for a short-term certificate to generate the identity signature. When the certificate is received, Browser M generates a digital signature over the SRTP keying material to be used to establish the Peer Connection. This signature is sent over the signaling channel with the SDP object to the Web Server. The Web Server forwards the SDP object and the identity signature to Browser T.

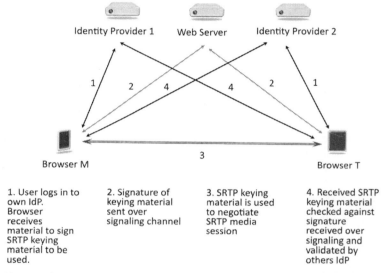

| 1. User logs in to own IdP. Browser receives material to sign SRTP keying material to be used. | 2. Signature of keying material sent over signaling channel | 3. SRTP keying material is used to negotiate SRTP media session | 4. Received SRTP keying material checked against signature received over signaling and validated by others IdP |

1) User logs in to own IdP. Browser receives material to sign SRTP keying material to be used
2) Signature of keying material sent over signaling channel
3) SRTP keying material is used to negotiate SRTP media session
4) Received SRTP keying material checked against signature received over signaling and validated by others IdP

Figure 13.7 Steps in using an Identity Provider in WebRTC

The user at browser T has an account with Identity Provider 2, and has configured her browser to use Identity Provider 2 as her identity provider. The user signs in to Identity Provider 2. Upon receipt of the SDP object, Browser T contacts Identity Provider 2 for a short-term certificate for generating the identity signature. The SDP object is generated, and a signature generated of the DTLS fingerprint to be used for the session.

Both are sent over the signaling channel which forwards them to Browser M. Browser M and Browser T begin ICE hole punching, then the DTLS handshake. When DTLS is established, each browser checks the fingerprint used to establish the DTLS connection with the signature over the SDP object. The certificate used to sign the identity signature is verified with the other's Identity Provider. If all checks out, the Peer Connection is authenticated and the identity asserted by the Identity Provider can be displayed as an authenticated identity.

Note that this identity assertion is generated and checked by the browser. The Web server plays no role, on either the downloaded local JavaScript or on the server code itself. The only role the Web server could provide would be to block the identity signature exchange. Note that the Web Server might also provide an identity indication, which may or may not match the one provided by the Identity Provider.

Needless to say, if a user wants privacy in a session, or to not to have their identities linked across multiple WebRTC sites, they should not enable this identity service.

So far, Mozilla has shown the most interest in the Identity Provider mechanism and will likely have the first browser supporting it. Depending on its utility and adoption by WebRTC developers, other browsers may add support for it in the future.

See Section 8.3.1.5 for information about the Identity Provider APIs.

13.5 Enterprise Issues

Enterprises typically use border security to control what Internet traffic flows across their boundaries. For general IP traffic, firewalls are often utilized. Firewalls are points of policy enforcement for IP access. The simplest access rules are one-way filtering. In general, incoming packets from the Internet are blocked unless they are responses to requests sent from inside the enterprise. Other rules can be set up for particular IP addresses, ports, and transports. The combination of local and remote IP addresses, local and remote ports, and transport protocol (e.g. UDP or TCP) is often referred to as a 5-tuple for the five data points that can characterize a particular protocol. Some protocols always use a particular port, allowing for 5-tuple rules to be used for a particular protocol. For example, web browsing typically uses TCP port 80, so opening port 80 in a firewall can be used to enable web browsing, and blocking port 80 can restrict web browsing. Media flows such as those established by WebRTC, or SIP, or Jingle do not use well-known or registered ports. As such, they cannot be allowed or blocked simply by 5-tuple filtering rules.

For particular application traversal through firewalls, Application Layer Gateways or ALGs are used. For Internet Communications, specialized

ALGs known as Session Border Controllers or SBCs are used. Typically, they use a signaling channel, such as SIP or Jingle, to authorize the resulting media flows, such as RTP or SRTP. The SBC is typically placed next to the firewall in a trusted connection known as a DMZ (for demilitarized zone, a buffer region used around national borders to prevent direct interaction between opposing military forces.)

An SBC uses the signaling channel to apply policy. For example, based on the destination IP address or URL, a particular type of media communication can be allowed or blocked. In addition, other policies can be applied, such as whether the media is recorded and archived.

With WebRTC, there is no standardized signaling channel, so a device such as an SBC is limited in what it can do in general, unless a standardized signaling protocol is used. Even if a WebRTC application uses a signaling protocol within the JavaScript, this will not necessarily be accessible to an SBC, as it could be transported over a Secure HTTP or Secure WebSocket connection and mixed in with all the other web traffic going in and out of the enterprise.

For a more in-depth discussion of enterprise WebRTC issues, see [IEEE-COMS].

13.6 Privacy

There are a number of areas in WebRTC that relate to privacy. Identity privacy, IP address privacy, and browser fingerprinting are all important. Useful guidelines for Internet protocols are in [draft-iab-privacy-considerations].

13.6.1 Identity Privacy

Identity privacy in WebRTC means that a user can visit a website and use WebRTC and not have their identity compromised. Normally web sites using WebRTC will use and share identity information as part of the service. However, a web site might promise anonymous or private communication using WebRTC. Of course, a web site needs to know one's identity in order to share it, although even IP addresses can provide some level of identity information. Once a user has signed in to a web site, there is no protocol or API way to enforce an anonymous or private WebRTC session. This is analogous to the PSTN, where the telephone network always knows a caller's identity. While the user can select to block delivery of their identity, this won't always be the case, such as a call to a toll free (8xx) number in which the caller identity is always delivered regardless of the caller's indication.

It is also somewhat obvious that if a private or anonymous WebRTC session is established, that an Identity Provider should not be used.

Identity information could also be leaked in the signaling channel. For example, a SIP `INVITE` request might contain the non-anonymized SIP URI of a user.

13.6.2 IP Address Privacy

Privacy on the Internet is a very complicated subject, and even privacy in web browsing is also very involved. This book does not discuss topics such as web cookies. However, there is one aspect of privacy that WebRTC affects which we will discuss here: IP address privacy.

Whenever a browser connects to a web sever, the web server knows the IP address of the browser. In most cases, it is actually just the public IP address of the outer-most NAT that the browser is connecting through. For example, in Figure 3.7, if either the mobile or the tablet access a web page, the web server will get the IP address 203.0.113.4 and not the individual IP address that would distinguish the mobile from the tablet. However, this IP address can reveal a lot about the user, such as location information which is commonly used for location specific ads and search results. There are some services which allow a browser to connect to a server without revealing this information. One such example is The Onion Router [TOR], an anonymizing service for browsing. In general, though, a web server always knows the IP addresses of the browsers that connect to it, and it can do anything with this information including log it, store it, or share it with anyone. For example, there are sites that display this information for troubleshooting purposes [WHATSMYIP] or to correlate anonymous postings. WebRTC does not change any of these well-known web properties.

However, if WebRTC is used to establish direct browser-to-browser media flows, then each browser can learn the IP address of the other browser. This can be true even if the session is not established or is refused by the other party. This information can also include the inside IP address, the private IP address, if this address was shared as a candidate address for hole punching. This is a new privacy exposure introduced by WebRTC that could potentially be used to obtain new information about other users.

If privacy is important in the WebRTC application, there are a number of possible ways to improve the situation:

1) A browser could only send one IP address candidate, that of a TURN server, discussed in Section 9.2. This would allow the other browser to learn where the TURN server is located but not the actual browser using the TURN server.
2) A virtual private network, VPN, service could be used and only the VPN IP address shared as a candidate.
3) A browser might choose not to share the private IP address as

a candidate. The browser would instead share the public IP address, which might be that of a service provider or enterprise, but not reveal the individual user or computer behind it.

4) A web server could have a policy of intentionally relaying all media traffic, using a TURN server for example. However, users must trust the web site to do this for them.

In the signaling channel, IP address information can be leaked in the content of the signaling message or in the transport of the signaling message. For example, a WebSocket Proxy will learn the IP address of browsers that use it for WebRTC. Since the SDP object will contain ICE IP address candidates, this also provides IP address information. This also provides private IP address information, something not normally known by a web server which normally only sees the IP address of the outside NAT.

It is very important to note that in all web browsing cases, some IP address must be shared with both the web server and the other web browser. The only question is which IP address and how much information this reveals about the user.

13.6.3 Browser Fingerprinting

Browser fingerprinting is the process of trying to identify a particular browser by its capabilities and features. The more information about a browser that a web site can learn, the easier fingerprinting can be. Fingerprinting can be used for tracking that circumvents a browser's cookie policy, for example. The EFF performed a survey of the uniqueness of web browsers using an online test tool [PANOPTICLICK]. In their published report [EFF-FINGER], they list the top sources of browser fingerprinting as plug-ins, fonts, browser, accepted methods, screen resolution, time-zone, and cookies enabled. A discussion from a W3C plenary considers this topic [FINGERPRINT].

WebRTC provides much more information about a browser that could be used for fingerprinting, such as supported media types, codecs, network interfaces, and labels for the cameras, microphones, and speakers, etc.

13.7 ZRTP over Data Channel

The ZRTP protocol [RFC6189] can be run over the data channel to verify that there are no Man-in-the-Middle (MitM) attackers in the media session or data channel connection [draft-johnston-rtcweb-zrtp]. This is shown in Figure 13.8. Essentially, this approach replaces a third party such as an Identity Provider with regard to verifying the fingerprints of the self-signed certificates used to establish the DTLS connection. Instead, after the

DTLS connection is established, a data channel is established and a ZRTP session is established over the data channel. In the process, the DTLS fingerprints are compared, and if the fingerprints match, it indicates that there is no MitM attacker.

By comparing the Short Authentication String (SAS) displayed on each browser, the users can verify that there is no MitM attack on ZRTP.

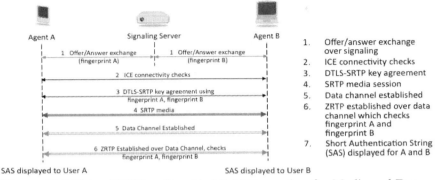

Figure 13.8 Using ZRTP to Provide MitM Protection for Media and Data Channel

13.8 Summary

WebRTC security is a very important topic that will receive much attention as this new technology rolls out. WebRTC can make use of existing web security features such as secure HTTP. It also has built-in security in the media path. It can also make use of browser identity approaches through the Identity Provider mechanism.

It is important that WebRTC browsers support auto updates so that users have the latest patches and updates.

13.9 References

[draft-ietf-rtcweb-security]   http://tools.ietf.org/html/draft-ietf-rtcweb-security

[draft-ietf-rtcweb-security-arch]   http://tools.ietf.org/html/draft-ietf-rtcweb-security-arch

[APPLIED-CRYPTO]   http://www.amazon.com/Applied-Cryptography-Protocols-Algorithms-Source/dp/0471117099

[HTTPS-EVERY] https://www.eff.org/https-everywhere

[DANE] http://www.internetsociety.org/deploy360/resources/dane/

[DNSSEC] http://tools.ietf.org/html/rfc4033

[VOIP-SEC] http://www.amazon.com/Understanding-Security-Artech-Telecommunications-Library/dp/1596930500

[CORS] http://www.w3.org/TR/cors/

[XHR-API] http://www.w3.org/TR/XMLHttpRequest/

[RFC3711] http://tools.ietf.org/html/rfc3711

[RFC4568] http://tools.ietf.org/html/rfc4568

[IEEE-COMS] Alan Johnston, John Yoakum and Kundan Singh, Taking on WebRTC in an Enterprise, IEEE Communications Magazine, Vol. 51, No. 4, April 2013

[draft-iab-privacy-considerations]   http://tools.ietf.org/html/draft-iab-privacy-considerations

[TOR]   http://theonionrouter.com

[WHATSMYIP]   http://whatismyipaddress.com

[PANOPTICLICK] https://panopticlick.eff.org/

[EFF-FINGER] https://panopticlick.eff.org/browser-uniqueness.pdf

[FINGERPRINT] http://www.w3.org/wiki/Fingerprinting

[RFC6189] http://tools.ietf.org/html/rfc6189

[draft-johnston-rtcweb-zrtp]   http://tools.ietf.org/html/draft-johnston-rtcweb-zrtp

14 IMPLEMENTATIONS AND USES

Web browsers are at various stages of supporting WebRTC APIs and protocols. This information changes rapidly, so always do some searching of official documentation to determine the exact support of WebRTC. This information is presented in alphabetical order. Another view of this is available at [READY-YET].

14.1 Browsers

14.1.1 Apple Safari

No information yet. Note that iOS WebRTC applications are being written using Objective C APIs and using the SDK from Google.

14.1.2 Google Chrome

Support for `RTCPeerConnection`, `getUserMedia()`, `MediaStreams` and `DataChannels`, is available in standard Chrome [CHROME]. VP8, Opus, STUN, and TURN are supported. Google Chrome for Android [CR-ANDROID] also supports WebRTC.

Chrome has useful tools for WebRTC developers in the Tools/Developer Tools menu. Also, `chrome://webrtc-internals` provides a wealth of useful information including JavaScript state and media information.

For details on this, as well as the most up-to-date status on Chrome support of WebRTC, please visit http://www.webrtc.org/chrome.

14.1.3 Mozilla Firefox

Firefox FIREFOX] supports `RTCPeerConnection`, `getUserMedia()`, `MediaStreams`, and `DataChannels`, on by default. Firefox supports VP8, Opus, and STUN, but not TURN. For the most recent documentation on

WebRTC support in Firefox, see http://developer.mozilla.org/en-US/docs/WebRTC . Firefox 24 for Android also supports WebRTC. Firefox OS [FIREFOX-OS] will also support WebRTC.

14.1.4 Microsoft Internet Explorer

No information yet. However, projects such as webrtc4all [WEBRTC4ALL] aim to provide a temporary solution. Note that [WEBRTC4ALL] uses a different API prefix than either Chrome or Mozilla which isn't part of the adapter.js library. As a result, the demo application in this book will not work without modification.

Microsoft has published several versions of an alternative API document [CU-RTC-WEB]. Discussions about integrating this into the existing standards work are ongoing. As a result, it is not yet clear whether or how much of the existing WebRTC APIs will be supported in Internet Explorer.

14.1.5 Opera

Opera 20 [OPERA] supports `RTCPeerConnection`, `getUserMedia()`, `MediaStreams`, and `DataChannels`, on by default. It is built on top of the Chromium browser that Chrome is built on top of. However, at the time of publication Opera does not work with the demo application in this book in all configurations.

14.2 Other Use Cases

Google has made their Chrome WebRTC implementation available as a downloadable and embeddable SDK. It is likely that this SDK will find its way into many non-browser devices.

A plethora of APIs have been developed on top of WebRTC. EasyRTC [EASYRTC] is a toolkit composed of prebuilt web applications, server components, code snippets, etc. that are designed to be easy to put together to start using WebRTC today, even as the standard changes. The Open RTC (ORTC) API [ORCA] was originally created as a competitor to WebRTC, but its focus now is on being an API that can be implemented easily on top of WebRTC 1.0 or implemented natively. It attempts to avoid the offer/answer model used in WebRTC. Note that this work is currently being done in a W3C Community Group, which is a non-standards-track group.

There are other many other WebRTC-related communication API providers. One that is worth mentioning is Phono. Phono [PHONO] started life as an API to make it easy to create a SIP softphone, but it quickly evolved into the "jQuery of communications", with both jQuery and JavaScript implementations that make it almost trivially easy to establish communication with a server or another Phono implementation. Developed before WebRTC, it still supports its JavaScript and Adobe Flash plugins for getting access to the microphone, while now supporting the WebRTC APIs as well.

14.3 STUN and TURN Server Implementations

A very good standards-based open source STUN and TURN server is rfc5766-turnserver [TURNSERVER]. This is the TURN server used for the demo application in this book. Step-by-step instructions on how to setup this TURN server are available at http://webrcbook.com/turnserver .

14.4 References

[READY-YET]   http://iswebrtcreadyyet.com/

[WEBRTC4ALL]   http://code.google.com/p/webrtc4all

[CHROME]   http://www.google.com/chrome

[CHR-ANDROID]
    http://www.google.com/intl/en/chrome/browser/mobile/android.ht
ml

[FIREFOX]   http://www.firefox.com

[FF-OS]   http://developer.mozilla.org/en-US/Firefox_OS

[CU-RTC-WEB]   http://lists.w3.org/Archives/Public/public-webrtc/2012Oct/att-0076/realtime-media.html

[OPERA]   http://www.opera.com

[EASYRTC]   http://www.easyrtc.com

[ORCA]   http://www.w3.org/community/orca/

[PHONO]   http://phono.com

[TURNSERVER]   http://code.google.com/p/rfc5766-turn-server/

APPENDIX A – THE W3C STANDARDS PROCESS

The World Wide Web Consortium is developing the standard APIs for WebRTC. Besides the WEBRTC Working Group, there are a number of other W3C working groups and task groups working on WebRTC.

A.1 Introduction to the World Wide Web Consortium

The World Wide Web Consortium (W3C) [W3C] was established by Tim Berners-Lee, the creator of HTML, to promote the development of HTML and other web technologies. Over time, W3C has built up processes that make it a proper Standards Development Organization (SDO), including a focus on consensus, processes for dispute resolution, handling of non-member comments, implementability testing, permanent storage of and access to discussions, resolutions, and official development drafts of specifications. W3C is a membership organization – only members can create Working Groups, and some Working Groups are restricted such that only members can attend meetings and calls. However, all official documents and final discussions are publicly available on the web without charge. All discussions in the WEBRTC Working Group are public.

Although W3C has a variety of group structures for discussing specifications, only a Working Group leads to an officially sanctioned W3C standard, known as a W3C Recommendation. Recommendations are published in (what else?) HTML format. W3C Working Groups are loosely organized into Activity Domains, but that is primarily for internal W3C administration reasons and has little impact on the direction of the group. In addition, there are Task Forces which are informal collaborations between two or more Working Groups. The Media Task Force that is developing the "Media Capture and Streams" document is one such task force.

The two most important factors in W3C standard development are the specification development stages and the focus on consensus. Specifications in W3C, referred to as Technical Reports, progress through the following stages of maturity:

1) First Public Working Draft
2) Working Draft
3) Last Call Working Draft (LCWD)
4) Candidate Recommendation
5) Proposed Recommendation
6) Recommendation

The first three stages together indicate that a Technical Report is not yet complete technically and does not yet represent broad consensus. The last three stages together indicate that the specification is believed to be technically complete and has had broad review.

More specifically, a specification begins its public life as a First Public Working Draft. At this stage there is no consensus, only an Intellectual Property commitment. There are then any number of Working Drafts released regularly by the Working Group as it hashes out the technical contents of the specification. Although an efficient and effective group will plan to build consensus as it develops these Working Drafts, officially, a Working Draft does not represent consensus and must be cited as a Work in Progress.

Once the Working Group believes a specification is technically complete, it publishes the document as a Last Call Working Draft (LCWD). Interestingly, this is often the first time that other W3C groups will review the draft, so it is not unusual to have more than one LCWD before moving forward. It is also the first time that a record must be kept of the disposition of every public comment – the specification may not move forward until every comment has been addressed to the satisfaction of the commenter, except in unusual circumstances.

After passing the LCWD stage, the next step is to produce a Candidate Recommendation document containing a detailed Implementation Report Plan, which is typically a list of assertions and tests along with a plan for how many implementations of each feature are required in order to progress. The goal at this stage is not to test implementations, but to ensure that there have been enough implementations to confirm that the specification is implementable and, ideally, that implementations will be interoperable. Any specification changes beyond clarifications and editorial changes will cause the document to move back to the Working Draft stage to again ensure sufficient review and consensus. After receiving sufficient implementations according to the plan, and with no major changes needed, the Technical Report can move to the penultimate stage, the Proposed Recommendation. This stage is largely a formality and is, in fact, out of the hands of the Working Group. Assuming there are no public objections within this stage (typically a month), the Report moves automatically to the Recommendation stage.

Any discussion of W3C process would be insufficient if it did not include a discussion of consensus. W3C takes the consensus requirement very seriously, requiring that every objection be addressed if at all possible. Although the IETF only requires rough consensus, W3C requires full consensus. While this can increase the time needed to produce a Recommendation, it reduces the likelihood that the document will knowingly alienates a sizeable fraction of the intended users.

A.2 The W3C WEBRTC Working Group

The main working group in W3C for WebRTC is the WEBRTC Working Group [WEBRTCWG]. Although efforts to create the IETF RTCWEB and the W3C WEBRTC groups began at the same time, it took significantly longer to get the WEBRTC group going. The issue, in this case, was to agree on what to use as a starting document. The WHATWG [WHATWG] is an independent organization that makes suggestions for the direction of HTML development by creating a modification of HTML itself. One such modification was an extension to set up media connections (known as a "Peer Connection") between two browsers. It took a substantial amount of time to work out the copyright issues, but eventually W3C developed a copyright statement that allowed the WEBRTC Working Group to use the WHATWG's PeerConnection text as a starting point for the group's work.

A.3 How WEBRTC relates to other W3C Working Groups

WebRTC's goal is to define APIs for setting up direct browser-to-browser media connections. It is not the goal of WebRTC to define what media is, how media will or could be used by the near or far end, or how it relates to the existing capabilities of HTML. While there are aspects of media synchronization that do need to be defined by WebRTC because of the need to choose synchronized or asynchronous transports, the other aspects listed above are handled by other groups within W3C. Some related groups are listed below.

> Media Capture Task Force [MEDIAWG] - The Media Capture Task Force is comprised of members of two W3C Working Groups: WEBRTC and Device APIs. The goal of this group is to jointly define getUserMedia(), the API call used to request local media (access to a camera, microphone, speaker,

etc.). Additionally, this group is defining the core of the `MediaStream` interface since it is of relevance to both groups.

HTML [HTMLWG] - Clearly the HTML Working Group focuses on the development of the Hyper-Text Markup Language, the language that is the foundation of the World Wide Web. Although there is no direct working relationship between the WEBRTC and HTML WGs, many of the participants in the WEBRTC group are active participants in or followers of the HTML WG. More importantly, WebRTC participants understand that the WebRTC APIs must be consistent with and integrate well with existing HTML APIs and markup. The current version of HTML is HTML5.

Audio [AUDIOWG] - The Audio Working Group develops APIs for more advanced audio manipulation within HTML. Although there is no direct connection between the WEBRTC and Audio WGs, the Audio Working Group has use cases that affect the `MediaStream` and `getUserMedia` interfaces being defined by the Media Capture Task Force.

A.4 References

[W3C]   http://www.w3c.org

[WEBRTCWG]   http://www.w3.org/2011/04/webrtc

[WHATWG]   http://www.whatwg.org

[MEDIAWG]   http://www.w3.org/wiki/Media_Capture

[HTMLWG]   http://www.w3.org/html/wg

[AUDIOWG]   http://www.w3.org/2011/audio

APPENDIX B – THE IETF STANDARDS PROCESS

The Internet Engineering Task Force is developing standard protocols for WebRTC. Besides the RTCWEB Working Group, there are a number of other IETF working groups working on WebRTC.

B.1 Introduction to the Internet Engineering Task Force

The Internet Engineering Task Force (IETF) [IETF] is the international standards body responsible for protocol standardization on the Internet. The IETF has standardized protocols such as IP, TCP, UDP, DNS, SIP, RTP, HTTP, and SMTP to name some popular ones. The IETF publishes its standards documents as the numbered series known as "Request for Comments" or RFCs. Note that not all RFCs are IETF documents. Also, not all IETF RFCs are standards documents. Before they are finalized and approved as RFCs, working drafts of standards documents are known as "Internet-Drafts".

Work in the IETF is primarily done over email using mailing lists. There are separate mailing lists for each Working Group. Much of the work on WebRTC in the IETF is discussed in the RTCWEB Working Group, although related work is also happening in other working groups.

There are no membership fees, and anyone can contribute to the work by subscribing to a mailing list, sending comments, writing Internet-Drafts, or attending face-to-face IETF meetings. Work is organized into areas known as Working Groups.

The normal process steps for an IETF document are listed below:

1) Submission of individual Internet-Draft
2) Adoption of a Working Group document
3) Working Group Last Call (WGLC)

4) IETF Last Call
5) Approval by IESG as an RFC.

Internet-Drafts are working documents submitted to the IETF via email or the online form on the IETF website. Internet-Drafts must meet specific formatting requirements and have intellectual property and copyright declarations. Internet-Drafts are frequently updated, and automatically expire after six months if they are not updated or finalized as an RFC. The initial version is -00 (counting from zero) and is incremented for each update. As an individual draft, the authors can include any content they like in their draft. Internet-Drafts are identified by their filename, which always begin "draft-lastname-wgname" where "lastname" is the last name of the principle author or editor, and "wgname" is the name of the working group where the work is likely to be discussed. The rest of the filename is a hyphenated version of the title or content. For example, draft-burnett-rtcweb-constraints-registry is an individual Internet-Draft, written by Daniel C. Burnett for the RTCWEB working group about a constraints registry.

Since WebRTC is a work in progress, many of the documents discussed in this book are Internet-Drafts, and as such their content may have changed. The hyperlinks in this book will automatically take you to the latest version. However, the document name may have changed or documents may have been merged together or split into multiple documents.

Working Groups in the IETF are chartered to produce documents to meet specific protocol milestones. Working Groups "adopt" a draft as a starting point towards producing a consensus document to meet a particular milestone. The authors or editors of the draft are expected to try to reflect working group consensus in the draft from this point on. When the draft is revised, the filename will change to "draft-ietf-wgname", dropping the author name. Since the filename has changed, the version resets to -00. Working group documents tend to get wider review, agenda time at face-to-face IETF meetings, and listings on Working Group pages and summaries.

Once Working Group chairs believe an Internet-Draft is complete and represents the consensus of the group, they will call for a Working Group Last Call (WGLC) for final reviews and comments. If there are significant changes or updates as a result, there may be additional WGLCs for the document. After this process is completed and the chairs believe the draft has "rough consensus" they will move the document towards IETF-wide final review in an IETF Last Call. Upon completion, the members of the Internet Engineering Task Force Steering Committee (IESG) vote. If the vote is successful, the Internet-Draft will be approved and put into the RFC

Editor's queue. After a few months, the draft will be assigned an RFC number and published as an RFC.

There are a number of types of RFCs published by the IETF. The most common are Proposed Standards (PS) and Informational documents. Proposed Standards are actual IETF protocol standards. Informational RFCs do not define protocols or standards but instead document requirements, issues, or the motivation behind protocols. Some WebRTC documents will be published as Informational RFCs, although most will be published as Proposed Standards.

B.2 The IETF RTCWEB Working Group

The main Working Group for WebRTC in the IETF is the RTCWEB Working Group [RTCWEB WG], short for Real-Time Communications Web. However, the WebRTC work encompasses a number of areas, and as such the work is spread across a number of working groups. In addition to Internet-Drafts (working standards documents), WebRTC references other IETF RFCs (Request for Comments, the finished standards documents). Both are also listed and explained in this book.

B.3 How RTCWEB relates to other IETF Working Groups

Besides the work in the RTCWEB Working Group, there is active work relating to WebRTC being done in other working groups, which are listed below.

AVTCORE [AVTCOREWG] - The Audio Video Transport Core Working Group (AVTCORE) standardizes extensions to the Real-time Transport Protocol (RTP), which is used by WebRTC. This is the group responsible for defining how different types of media can be synchronized and sent together.

MMUSIC [MMUSICWG] - The Multiparty Multimedia Session Control Working Group (MMUSIC) standardizes extensions of the Session Description Protocol (SDP), which is used by WebRTC.

RMCAT [RMCATWG] – The RTP Media Congestion Avoidance Techniques Working Group is developing congestion control for RTP media over UDP transport. Requirements, feedback information in RTP or RTCP packets, and congestion control algorithms are being developed. These approaches will be used by WebRTC to ensure that widespread use of WebRTC will not cause excessive congestion on the Internet, and so that WebRTC media sessions can avoid congestion for the best user experience.

TRAM [TRAMWG] – The TURN Revised And Modernized Working Group is developing STUN and TURN extensions, many of which, relate to WebRTC. They relate to new transports, authentication methods, and general extensions.

B.4 References

[IETF]   http://www.ietf.org

[RTCWEBWG]   http://tools.ietf.org/wg/rtcweb

[AVTCOREWG]   http://tools.ietf.org/wg/avtcore

[MMUSICWG]   http://tools.ietf.org/wg/mmusic

[RMCATWG]   http://tools.ietf.org/wg/rmcat

[TRAMWG]   http://tools.ietf.org/wg/tram

APPENDIX C – GLOSSARY

ABNF – Augmented Backus-Naur Format. This is the meta-language used to define the syntax of text-based Internet protocols such as SDP and URLs. Originally defined in RFC 822, the most recent specification is RFC 5234.

API – Application Programming Interface. APIs are interfaces used by software components to communicate with each other.

HTML5 – The latest version of Hyper-Text Markup Language, the markup language used on the World Wide Web for web pages and applications. HTML originally defined simple markup tags in XML. Today, HTML5 supports Cascading Style Sheets (CSS) and scripting such as JavaScript. WebRTC is the part of HTML5 that deals with real-time voice, video, and data streams in browsers.

JavaScript – An interpreted scripting programming language used on web pages. Despite the name, it is quite different from Java. Today, most advanced web pages and applications use JavaScript. Technically, JavaScript is an implementation of the ECMA-262 (ECMAScript) standard. In practice, the terms JavaScript and ECMAScript are used interchangeably.

Jingle – A multimedia signaling protocol, which is an extension of XMPP (Extensible Messaging and Presence Protocol, RFC 6120, also known as Jabber). Jingle is defined by XEP-0166. Jingle uses RTP/SRTP for media, ICE NAT traversal, and supports mapping of media information to SDP.

NAT - Network Address Translation. NAT is a function often built into Internet routers or hubs that map one IP address space to another space. Usually, NATs are used to allow a number of devices to share an IP address, such as in a residential router or hub. NATs are also used by enterprises or service providers to segment IP networks, simplifying control and administration. Many Internet protocols, especially those using TCP transport or a client/server architecture, have no difficulty traversing NATs. However, peer-to-peer protocols and protocols using UDP transport can have major difficulties. NAT traversal in WebRTC uses the ICE protocol. For details of how NAT and hole punching works, see Chapter 10 of <u>SIP: Understanding the Session Initiation Protocol</u>, 3rd Edition. NAT is also sometimes used to refer to Network Address Translator.

Offer/Answer – Media negotiation is the way in which two parties in a communication session, such as two browsers, communicate and come to agreement on an acceptable media session. Offer/answer is an approach to media negotiation in which one party first sends to the other party what media types and capabilities it supports and would like to establish – this is known as the "offer". The other party then responds indicating which of the offered media types and capabilities are supported and acceptable for this session – this is known as the "answer". This process can be repeated a number of times to setup and modify a session. While the term offer/answer is general, when used in WebRTC, it usually refers to RFC 3264 which defined the Offer/Answer Protocol, a usage of SDP by SIP. Offer/Answer must be studied in order to understand how exchanging SDP session descriptions can be used to negotiate a media session with WebRTC. For examples of SDP offer/answer, see Chapter 13 of <u>SIP: Understanding the Session Initiation Protocol</u>, 3rd Edition.

Node.js – The WebRTC APIs operate on the client side, in the web browser. They are JavaScript APIs that make use of the event loop built into the browser for handling the asynchronous input and output that is the hallmark of a Web GUI. WebRTC has quite a number of methods that take time

302

to execute and are thus structured to execute application developer-provided callbacks when complete. Node.js, often referred to as just "Node", is a JavaScript interpreter and an event loop rolled together, along with modules for networking and file access and a convenient module/package management system. Traditional web servers spawn a new process for each request that is handled by PHP, Perl, or other languages. For isolated pages this is fine, but for services where the requests are related (or even connected) and still asynchronous, coordination among the different running request handlers can be tricky, requiring a shared database, a shared file system, or explicit interprocess communication. Node's http server, on the other hand, uses a single process thread to handle all incoming requests. Each request is queued and handled via the event loop. Thus, programming a web server in Node is similar to programming a dynamic web page in a browser – every code snippet is initiated by etiher an event or a callback, and all code must ensure that it does not block. In return for this programming style requirement, all requests are handled within the same memory and process space, allowing for much easier control of and synchronization across multiple requests. When used with web pages containing WebRTC APIs, Node is convenient for handling both page requests and XHR pushes/requests, able to maintain state about the various browsers using it as the signaling gateway between the browsers.

Peer Connection – This term is used to refer to a direct connection set up between two "peers", two web browsers in the context of WebRTC, for the purpose of transporting audio, video, and data. Such a connection is established using the RTCPeerConnection and related APIs.

SIP – Session Initiation Protocol. SIP is an application level signaling protocol used for Internet Communications, Voice over IP, and video. SIP is defined by RFC 3261 and uses SDP session descriptions as defined by the offer/answer protocol.

WebSocket – The WebSocket protocol establishes a long-lived bi-directional TCP connection between a web browser and a web server, opened by the browser using HTTP.

APPENDIX D – SUPPLEMENTARY READING AND SOURCES

For online training and certification relating to WebRTC, we recommend WebRTC School:

http://www.webrtcschool.com

For background on HTML5 and JavaScipt, we recommend the easy-to-follow tutorials at:

http://www.w3schools.com

For background on an Internet communication signaling protocol such as Session Initiation Protocol, we recommend:

Johnston, Alan B, SIP: Understanding the Session Initiation Protocol, Artech House, Boston, 2009, 283 pages, 3rd Edition. ISBN-13:978-1607839958

This book also discusses NAT traversal and hole punching, SDP session descriptions, and SDP offer/answer.

Sinnreich, Henry and Alan B. Johnston, Internet Communications using SIP: Delivering VoIP and Multimedia Services with Session Initiation Protocol (Networking Council Series), John Wiley and Sons, New York, 2005, 298 pages, 2nd Edition. ISBN-13:978-0471776574

For background on RTP and media transport, we recommend:

Perkins, Colin, <u>RTP: Audio and Video for the Internet</u>, Addison-Wesley Professional, New York, 2003, 432 pages. ISBN-13:978-0672322495

For Internet Communications security for VoIP and video, we recommend:

Johnston, Alan B. and D. Piscitello, <u>Understanding Voice over IP Security</u> , Artech House, Boston, 2006, 276 pages, ISBN-13: 978-1596930506

For an entertaining fictional account of cybercrime and hacking that also happens to teach the basics of computer and Internet security, we recommend:

Johnston, Alan B, <u>Counting from Zero</u>, 2011, 281 pages, paperback ISBN-13:978-1461064886 or Kindle eBook

INDEX

307

ABOUT THE AUTHORS

Dr. Alan B. Johnston has over thirteen years of experience in SIP, VoIP (Voice over IP), and Internet Communications, having been a co-author of the SIP specification and a dozen other IETF RFCs, including the ZRTP media security protocol. He is the author of four best selling technical books on Internet Communications, SIP, and security, and a techno thriller novel "Counting from Zero" that teaches the basics of Internet and computer security. He is on the board of directors of the SIP Forum. He holds Bachelors and Ph.D. degrees in electrical engineering. Alan is an active participant in the IETF RTCWEB working group. He is currently a Distinguished Engineer at Avaya, Inc. and an Adjunct Instructor at Washington University in St Louis. He owns and rides a number of motorcycles, and enjoys mentoring a robotics team.

Dr. Daniel C. Burnett has more than a dozen years of experience in computer standards work, having been author and editor of the W3C standards underlying the majority of today's automated Interactive Voice Response (IVR) systems. He has twice received the prestigious "Speech Luminary" award from Speech Tech Magazine for his contributions to standards in the Automated Speech Recognition (Voice Recognition) field. As an editor of the PeerConnection and getUserMedia W3C WEBRTC specifications and a participant in the IETF, Dan has been involved from the beginning in this exciting new field. He is currently the Chief Scientist at Tropo and Director of Standards at Voxeo, an Aspect Company. When he can get away, Dan loves camping both with his family and with his son's Boy Scout Troop.

Follow Alan and Dan on Twitter as @alanbjohnston and @danielcburnett and on Google+ as alanbjohnston@gmail.com danielcburnett@gmail.com.

For information on future editions along with updates and changes since publication, visit http://webrtcbook.com

Facebook http://www.facebook.com/webrtcbook
Google+ http://plus.google.com/102459027898040609362

315

Also by Alan B. Johnston:
Counting from Zero

Can a security expert save the Internet from a catastrophic zero day cyber attack by a network of zombie computers, known as a botnet? At what cost? Unfolding across three continents, this novel gives a realistic insider's view of the thrust and parry world of computer security and cryptography, and the very real threat of botnets.

"Credible and believable, this story is told by a subject matter expert. I could not wait to find out what happened next."
- Vint Cerf, Internet pioneer

"The threat to the Internet from worms, viruses, botnets, and zombie computers is real, and growing. **Counting from Zero** is a great way to come up to speed on the alarming state of affairs, and Johnston draws you in with his story and believable cast of characters."
- Phil Zimmermann, creator of Pretty Good Privacy (PGP) the most widely used email encryption program

"**Counting from Zero** brings Dashiell Hammet and Raymond Chandler into the computer age."
- Diana Lutz

WebRTC School

Learn and Qualify

The WebRTC School is the web's premier location for WebRTC Integrator and Developer education. Associated with the training programs are the industry supported certifications, the WebRTC School Qualified Integrator (WSQI™) and WebRTC School Qualified Developer (WSQD™). For more information and online demos, please visit:

http://www.webrtcschool.com

WebRTC | **WSQD™**
WebRTC School
Qualified Developer

WebRTC | **WSQI™**
WebRTC School
Qualified Integrator

Made in the USA
Middletown, DE
25 May 2016